Initia
of
Theosophical Masters

SUNY Series in
Western Esoteric Traditions

David Appelbaum, Editor

Map of Indian subcontinent, 1886

Initiates of Theosophical Masters

K. Paul Johnson

STATE UNIVERSITY OF NEW YORK PRESS

Production by Ruth Fisher
Marketing by Nancy Farrell

Published by
State University of New York Press, Albany

Printed in the United States of America

For information, address the State University of New York Press, State University Plaza, Albany, NY 12246

Library of Congress Cataloging-in-Publication Data
Johnson, K. Paul, 1953–
Initiates of theosophical masters / K. Paul Johnson.
p. cm. — (SUNY series in Western esoteric traditions)
Includes bibliographical references and index.
ISBN 0-7914-2555-X (alk. paper). — ISBN 0-7914-2556-8 (pbk. : alk. paper)
1. Blavatsky, H. P. (Helena Petrovna), 1831–1891—Friends and associates. 2. Theosophists—Biography. 3. Theosophy—History—19th century. 4. Great White Brotherhood. I. Title. II. Series.
BP585.B6J62 1995
299'.934'0922—dc20
[B] 94-34609
CIP

10 9 8 7 6 5 4 3 2 1

Dedicated to the cyberspace communities of theos-l, Talisman, alt.religion.eckankar, and misc.writing.

CONTENTS

LIST OF ILLUSTRATIONS

THE INITIATES

Helena Petrovna Blavatsky Russian occultist, world traveler, journalist, co-founder of the Theosophical Society, author of *Isis Unveiled, Caves and Jungles of Hindustan, The Secret Doctrine, The Voice of the Silence* and *The Key to Theosophy.*

Henry Steel Olcott American Theosophist, president-founder of the Theosophical Society, retired Army colonel, champion of world-wide Buddhist revival.

S. Ramabadra Ramaswamier Hindu disciple of Blavatsky who followed her to Darjeeling and beyond on a crucial 1882 journey.

Keshava Pillai South Indian *chela* of Mahatmas Morya and Koot Hoomi, also involved in HPB's journey to Darjeeling.

Mohini Chatterji Bengali intellectual, lawyer, Theosophical propagandist in Europe and India.

William T. Brown Scottish Theosophist who accompanied Olcott and Damodar on their 1883 pilgrimage to Lahore and Jammu.

Babaji South Indian Theosophist with multiple aliases, alleged to be a disciple of Mahatma Koot Hoomi.

Godolphin Mitford English eccentric who joined the TS while employed by the native state of Bhaunagar; "Mirza Moorad Ali Beg."

Damodar Mavalankar Maratha Brahmin youth who renounced caste and family for Theosophy and later vanished en route to Tibet.

Prince Harisinghji Rupsinghji Gujerati Theosophical leader in correspondence with Mahatma Koot Hoomi.

T. Subba Row Vedanta scholar, young Madras lawyer, alleged disciple of the Master Morya.

Norendro Nath Sen Bengali editor, president of the Calcutta branch TS.

Rai Saligram Guru of a Radhasoami sect, discussed in the *Mahatma Letters* as an acquaintance of A. P. Sinnett.

Alfred Percy Sinnett English author of *The Occult World* and *Esoteric Buddhism*, editor of the Allahabad *Pioneer*, primary recipient of letters from Koot Hoomi and Morya, later vice-president of the TS.

Allan Octavian Hume Retired Anglo-Indian civil servant, founder of the Indian National Congress, correspondent of the Theosophical Masters.

Muhammad ʿAbduh Jamal ad-Din's preeminent disciple, Grand Mufti of Egypt after his return from political exile.

Adib Ishaq Syrian Christian journalist, political reformer, linked with Jamal ad-Din in Cairo.

Ernest Renan French Orientalist and author, opponent of dogmatic Christianity, associated with Jamal ad-Din in Paris.

Wilfrid Scawen Blunt English explorer, poet, politician, Muslim convert, allied with Jamal ad-Din for many years.

Henri Rochefort French journalist, revolutionary, supporter of Jamal ad-Din.

Edward Granville Browne English scholar of Persian literature and history, associate of Afghani supporters as well as Babi and Bahaʾi leaders.

ʿAbduʾl Baha Persian Bahaʾi leader, for many years a political prisoner, later linked with Theosophists during travels in the West.

Anagarika Dharmapala Sinhalese champion of Buddhist revival, founder of the Maha-Bodhi Society.

Esper Ukhtomskii Russian prince, explorer, Buddhist convert, admirer of Blavatsky and Olcott.

Agvan Dorzhiev Buryat Mongol tutor of the 13th Dalai Lama, allied with Russian interests.

George I. Gurdjieff Greek/Armenian magus, world traveler, teacher of "Fourth Way" philosophy and practice.

Peter Demian Ouspensky Russian author of *In Search of the Miraculous*, chief chronicler of Gurdjieff.

Lady Hester Stanhope English noblewoman, student of Middle Eastern occult lore, resident in Lebanon.

Isabelle Eberhardt Russian/Swiss travel writer, Muslim convert, initiate of Algerian Sufis.

Alexandra David-Neel French explorer and Orientalist, the first Western scholar to penetrate Lhasa in Tibetan disguise.

Alice Cleather English disciple of Blavatsky's "Inner Group," later initiated into Tibetan Buddhism.

Annie Besant Second president of the Theosophical Society, leader of Indian political reform, adoptive mother of J. Krishnamurti.

ACKNOWLEDGMENTS

The emergence of the Theosophical History Centre in London in 1985 was crucial to the writing of this book. Its founder Leslie Price encouraged my investigation of Gurdjieff's links to Theosophy and Sufism, and published the resulting monograph. In 1989 the Centre became the Theosophical History Foundation, directed by James A. Santucci of California State University—Fullerton. He published my preliminary investigation of Theosophical connections to Bahaʾi history in 1992 in the journal *Theosophical History.*

Part One was enhanced greatly by materials provided by Michael Gomes and critiques of my previous work made by Daniel Caldwell. David Christopher Lane reviewed the entire manuscript with particular attention to the portion on Radhasoami. Part Two draws upon criticisms and suggestions made by several Bahaʾi historians. Christopher Buck, Juan R. I. Cole, Michael McCarron, Brent Poirier, and Robert H. Stockman each read the entire section and made several corrections and suggestions. Richard Hollinger and Robert H. Stockman provided helpful source material. Part Three follows leads suggested by Joscelyn Godwin and Jeffrey Somers, and draws upon material provided by Michael Gomes. Part Four relies in part on research conducted in France, which was facilitated by the officials of the Paris headquarters of the Theosophical Society. Jerry Hejka-Ekins provided advice and citations related to the Judge case, treated in Part Four. Brenda Fincher assisted in proofreading.

I thank Cornell University Press for permission to quote passages from Abbas Amanat's *Resurrection and Renewal* (1989). The illustration of the 1884 TS convention was provided by Elisabeth Trumpler of the Olcott Library in Wheaton, Illinois, and Steve Schweizer of the Audio-visual Department of the Theosophical Society in America, under the direction of John Algeo, President.

Libraries consulted in the United States include Cabell Library at Virginia Commonwealth University; Davis Library at the University of North Carolina; Halifax County/South Boston Regional Library, Meherrin Regional Library, Old Dominion University

Library, Perkins Library at Duke University, and the Walter Cecil Rawls Library & Museum. In India: the Adyar Library and Research Centre, the Asiatic Society Library in Bombay, the Nehru Library in New Delhi, and the Jammu & Kashmir State Archives. In France: the Bibliothèque Nationale, the Paris Préfecture of Police, the Theosophical Society's library, and the Archives d'Outre-Mer in Aix-en-Provence.

I thank everyone involved with the book at SUNY Press for their kindness and professionalism.

Prologue: Initiation in Theosophical History

Helena Petrovna Blavatsky is proclaimed by her disciples as the greatest occult initiate in the history of Western civilization. What do Theosophists mean by this claim? Her posthumously published *Theosophical Glossary* provides this definition of "initiate":

> The designation of anyone who was received into and had revealed to him the mysteries and secrets of either Masonry or Occultism. In times of antiquity, those who had been initiated into the arcane knowledge taught by the Hierophants of the Mysteries; and in our modern days those who have been initiated by the adepts of mystic lore into the mysterious knowledge, which, notwithstanding the lapse of ages, has yet a few real votaries on earth.[1]

Blavatsky's life was devoted to a search for these "adepts of mystic lore," beginning in her childhood in Russia. In the home of her grandparents she encountered the occult library of her maternal great-grandfather, Prince Pavel Dolgorukii, a prominent Rosicrucian Freemason in the years before Catherine II closed the lodges. In her adolescence, she admired Prince Aleksandr Golitsyn, a magician and Freemason who encouraged her growing interest in esotericism. After fleeing her 42-year-old husband Nikolai at the age of eighteen, HPB went to Istanbul and then to Cairo, where she met Paolos Metamon, a Coptic occultist with whom she was mysteriously linked for twenty years. Around the same time, she met Albert Rawson, an American artist, author, and explorer, with whom she traveled widely in the Near East, Europe, and America. Rawson, an Orientalist and leader in Egyptian Masonry, later joined the Theosophical Society in New York. HPB spent much of her thirties in the company of Agardi Metrovitch, a Hungarian opera singer and member of the radical Carbonari. Metrovitch was a disciple of Giuseppe Mazzini, prophet of Italian nationalism, with whom HPB was associated in the 1850s in London. Although she visited India around 1856 and again in 1869, her acquaintance with spiritual teachers during this period remains undocumented. In the early 1870s, she went to Cairo, where she was associated with a group she would later call the Brotherhood of Luxor. Most eminent among these mentors was Jamal ad-Din "al-Afghani," an Iranian political organiser, religious reformer, and leader of subversive movements throughout the Muslim world, whose travels paralleled those of HPB for thirty years. One of his closest colleagues was James Sanua, an Egyptian playwright and journalist of Italian-Jewish background, later exiled to Paris, where he spent most of his life. For many years, Sanua maintained close ties with Lydia Pashkov, a Russian travel writer and friend of Blavatsky, who accompanied her on a long Syrian journey in 1872. An important secret sponsor of Blavatsky's later career was Raphael Borg, a British diplomat in Egypt, who had recruited Afghani and Sanua as members of a Cairo Masonic lodge.

After HPB went to New York in 1873, she was visited there by Pashkov, and also by a Cypriot magician who called himself "Ooton Liatto" and who seems to be the inspiration for her references to "the Master Hilarion." Almost immediately upon her arrival in New York, Blavatsky set out to make a name among Spiritualists. She met Henry Steel Olcott at a series of seances in Chittenden, Vermont, conducted by William and Horatio Eddy, noted for their materialization phenomena. Olcott, captivated by her talk of distant lands and occult secrets, soon fell completely under her spell. Assuring him that she was the agent of a secret brotherhood of initiates, Blavatsky transmitted letters to Olcott from various adepts beginning in the summer of 1875. The first, from Tuitit Bey of the Brotherhood of Luxor, opens:

> Brother Neophyte, we greet thee.
>
> He who seeks us finds *us.* TRY. Rest thy mind—banish all foul doubt. We keep watch over our faithful soldiers. Sister Helen is a valiant trustworthy servant. Open thy spirit to conviction, have faith and she will lead thee to the Golden Gate of truth.[2]

Within a few months, Olcott and Blavatsky founded the Theosophical Society, whose other cofounders included Charles Sotheran, an English immigrant to New York who was a noted journalist and

Socialist. Sotheran was also a prominent Mason and Rosicrucian, associated with Rawson in several secret societies.

Soon after the establishment of the Theosophical Society, Blavatsky and Olcott were visited by James Peebles, an American Spiritualist traveling lecturer who had recently returned from India and Ceylon. He introduced them to leaders of the Indian reform group the Arya Samaj, and of Sinhalese Buddhism, both of which were crucial to the Theosophists' decision to move to Bombay at the end of 1878. Blavatsky and Olcott arrived in India regarding the leader and founder of the Arya Samaj, Swami Dayananda Sarasvati, as a Master of the Great White Brotherhood. In their first year in India, Blavatsky began to write for Mikhail Katkov, a Moscow newspaper editor. Katkov was also a political conspirator, who encouraged a Russian attack on British India.

The central figure in Blavatsky's *Caves and Jungles of Hindustan,* a travel book published serially by Katkov, is "Gulab-Singh," a Hindu ruler who seems modeled on Maharaja Ranbir Singh of Kashmir. Ranbir appears under his own name in another series of Russian articles by Blavatsky entitled *The Durbar in Lahore.* Substantial evidence suggests that "Master Morya" of Theosophical tradition may be a fictionalization of the maharaja; conflicting elements of the Morya persona seem to be derived from Thakur Daji Raja of Wadhwan. Another character in *Caves and Jungles* is "Ram-Ranjit Das," a Sikh official at the Golden Temple in Amritsar. The same figure appears in later Theosophical literature as the Master "Koot Hoomi Lal Singh." His most persuasive historical analogue appears to be Sirdar Thakar Singh Sandhanwalia, founder of the Singh Sabha, a Punjabi Sikh reform organization allied with the Theosophical Society. The Singh Sabha's co-founder, Bhai Gurmukh Singh, was a leading Sikh intellectual with documented Theosophical associations. His colleague Sirdar Dayal Singh Majithia, a philanthropist, journalist, and political leader, might be the basis for Blavatsky's references to a Master "Djual Kul" associated with Morya and Koot Hoomi.

In 1885, Blavatsky left India forever, following the investigation of her alleged psychic phenomena by Richard Hodgson, sponsored by the Society for Psychical Research. Hodgson concluded that all of Blavatsky's phenomena were fraudulent and her Masters nonexistent. In a series of letters allegedly written by Morya and Koot Hoomi to the Englishmen A. P. Sinnett and A. O. Hume, they portrayed themselves as residents of Tibet who frequently traveled in North India. After her departure from India, Blavatsky lived briefly in Italy, Germany, and Belgium, before settling in

London in 1887. Before her death there in 1891, she completed three books that established her reputation as the most comprehensive occult writer of her time: *The Secret Doctrine, The Key to Theosophy,* and *The Voice of the Silence.* The latter, as well as some material left unpublished at her death, revealed HPB's familiarity with Tibetan Buddhism. Olcott's close friendship with the Bengali explorer Sarat Chandra Das, who had penetrated Tibet in the early 1880s and returned with more than two hundred manuscripts, seems to have provided HPB with abundant source material for her later writings.

This summarizes the major conclusions about Blavatsky's Masters presented in *The Masters Revealed,* of which the present work is a sequel. The questions pursued in that book are, "Who were the Theosophical Masters, and in what sense was Blavatsky their agent?" In the present series of investigations, the focus is on the disciples of these adepts. How were they influenced by their relations with the Masters, and what cultural impact did they have in the role of occult initiates?

At the outset, it may be helpful to explore the nature of Blavatsky's status as an initiate, and the historical consequences of its ambiguity. Of the many traditions with which she became familiar, only a few give evidence of formal initiation. The Masonic Rite of Memphis, which claimed many of HPB's mentors as members, formally granted her a diploma through its Rite of Adoption. This was arranged through Charles Sotheran and John Yarker. According to Albert Rawson, both he and HPB were initiated into the secret teachings of the Druze, an offshoot of Isma^{c}ili Shi^{c}ism. In 1880, Blavatsky and Olcott were formally admitted to Sinhalese Theravada Buddhism in the pansil ceremony, performed at a large public gathering in Kandy. It is likely that in the 1850s she was a formal member of a Carbonari secret organization, Mazzini's *Jeune Europe.* Apart from these examples, it is difficult to identify points in HPB's life at which she was formally accepted as a member of any religious or occult tradition. The traditions most highly praised in her writings are the Kabbalah, the Vedanta, and Mahayana Buddhism. While it is possible to identify Master figures from whom she derived information on these subjects, her relationships with them seem to have been informal and usually secret. The synthesis presented in Blavatsky's writings as *the* ancient occult tradition was in fact her own understanding of materials gathered from diverse sources. By insisting on her role as *the* agent of *the* Masters who were guardians of *the* occult tradition, HPB mythologized herself. In fact, she was occasionally *an* agent of *some* Masters who often did not know one another and whose common denominator was acquaintance with her. To René Guénon and his Traditionalist followers, this makes Blavatsky a fraud and Theosophy a counter-initiatory snare. According to Seyyed Hossein Nasr, the "whole message" of Guénon, one of HPB's most vociferous critics, is "in fact based upon not only the theoretical grasp of tradition but the necessity of living within an orthodox, traditional way, without which no metaphysical truth can possess efficacy . . . There is for him no spiritual realization possible outside tradition and orthodoxy."[3]

Mircea Eliade defines initiation more usefully as "a body of rites and oral teachings whose purpose is to produce a radical modification of the religious and social status of the person to be initiated."[4] He distinguishes three types of initiation, two of which apply to Blavatsky and her successors. The most common initiations are rites of passage required of all members of a society at given points in the life cycle. The other categories are rites of entry into secret societies, and personal ecstatic experiences that occur "in connection with a mystical vocation."[5] Themes common to all three types are isolation, death and rebirth, and learning secret teachings. What is distinctive (and from Guénon's perspective disqualifying) about the initiations of HPB and her successors is that the secret societies involved were often recently created groups with political agendas, and that mystical vocations were intertwined with political ones. Sometimes the groups were ad hoc and short-lived. While not all the experiences described in this book may be initiatory according to textbook definitions, they did involve learning secrets that led to transformations of social and religious identity.

The initiations experienced by Blavatsky were rarely traditional or orthodox, yet she managed to acquire as spiritual mentors many of the most important figures of her time. Swami Dayananda, Jamal ad-Din, and Thakar Singh were the most influential late-nineteenth century reformers of Hinduism, Islam, and Sikhism respectively. That her relationships with these and other Master figures were temporary is not acknowledged by her self-portrayal as the lifelong pupil of a single Master teaching a single tradition. But her status as an *occult* initiate implies that her relationships with her Masters were wrapped in secrecy. Theosophy and its offshoots still suffer the consequences of HPB's secrecy and disinformation. Nonetheless, a genuine and unprecedented spiritual transmission occurred between East and West through the efforts of Blavatsky and her Masters.

The question of authority in the Theosophical Society has always been confused by contradictory claims. On one hand, the

Masters' wisdom is allegedly eternal and authoritative, and their orders, while not infallible, are regarded with religious awe. On the other hand, Theosophical literature is filled with assertions of the autonomy of individual conscience, and denials that spiritual authority can exist apart from each individual's higher self. This made the positions of Blavatsky and Olcott particularly anomalous. Their personal acquaintance with the Masters gave them, especially HPB, a derivative authority and charisma. In HPB's case, her own charisma, based on psychic phenomena, was a large drawing card for the early Theosophical Society. Yet their vows of secrecy prevented them from giving proof of their claims about the adepts, which led to continual resentment and rebellion among impatient members, and disbelief among outsiders.

Conflicts over the authority of the Masters and their disciples arose during HPB's lifetime, particularly between her and Olcott. After she left India in 1885, Olcott no longer felt indebted to her for his contacts with the Masters; indeed, he, rather than HPB, was to enjoy many more years of association with numerous Asian religious teachers. After her return to Europe, HPB was disdainful of Olcott's presidential authority, and resentful of his diminished respect for her. She blamed him for the debacle of the SPR investigation, and he blamed her with reciprocal vehemence. When she created an Esoteric Section in 1888, Olcott's resistance was so great that he threatened to resign, something he would do again in 1890 to force HPB to relent in her demands. Bruce Campbell, in *Ancient Wisdom Revived,* attributes their strained relations to the conflict between charismatic authority and authority of office.[6] Olcott, although a better orator, was by no means HPB's intellectual equal. The combination of her erudition and her charisma enabled her to overcome every challenge from Olcott and others, and by the time of her death, HPB was viewed by her disciples in even more exalted terms than before her denunciation by Hodgson.

After HPB's death, the Esoteric Section (soon renamed the Eastern School of Theosophy) was to become a fertile source of personality conflicts. First, Annie Besant and William Q. Judge, whom HPB had appointed as co-heads of the EST, joined forces against Olcott and succeeded in obtaining his resignation. Rumors circulated to the effect that the discovery of Olcott's sexual liaisons was used to induce the resignation, which was soon withdrawn, allegedly on orders of the Masters. But part of Judge's hold on Besant was the Mahatma letters he was writing to her under the alleged inspiration of M and KH. They warned her not to go to

India, as Olcott was allegedly plotting to harm her.[7] Besant eventually rejected Judge as a mentor, and complained to Olcott that she had been deceived by phony Mahatma letters. This led to an abortive attempt to demand Judge's resignation as vice-president of the TS, which collapsed when he defended himself by pointing out that the society had no official position on the Masters' existence, and thus could not proceed in its case against him.

Although the impasse left the anti-Judge forces in disarray, within a year the break became an open schism when Judge and Besant expelled each other as Outer Heads of the EST. In 1895, Judge's American Section of the TS declared autonomy, with only a small remnant remaining loyal to Adyar. Lodges in many other countries followed suit. After Judge died in 1896, his closest disciples turned to Katherine Tingley as his successor. In 1897, she led a crusade around the world, challenging Annie Besant for preeminence as a Theosophical orator. While in the Darjeeling area, she slipped away from her companions and returned with a story of having met Master M on the side of a mountain. This succeeded in endowing her with initiatory charisma, and in early 1898 she transformed her organization into the "Universal Brotherhood and Theosophical Society," in which she had near-dictatorial powers. Tingley was succeeded as Leader in 1929 by Gottfried de Purucker, a scholar and linguist whose presentation of Theosophy was far more intellectually oriented. Purucker claimed astral visits from the Masters M and KH shortly after his succession, but was more discreet thereafter. His comments about initiation were less dramatic than those being made in other quarters at the time: "Initiation is always self-conferred, and all the teacher does is to point the way, and the pitfalls, and give the warnings and sometimes to give the magic touch of that which will free the stumbling block in the mind of the querent."[8] After his death and the move from Point Loma to the Los Angeles area, the Judge/Tingley/Purucker TS closed its Esoteric Section in 1950.

A third major Theosophical group was led by Robert Crosbie, who had been expelled from Point Loma by Tingley in 1904. Crosbie's United Lodge of Theosophists appealed to disaffected members of the Adyar and Point Loma groups, offering an impersonal approach to Theosophy. Proclaiming itself free of "constitution, by-laws, or officers," the ULT preserved Theosophy as taught by Blavatsky and Judge, rejecting all claims and counterclaims about the Masters. But it, too, was subject to sectarian division, as in the 1930s, Crosbie's widow and a group of disaffected members sued the leadership in an unsuccessful attempt to take over the organization. The ULT had its own esoteric section, but its existence has been a closely guarded secret.

Another group that broke from the Judge/Tingley TS is the Temple of the People, founded in 1898 in Syracuse, New York, by Francia LaDue and William H. Dower. The Temple, which published messages from the Masters channeled by LaDue and Dower, moved in 1903 to Halcyon, California. There it built a spiritual community that remains the headquarters of the international Temple organization.

In 1907, Olcott died after nominating Annie Besant as his successor. Although she was elected by a huge majority, a number of prominent Theosophists were already repelled by her relationship with Charles W. Leadbeater, who had been accused of sexual abuse by two pubescent boys. When two Besant supporters testified to apparitions of the Masters at Olcott's deathbed, during which they allegedly appointed Besant as successor, such stalwarts of the society as G. R. S. Mead and A. P. Sinnett resigned in protest. Sinnett, however, was later to return and serve as international vice-president in his final years.

Throughout Besant's presidency, her beliefs and activities were dominated by Leadbeater's influence. With her encouragement, he elaborated the Theosophical teachings about the Masters so freely as to virtually obliterate memory of the human "adept brothers" portrayed by Blavatsky. Leadbeater's Masters are a schematized hierarchy of superhuman cosmic personalities with titles and formal job descriptions, as explained by his biographer Gregory Tillett:

> The seven Masters principally concerned with the government of the world on the inner planes exist on the level of the Sixth Initiation, the Chohan initiation; but above them stand the three principal Officers in the administration of the world from an occult point of view, the Mahachohan, the Bodhisattva and the Manu. These are on the level of the Seventh Initiation. The Eighth is that of the Buddha, above whom comes the Lord of the World. At the very top of the Occult bureaucracy stands the Trinity of the Logos of our solar system . . . [9]

Leadbeater's fertile imagination had taken every possibility inherent in HPB's Theosophy and twisted it into an ecclesiastical model of the universe. As a former curate, he was soon to fulfill his lost possibilities by becoming a bishop in the Liberal Catholic Church, which Theosophists dominated after 1916. Leadbeater, future TS President George Arundale, and James Wedgwood were leading bishops in the Church, which was only one of many spinoffs competing for Theosophists' attention during Besant's presidency. The greatest propaganda success in the history of the Theosophical movement was Leadbeater's brainstorm, the boy-Messiahship of Jiddu Krishnamurti. In 1909, Leadbeater recognized around the young son of a TS staff member the luminous aura which proved him to be a vehicle of some great Master. Annie Besant had apparently been waiting for just such an event. On 31 December 1908, she announced in a lecture at Madras that the Bodhisattva would soon take possession of a human agent:

> Among the mightiest of the hierarchy is His place, Teacher and Guide, whom even the Masters call their ROCK OF AGES. High above Them, They bow before Him, and yet he will deign once more to tread our mortal ways.[10]

For twenty years, Krishnamurti was promoted around the world by Mrs. Besant, his adoptive mother, as the savior of human civilization. The most febrile period of the Krishnamurti craze came in 1925 when Arundale and Wedgwood had revelations from the Masters during a TS Summer camp in the Netherlands. Leadbeater was far away in Australia and unable to interfere with the freelance clairvoyance. Mrs. Besant, who was at the camp, was prevailed upon to announce to the large gathering that she, Leadbeater, C. J. Jinarajadasa, Wedgwood, and several other TS worthies had been selected to serve as the twelve apostles to Krishnamurti's Jesus. Leadbeater was furious at the unauthorized revelations, and the ever trusting Mrs. Besant was dismayed and confused. Krishnamurti, characteristically, was torn between love for Mrs. Besant and disgust with Arundale and Wedgwood. Despite the internal disarray of the TS, it reached its peak membership of 45,000 by 1928. In 1929, publicly rejecting the phantasmagoria that had surrounded him, Krishnamurti disbanded the Order of the Star in the East, which had been created to welcome his coming. He explained his reasons to a large audience on 3 August:

> I maintain that Truth is a pathless land, and you cannot approach it by any path whatsoever, by any religion, by any sect . . . I do not want followers, and I mean this. The moment you follow someone you cease to follow Truth . . . You can form other organizations and expect someone else.[11]

The Adyar TS in the fifty years after the deaths of Besant and Leadbeater lived to some extent in the shadow of Krishnamurti, who became immensely popular in India and the West. Public proclamations of occult initiation ended in the TS with the deaths of Besant and Leadbeater, but Theosophy's reputation has yet to recover from their excesses, of which Krishnamurti was a constant reminder. Within Theosophical ranks, the subject of Masters and initiations evokes considerable ambivalence and disagreement.

Ambivalence about claims to initiatory status and authority was a prominent feature of the movement surrounding Krishnamurti. Although he disclaimed the title of World Teacher, he never discouraged his followers from treating him as a great guru, and took for granted the benefits of such an exalted position. An insider's account of his later life is provided by Radha Rajagopal Sloss in *Lives in the Shadow with J. Krishnamurti.* Sloss, daughter of the couple most closely associated with Krishnamurti after his defection from Theosophy, reveals that her mother carried on an adulterous relationship with him which they concealed from her husband for many years. All this was occurring while Desikacharya Rajagopal was acting as Krishnamurti's business manager and general factotum, living a celibate life which he believed to be in accord with his guru's teachings. When, after twenty years, the true state of affairs was revealed, Rajagopal remained in his position but was permanently embittered and disillusioned. His wife Rosalind continued her secret affair with Krishnamurti even after admitting the betrayal and assuring her husband it had ended. Several years later, Krishnamurti became involved with an Indian woman, and the affair with Rosalind came to an end. Subsequently both Rajagopals were estranged from Krishnamurti, which was exacerbated by a series of lawsuits against them that ended only after the death of Krishnamurti.

Although he explicitly rejected belief in Masters and world teachers, there was an undercurrent among his disciples of conviction that he was in fact the exalted being Leadbeater had proclaimed him to be, and only denied it out of modesty. This allowed loyal Theosophists to be Krishnamurti disciples, reconciling the apparent contradiction by a distinction between his exoteric statements and the esoteric reality of his messianic status. The meaning of Krishnamurti's role has received little overt attention from Theosophical writers, leaving the movement in ambiguity and confusion over an issue absolutely central to its twentieth century history.

The relationship between Krishnamurti and the TS came full circle with the election of his disciple Radha Burnier as president of the society in 1980. Pupul Jayakar's biography of Krishnamurti reveals that in November 1979, Burnier was undecided about running for the office, which had been vacated by the recent death of John B. S. Coats. At breakfast on the morning of the 28th, Krishnamurti asked Burnier if she planned to run, and seemed disturbed when she replied that she was undecided:

> He said, "What do you mean by you do not know?"
>
> Suddenly, the atmosphere grew charged with a new energy. Krishnaji said, "Mrs. Besant intended the land at Adyar to be meant for the teaching [of Krishnamurti]. The Theosophical Society has failed, the original purpose is destroyed." He spoke of the true religious spirit that probed, questioned and negated . . . "Can we do something about it?" he asked.[12]

At Krishnamurti's urging, Burnier decided to run for the presidency, which she won easily. In November 1980, a half-century of estrangement came to an end with his first return to the TS Headquarters since Mrs. Besant's death. Accompanied by Jayakar and Burnier, Krishnamurti was welcomed at the gate with garlands of pink roses. Together, he and Burnier walked through the grounds to the beach where he had been discovered by Leadbeater. Throughout his stay in Madras, he visited the TS daily.[13] Yet despite her frequent expressions of veneration for Krishnamurti, Burnier's presidency has not brought any marked change in TS attitudes about the Masters. Indeed, like Besant, she simultaneously serves as Outer Head of the Esoteric Section (renamed to its original title after the Judge secession), which Krishnamurti had advised Besant to close. The contemporary ES preserves Leadbeater's secret teachings and provides devout Theosophists with techniques for becoming disciples of the hierarchy of adepts. An article by Burnier in the January/February 1994 *American Theosophist* invokes the same Masters whom Krishnamurti had rejected:

> May Those who are the embodiments of Love immortal bless with their help and guidance this Society founded to be a channel for their work. May They inspire it with Their wisdom, strengthen it with Their power, and energize it with Their activity.[14]

Scholarly discussion of the Theosophical movement has been dominated by the assumption that Blavatsky invented her Masters. Theosophical writers have generally accepted HPB's claims with little scrutiny, and minimized subsequent conflicts over initiatory status. The present study is based on the conclusion, reached in *The Masters Revealed,* that the Theosophical Masters were historical persons who had been mythologized by HPB, but who in fact were her teachers and advisors. This raises the question of what other historical figures were genuine disciples of these Masters, and how historical reality compares with the initiatory legends of Theosophy and its offshoots. The following pages offer some tentative answers.

Part One examines evidence concerning the native Indian rulers and young disciples who became Theosophists in the 1880s. Primary sources provide extensive clues to the reasons for their rapid disaffection from the Society, despite their knowledge of the Masters behind the scenes. This section closes by comparing and contrasting Theosophy with other nineteenth-century Indian religious reform movements, in order to reveal the historical context in which the chelas were recruited.

Jamal ad-Din "al-Afghani" played the role of spiritual Master or political mentor to a varied international cast of characters. Part Two identifies the most significant of Afghani's disciples. The careers of Muhammad ʿAbduh, Wilfrid Scawen Blunt, and Edward Granville Browne are reviewed among examples of Afghani's influence. Afghani's complicated relationship with the Babi and Bahaʾi movements is explored, and the historical links between Bahaʾis and Theosophists are examined.

The question of successorship has provided continual conflict within the Theosophical movement. Yet it may be among Buddhists rather than Theosophists that the most effective successors to HPB can be found. In Part Three, Theosophy's relationship to the revival of Buddhism is reviewed, with special emphasis on the careers of Anagarika Dharmapala and Esper Ukhtomskii. A new occult movement, often called the Fourth Way, was established by George Ivanovitch Gurdjieff in the early twentieth century, based on sources linked to Blavatsky. The relationships between Theosophy and the Fourth Way are explored with emphasis on Gurdjieff's initiatory claims.

Part Four examines the careers of a series of European women who became pupils of Eastern spiritual teachers. Lady Hester Stanhope spent many years in Syria, awaiting the coming of the Mahdi. After HPB's death, Alexandra David-Neel was the most renowned Western woman to penetrate the secrets of Tibet. Her friend Mirra Alfassa became the quasi-divine consort of Sri Aurobindo in his Indian ashram. Isabelle Eberhardt, a convert to

Islam, showed great literary promise before her early death in a desert flood. Alice Cleather was a personal pupil of HPB who in later life traveled extensively in India, China, and Mongolia. Her quest for the Masters combined Buddhism and Theosophy in a way that has inspired Theosophists throughout the twentieth century. Part Four concludes with an examination of initiatory links between Annie Besant and Colonel Olcott.

In closing, it must be stressed that the present study is a selective investigation. The figures profiled in the following pages are by no means the only ones who might be nominated as initiates of the Theosophical Masters. When a linear model of initiatic succession is supplanted by an inductive approach based on historical evidence, possible "successors" appear in multitudes. Several avenues of inquiry have been deemed outside the scope of this investigation, although they merit further examination. The Rites of Memphis and Mizraim, the Hermetic Brotherhood of Luxor, and the Societas Rosicruciana in America all survive to the present, and can be considered successors to the work of HPB and some of her Masters. Franz Hartmann provides a link between Theosophy and the Ordo Templi Orientis, while both he and John Yarker were linked to the TS and to neo-Rosicrucian groups. HPB's friend Wynn Westcott was a central figure in the Hermetic Order of the Golden Dawn. Through such figures, much of the Western magical revival, with its "Secret Chiefs," can be seen as deriving in part from the Theosophical impetus. These developments, however, are excluded from consideration here for two reasons. There is already a substantial body of literature placing HPB in the context of Western esotericism, most recently including Joscelyn Godwin's *The Theosophical Enlightenment* and Antoine Faivre's *Access to Western Esotericism.* Also, these post-Blavatskian developments in Western esoteric movements are relatively peripheral to Theosophical history, although important in their own right.

Some readers may be surprised by the omission of many claimants to paranormal communication with the Theosophical Masters. Morya and Koot Hoomi have been cited as sources by several "channelers," among whom Elizabeth Clare Prophet is today best known. Prophet, whose alleged sources include many figures outside the Theosophical pantheon, derives much of her inspiration from the "I Am" movement. Founded in the 1930s by Guy and Edna Ballard, the "I Am" teachings emphasized transmission from the Master St. Germain. In subsequent decades, HPB's Master Hilarion was channeled by Canadian medium Maurice Cooke. Helena Roerich, wife of the artist Nicholas, wrote a series of "Agni

Yoga" books based on alleged transmissions from Morya. Most prolific among such channelers was Alice Bailey, who produced a huge volume of teachings from "the Tibetan," Djual Kul (who is identified in *The Masters Revealed* as Punjabi rather than Tibetan). The English composer Cyril Scott believed himself for many years in paranormal contact with the Master Koot Hoomi. But no such alleged pupils of Theosophical Masters appear in the following pages, because their initiations are inaccessible to historical investigation. A crucial criterion for inclusion is historical evidence of contact with Theosophical Masters; claims of paranormal contact alone are insufficient.

One might argue that the disciples of Swami Dayananda who guided the Arya Samaj after his death, or leaders of the Singh Sabha in the twentieth century, or the sons and successors of the Theosophical maharajas should fall within the scope of this work. But what would be missing from such a criterion of inclusion are the crucial elements of pilgrimage and cultural marginality. The emphasis here is on those initiates whose quests for the Masters involved them in extensive travels which transformed their religious and social identities. What was new and unique about the TS was its role in cross-fertilizing Western and Eastern spirituality. Even the Indian chelas profiled in Part One were in quest of symbolic contact with other cultures. Disciples from southern, western, and eastern India all converged upon the northern frontier of their country seeking Masters who were closely identified with the Himalayas and Tibet, yet whose chief mouthpiece was a Russian. Although M was a Rajput and KH Punjabi, their leading Theosophical chelas were Bengali, Maratha, and Tamil. The charisma of Jamal ad-Din "al-Afghani" attracted disciples from around the world, all of whom regarded him as a source of exotic secret lore. Followers from Egypt, Syria, England, and France extolled the Persian sage for his role in changing their lives. Bahaʾi became a fully international faith within decades of its birth in Iran, and Theosophy played a hitherto unsuspected part in this accomplishment. The initiates in Parts Three and Four were all globetrotters who sought to transform themselves by plunging into foreign cultures. Olcott and Dharmapala played complementary roles in the dissemination of Buddhism in the West, each becoming an agent of international cooperation to that end. Esper Ukhtomskii, Alexandra David-Neel, George Gurdjieff, and Alice Cleather all penetrated the secret realms of Tibetan Buddhism and were transformed by the experience. Their journeys, like those of Isabelle Eberhardt and Mirra Alfassa, have evident links to HPB's previous pilgrimages.

In the weeks prior to the formation of the TS, Blavatsky wrote a passage in which she makes an explicit promise about the quest for spiritual enlightenment:

> One single journey to the Orient, made in the proper spirit, and the possible emergencies arising from the meeting of acquaintances and adventures of the traveller, may quite as likely as not throw wide open to the zealous student, the heretofore closed doors of the final mysteries. I will go farther and say that such a journey, performed with the omnipresent idea of the one object, and with the help of a fervent will, is sure to produce more rapid, better, and far more practical results, that the most diligent study of Occultism in books—even though one were to devote to it dozens of years.[15]

The initiatory journeys recorded in the following pages provide ample illustration of HPB's promise fulfilled.

Group of delegates to Convention of 1884 (Adyar). (L-R) Standing: Babaji, Gol. H. S. Olcott. Back row: Major-General H. R. Morgan; William T. Brown, T. Subba Row, HPB, Franz Hartmann, Rudolf Gebhard. Middle row: Norendro Nath Sen, Damodar Mavalankar, S. R. Ramaswamier, Judge P. S. Row. Front row: Bhavani Shankar, T. Vijayaraghavacharlu, Tukaram Tatya, V. C. Iyer. Courtesy of Theosophical Society Archives, Wheaton, IL.

PART ONE.

Patriotic Chelas

A key point of dispute between Theosophists and their opponents is the testimony of a handful of "chelas," disciples who claimed to have personal knowledge of the Masters' existence. Between 1880 and 1885, Damodar Mavalankar, T. Subba Row, "Babaji" Nath, Mohini Chatterji, Keshava Pillai, and S. Ramabadra Ramaswamier were all publicized as special pupils of the mysterious adepts. Several Europeans, including William T. Brown and Godolphin Mitford, as well as Colonel Olcott and Madame Blavatsky, were also in this select company. Despite the later defection of most of these witnesses, their testimony has been valued by Theosophists as evidence of the Masters' existence. On the other hand, critical writers have stressed their unreliability as witnesses. A closer look at these characters suggests political secrets behind the scenes of the society.

Hodgson's Mistake

The judgment of Richard Hodgson on HPB has stood unchallenged for most of the past century except by Theosophical true believers. Standard reference works have accepted his judgment of her as "neither . . . the mouthpiece of hidden seers, nor as a mere vulgar adventuress, [but] one of the most accomplished, ingenious, and interesting imposters in history."[1] The founder of the Theosophical History Centre, Leslie Price, published in 1985 an inquiry into the Hodgson report entitled *Madame Blavatsky Unveiled?* This was adapted from a lecture given to the Society for Psychical Research outlining the weaknesses of the case against HPB. In 1986, Vernon Harrison, a non-Theosophist expert in handwriting, published "J'Accuse," an analysis of the Hodgson Report, which draws attention to its weakest points. These are the veracity of HPB's accusers,

Alexis and Emma Coulomb, and the handwriting analysis of J. D. B. Gribble, who concluded that KH and HPB were the same person. In *Blavatsky and Her Teachers,* Jean Overton Fuller's linguistic analysis of incriminating letters produced by the Coulombs lends further weight to the evidence that they are forgeries. Future studies may probe more deeply into the paranormal phenomena discussed in the report, but progress is also being made in understanding the cultural bias inherent in Hodgson's approach. At the Fourth International Conference on Theosophical History in 1989, Joy Dixon, a graduate student at Rutgers University, presented a paper on the Hodgson report. She noted that Hodgson made racist assumptions leading to the dismissal of Indian witnesses. The confusion of technical and moral untrustworthiness is repeatedly made in the report. His bias, and that of the SPR leaders, was against HPB, due in part to her activities, which were totally in opposition to Victorian definitions of women's roles. In 1993, Dixon's studies were published as *Gender, Politics and Culture in the New Age: Theosophy in England, 1880–1935.* In light of the critiques which have emerged from these and other writers, it appears that Richard Hodgson's judgment on HPB will not be that of history.

Rather than questions of forgery and psychic phenomena, what make the Hodgson report relevant to the present study are its conclusions rejecting the reality of the Mahatmas and the reliability of various witnesses to their existence. While Hodgson's suspicion that HPB and the supposed chelas of the Masters were engaged in a massive fraud was understandable, it led him to two false conclusions: that the Masters were nonexistent, and that HPB's mission was to advance Russian interests. In both cases, he was profoundly mistaken. Evidence concerning the alleged "chelas" of the Mahatmas provides considerable proof that these Masters were real persons, and that Blavatsky's allegiance to them involved service to native Indian interests rather than to those of any foreign power.

Information about the Theosophical Society's relations with native Indian rulers and reformers makes it possible to understand the nature of Hodgson's mistake. It may be tempting to condemn Hodgson for his blindness, but the information available to him in the 1880s was so limited as to virtually insure that he reached false conclusions. Nevertheless, the shortcomings of his analysis are sometimes obvious. For example, Olcott's testimony is crucial to any investigation of the Masters, yet Hodgson began by rejecting Olcott as a witness because he had falsely denied knowing any

Hindus until HPB started making one appear phenomenally in New York. This obviously conflicts with his meeting of Moolji Thackersey and a Hindu friend on a transatlantic voyage in 1870, which Olcott later claimed that he had "momentarily forgotten." Moolji Thackersey is described by J. T. F. Jordens as "a wealthy mill-owner born in Kathiawar, [who] had visited England in the sixties and had played a prominent part in municipal politics, the widow-remarriage movement, and the crusade against the Vallabhacharya Maharajas . . . [who] strongly supported Dayananda right from the start."[2] Swami Dayananda Sarasvati was the leader of the Arya Samaj, a group with which the TS was allied when its founders decided to relocate in Bombay. Dayananda aimed to reform Hinduism and Indian society on the basis of his monotheistic interpretation of the Vedas. Olcott and Blavatsky had established correspondence with Thackersey after their Spiritualist friend James Peebles noticed a photograph of the wealthy Hindu that had been taking during the 1870 voyage. Peebles recognized Thackersey as someone he had met during his recent trip to India, and told HPB and Olcott about Thackersey's new guru, Dayananda. Correspondence with Thackersey led to acquaintance with Harischandra Chintamon and Shyamaji Krishnavarma, both leaders in the Arya Samaj. In the spring of 1878, less than a year before her arrival in Bombay, HPB wrote to Thackersey in reference to her hopes for the TS in India:

> Is our friend a Sikh? If so, the fact that he should be, as you say, "very much pleased to learn the object of our Society" is not at all strange. For his ancestors have for centuries been—until their efforts were paralysed by British domination, that curse of every land it fastens itself upon—battling for the divine truths against external theologies. My question may appear a foolish one—yet I have more than one reason for asking it. You call him a Sirdar—therefore he must be a descendant of one of the Sirdars of the twelve mizals, which were abolished by the English to suit their convenience—since he is of Amritsir *[sic]* in the Punjab?
>
> Are you personally acquainted with any descendant of Runjeet Singh, who died in 1839, or do you know of any who are? You will understand, without any explanation from me, how important it is for us to establish relations with some Sikhs, whose ancestors before them have been for centuries teaching the great 'Brotherhood of Humanity'—precisely the doctrine we teach.***

> As for the future "Fellows" of our Indian branch, have your eyes upon the chance of fishing out of the great ocean of Hindu hatred for Christian missionaries some of those big fish you call Rajahs, and-whales known as Maharajahs. Could you not hook out for your Bombay Branch either Gwalior (Scindia) or the Holkar of Indore—those most faithful and loyal friends of the British (?).[3]

This letter reveals several important facts about Blavatsky's political motivations. She is frankly hostile at this point to British rule of India, and seeks to ally her society with native rulers who share this feeling. Through Thackersey, she is developing an alliance with a Sikh Sirdar from Amritsar, who admires the objectives of the TS. Abundant evidence links this Amritsar Sirdar to the persona of Mahatma Koot Hoomi, who in *The Masters Revealed* is tentatively identified as Thakar Singh Sandhanwalia. This is relevant to HPB's search for a descendant of Ranjit (Runjeet) Singh, the Sikh maharaja who died in 1839. Thakar Singh was the cousin of Ranjit's son and successor Dalip Singh, who was deposed in early adolescence. The ex-maharaja converted to Christianity and lived as an English country squire, but Thakar was later instrumental in inducing Dalip's doomed attempt to regain his throne. At the time of Hodgson's investigation, Thakar was in London persuading his cousin to return to India. These facts suggest that Olcott's failure to mention Moolji to Hodgson may have been due to concern that it might lead to identification of some of the Theosophical adepts. Such suspicions did not occur to Hodgson, whose final conclusion on the President-Founder is:

> I cannot, therefore, regard Colonel Olcott's testimony as of any scientific value. In particular, his testimony to the alleged "astral" appearance in New York proves, in my opinion, no more than that he saw some one in his room, who may have been an ordinary Hindu, or some other person, disguised as a Mahatma for the purpose, and acting for Madame Blavatsky. And the same may be said for all of his testimony to apparitions of Mahatmas.[4]

Olcott had repeatedly testified to his normal contacts with Mahatmas as well to apparitions, which Hodgson failed to explain. The researcher began with a false distinction between Mahatmas and ordinary persons, derived from Theosophical literature. This led him to the false conclusion that the Masters did not exist. His mistakes were made possible in large part by the dubious veracity of many of the witnesses to the existence of the adept brotherhood.

Damodar Mavalankar was the Indian chela most explicitly accused of deception in Hodgson's report. Despite his youth, he had become manager of *The Theosophist* when it began publication in late 1879, soon after he joined the society. A wealthy Maratha Brahmin, Damodar renounced his caste, his family and his income in order to serve the cause of Theosophy. Damodar contributed many articles to *The Theosophist,* and introduced the use of the word *Mahatma* to describe the Theosophical adepts. He lived with Blavatsky and Olcott at the Bombay headquarters, and joined them on their December 1879 journey to North India.[5] It was on this trip that all three first met A. P. Sinnett and his wife Patience. Sinnett, editor of the Allahabad *Pioneer,* was Theosophy's most eminent Anglo-Indian convert. During an October 1880 visit to the Sinnetts in Simla, HPB performed an astounding series of paranormal phenomena which were reported in Sinnett's 1881 book *The Occult World.* During this visit, Sinnett received his first letters from the Master KH, beginning the correspondence for which both are best known. The overwhelming majority of his letters from the Mahatma were received in 1881 and 1882, and he wrote a second Theosophical book, *Esoteric Buddhism,* based on their teachings.

Second in rank among the Indian chelas was T. Subba Row, who met HPB and Olcott in April 1882, during their visit to Madras. Within the month, he became Corresponding Secretary of the newly-formed Madras branch of the TS. Subba Row was a Brahmin from the Coromandel coast north of Madras, and a promising young lawyer at the time of his encounter with Theosophy. He was undoubtedly the most intellectually capable among the Indian Theosophists, held in such high esteem by Blavatsky that she would later ask him to help her write *The Secret Doctrine.* He was an Advaita Vedantin, and thus a disciple of the same tradition as Maharaja Ranbir Singh.[6]

In May, the idea of moving the society's headquarters to Madras was first raised. That spring and summer, many omens indicated that North Indian links were weakening. Swami Dayananda first attacked the society publicly in March. In June, relations between Sinnett and his employer, Rattegan, began to worsen, leading to his eventual dismissal and return to England. Never again was the hand-picked recipient of Mahatma letters to be in a position of influence in Anglo-India.

By mid-1882, the Theosophical Society had made astounding progress in recruiting native rulers to its cause. Prior to its founders' arrival in India, they had secured the support of the maharajas of Kashmir and Indore. Sometime before the durbar in Lahore, in November 1880, the Sikh Maharaja Bikram Singh of Faridkot, patron of the Singh Sabha, had joined the ranks of TS sponsors. According to HPB's *The Durbar in Lahore,* Bikram Singh joined "Ram-Ranjit-Das" in welcoming the founders to the durbar, where they visited Ranbir Singh's encampment prior to the ceremonies. She described for her Russian readers an elaborate series of events culminating in the maharajas' exchange of gifts with the new Viceroy. At the conclusion of the durbar, Olcott proceeded to visit the Maharaja of Varanasi, whose motto, "There is no religion higher than Truth," was adopted by the TS. Neither Theosophical writers nor hostile biographers have paid adequate attention to the relationship between these maharajas and the TS founders. It seems incredible that two eccentric foreigners, without means or celebrity, could have gained entry into so many royal courts. Especially striking is the establishment of such sponsorship in advance of the founders' arrival in the country.

In June 1882, HPB and Olcott accepted an invitation from the Gaekwar of Baroda, visiting Daji Raja Chandra Singhji, Thakur of Wadhwan, *en route* back to Bombay. It was on this visit that Prince Harisinghji Rupsinghji, cousin of the Thakur, joined the TS at Daji Raja's home. Daji Raja was a Rajput prince whose early death ended a promising career. Wadhwan was fairly progressive and well-governed during his brief reign. His support for the TS was evidenced by his presidency of the Daji Raja Theosophical Society in Wadhwan, as well as by his attendance at annual meetings in Bombay.[7]

Pilgrimage to Darjeeling

In September 1882, a mysterious journey was undertaken by HPB. She departed from Bombay for Sikkim, passing through Varanasi, Calcutta, Chandernagar, and Cooch Behar. On 1 October, she wrote from Sikkim to her old friend Aleksandr Dondukov-Korsakov, military governor of the trans-Caucasian region. Her previous letters to Prince Dondukov-Korsakov were filled with exaggerations and falsehoods, for example claiming fifty thousand members of the TS when in fact there were fewer than one-tenth that number. In an outright fabrication, she claimed that a Sanskrit translation of *Isis Unveiled* had attained great literary success. Equally outrageous was her claim to have journeyed from New York in the early 1870s to Japan, to meet Master Morya. Yet despite their unreliability, these letters are valuable as evidence, often all that is available, for various aspects of HPB's life in India. Her contempt for her Theosophical disciples is repeatedly expressed, for example in her reference to "some fifty fools of all races, Hindus, Parsees, Mongolians and English, officials of the Society, on the way to attaining Nirvana and catching Parabrahm by the tail—at the foot of my personal pagoda."[8] Most intriguing is a partly fictional account of her travels dated 5 December 1881, which foreshadows her genuine journey the following year:

> Can you image *[sic]* it? These silly Englishmen began by spending enormous sums to run after the daughter of my father. The red-cheeked secret police with large yellow moustaches have followed me step by step for seven months, travelling about 5,000 kilometres by train, running after me from Bombay to the North of Hindustan in Rajputana, from there to Central India, then to the Punjab, Kashmir, and Darjeeling, where after seven months I left British territory and took leave of them with a thumb to my nose. They are not allowed to set foot on Tibetan territory and I went there *alone,* leaving the Hindus and Americans, my traveling companions, waiting for me at Darjeeling. I went to the monastery of my Lama friends, performing a pilgrimage "in worship of Buddha," as I wrote mockingly in the note I sent to the spy who had followed me. Returning after three weeks, I found my companions again and the spies who were waiting for my *dangerous* person.[9]

In fact, HPB's North Indian travels before the writing of this letter never took her anywhere near Darjeeling and certainly not beyond the frontier to a monastery. Nor were there any American travel companions. Yet within a year she was to actually make this journey, although its details remain unclear. In June 1882, she told the prince her intended itinerary:

> . . . I am going for two months to the North-West Province of India, then to Darjeeling, Bhutan, Assam, and much further into Tibet than the English are allowed to penetrate. Lamas from the Lamasery (monastery) of Tong-Douma will come to fetch me.[10]

Bhutan, Assam, and Tibet were no more than literary flourishes, but she did make it to Darjeeling in September. In her letter of 1

October, HPB gave Dondukov-Korsakov an elaborate description of her pilgrimage:

> As you see, my dear Prince, I am in the solitude of Ghum. And what is Ghum? It is a mountain in Sikkim and a monastery where Lamas live on their way to Tibet . . . no English are allowed to enter and I am *welcomed* . . . I went via Calcutta and Chandernagore to Cooch Bihar *[sic]* (the Rajah is a Theosophist) . . . A dozen Babu Theosophists from Calcutta accompanied me, together with three Buddhists from Ceylon and one from Burma . . . But instead of 15 people, only 5 followed me to Sikkim: the 4 Buddhists and one from Nepal—all the others were laid up . . . It was too late to go to Shigatse, the capital of the Tashi Lama, but I decided to go to the Lama Monastery, 4 days from Darjeeling . . . the chief Lama himself came and brought me tea with butter and all kinds of delicacies . . . he ordered me to be brought to his monastery . . . I remained there 3 days. I was only afraid they would not let me go away again. I lived in a small house at the foot of the walls of the monastery and I talked day and night with the monk Gylynjanic (also an *incarnation* of Sakya-Buddha) and I spent hours in their library where no woman is allowed to enter—touching testimony to my beauty and my perfect innocence—and the Superior publicly recognized in me one of the feminine incarnations of the Bodhisattva, of which I am very proud. I read to them a letter from Koot Hoomi in *The Occult World,* and the guides carried me back by another way to the bridge . . . and that is how I arrived in Sikkim where I find myself at present and where I am staying in another monastery, 23 miles from Darjeeling. Of course the English were very angry. I have heard long accounts of their wiles. They are doing their utmost to get into Tibet. They take boys, generally converts, teach them Tibetan, give them a Buddhist education and when they are ready, dress them up as Lamas, and give them a prayer wheel in which, instead of the prayer "Om mani padme hum," are hidden instruments. But not one of them was able to reach Lhasa, or even Shigatse . . . Then why did they let me pass? It is because I am an incarnation of Buddha.[11]

The compiler of the collection in which this letter appears notes that Ghum was in British India, not Sikkim, and that HPB was mistaken in claiming that no British spy had reached Lhasa or Shigatse. In fact, at that very moment Sarat Chandra Das, a Bengali explorer, and his companion Ugyen Gyatso, a lama from Sikkim, were in Shigatse preparing to return home to Darjeeling. The two were employed by the Bhutia Boarding School, which indeed trained young boys as future surveyors of Tibet. Considerable evidence links Das and Gyatso to the TS. Olcott was later on very cordial terms with Das, meeting him repeatedly in Darjeeling and supporting his Buddhist Text Society. On one of his trips to Darjeeling, Olcott was introduced to Gyatso by Das. Das, who returned from his year in Tibet with over two hundred sacred texts, appears to have supplied some of these to Blavatsky for use in her later writings, as suggested by internal evidence.

A peculiar event later in October 1882 suggests HPB's acquaintance with Das. For most of the rest of the month, she remained at Darjeeling, proceeding then to Allahabad, where she visited the Sinnetts, who were adrift after A.P.'s dismissal from editorship of *The Pioneer*. Just before HPB's arrival, Sinnett was visited by two chelas, "Darbhagiri Nath" and "Chandra Cusho." The visit of the two chelas is one of the more dubious missions carried out on behalf of the Mahatmas. Dressed in yellow robes, the two young Indians delivered letters from Master M, but were at a loss when Sinnett asked that they astrally transmit his latest letter to KH. Before departing, Babaji borrowed thirty rupees from Sinnett to replace the travel allowance he had lost *en route*. When KH returned the loan he called Babaji a "little wretch."[12] The use of parts of names of her genuine sponsors in her fictionalizations is a frequent feature of HPB's writings about the Masters. "Chandra Cusho" ("Cusho" being Tibetan for "Mister") seems to be a veiled allusion to Das.

S. Ramabadra Ramaswamier was a clerk from Tirunelveli in South India, on leave after a nervous breakdown. Following HPB on her travels, on October 5 he allegedly went from Darjeeling into Sikkim and penetrated twenty miles beyond the border, where he claimed to have met the Master M. Blavatsky's biographer Marion Meade interprets this as the hallucination of a madman, rather than a role played under direction of real Masters.[13] Ramaswamier's account is indeed inherently preposterous, but a closer look reveals it to have been inspired by HPB and her Masters. Published as extracts from a private letter to Damodar, Ramaswamier's tale begins:

> When we met last at Bombay I told you what had happened to me at Tinnevelly. My health having been disturbed by official

> work and worry, I applied for leave on a medical certificate, and it was duly granted. One day in September last, while I was reading in my room, I was ordered by the audible voice of my blessed Guru, M———Mararshi, to leave all and proceed immediately to Bombay, whence I was to go in search of Madame Blavatsky wherever I could find her, and follow her wherever she went. Without losing a moment, I closed up all my affairs and left the station. For the tones of that voice are to me the divinest sound in nature, its commands imperative. I travelled in my ascetic robes. Arrived at Bombay, I found Madame Blavatsky gone, and learned through you that she had left a few days before; that she was very ill; and that, beyond the fact that she had left the place very suddenly with a Chela, you knew nothing of her whereabouts. And now I must tell you what happened to me after I had left you.[14]

Ramaswamier continues his tale with the information that the mysterious voice directed him to Berhampur, where he attached himself to a party of Calcutta Theosophists, whose path he crossed entirely by accident. Their destination, after some discussion, becomes Darjeeling, where they plan to join HPB. They reach her at Chandernagar, after she has travelled into Sikkim to meet the Mahatmas. The entire party of Theosophists leaps onto the train with HPB, but they are mysteriously separated by a railway accident which is left unexplained. While all her pursuers were delayed by "accidents," Ramaswamier concludes, "It required no great stretch of imagination to conclude that Madame Blavatsky was perhaps, being again taken to the Mahatmas, who, for some good reasons best known to them, did not want us to be following and watching her. Two of the Mahatmas, I had learned for a certainty, were in the neighborhood of British territory; and one of them was seen and recognized by a person I need not name here, as a high Chutuktu of Tibet."[15] That the Masters are rarely even near British territory, much less actually in it, is the assumption conveyed to the reader. Ramaswamier's journey to Sikkim is a long, fanciful tale of a weak and fearful man, driven onward by his compulsion to find the Mahatma, encountering a leopard and wildcat *en route*, and supported by some "secret influence": "Fear of anxiety never once entered my mind. Perhaps in my heart there was room for no other feeling but an intense desire to find my Guru."[16]

As nightfall approached, Ramaswamier found a small hut, into which he was able to climb through an unlocked window. He was awakened from his sleep by men in the other room of the hut, who might have killed him if they thought him a burglar. Faith in the Master sustained him, and they left in the morning without disturbing him. The next morning, completely absorbed by his compulsion, he was almost oblivious to his surroundings when lo! in the distance, appeared a solitary horseman:

> From his tall stature and skill in horsemanship, I thought he was some military officer of the Sikkim Rajah. Now, I thought, I am caught! He will ask me for my pass and what business I have in the independent territory of Sikkim, and, perhaps, have me arrested and sent back, if not worse. But, as he approached me, he reined up. I looked at him and recognized him instantly . . . I was in the awful presence of him, of the same Mahatma, my own revered Guru, whom I had seen before in his astral body on the balcony of the Theosophical headquarters. It was he, the Himalayan Brother of the ever-memorable night of December last, who had so kindly dropped a letter in answer to the one I had given but an hour or so before in a sealed envelope to Madame Blavatsky, whom I had never lost sight of for one moment during the interval. The very same instant saw me prostrated on the ground at his feet. I arose at his command, and leisurely looking into his face, forgot myself entirely in the contemplation of the image I knew so well, having seen his portrait (the one in Colonel Olcott's possession) times out of number. I knew not what to say: joy and reverence tied my tongue. The majesty of his countenance, which seemed to me to be the impersonation of power and thought, held me rapt in awe. I was at last face to face with the Mahatma of the Himavat, and he was no myth, no "creation of the imagination of a medium," as some sceptics had suggested.
>
> His complexion is not as fair as that of Mahatma Kuthumi: but never have I seen a countenance so handsome, a stature so tall and so majestic. As in his portrait, he wears a short black beard, and long black hair hanging down to his breast: only his dress was different. Instead of a white, loose robe he wore a yellow mantle lined with fur, and on his head, instead of the turban, a yellow Tibetan felt cap, as I have seen some Bhutanese wear in this country.[17]

His only advice to the seeker was to wait patiently to become an accepted Chela. He promised that if HPB was allowed by the

Chohan (a chief among the Mahatmas) to visit Parijong the next year, then Ramaswamier could come along. When asked if an account of the meeting could be published, Morya urged his disciple to write it all in a letter to Damodar. After the Master returned from whence he came, the young Tamil returned to Darjeeling, where he arrived in complete exhaustion. HPB scolded him for his rashness, but she and the Bengali Theosophists pleaded with him to recount his story:

> They were all, to say the least, astounded. After all, she will not go this year to Tibet; for which I am sure she does not care, since she has seen our Masters and thus gained her only object. But we, unfortunate people! we lose our only chance of going and offering our worship to the Himalayan Brothers, who, I know, will not soon cross over to British territory, if ever, again.[18]

With this penultimate paragraph, the main goal of the letter is accomplished. The Masters of HPB are inhabitants of remote Tibet, whose Indian origins are far behind them. Although HPB and Olcott had repeatedly visited the northwestern and north central parts of India, attention was successfully diverted from any suspicion that the Mahatmas might reside in those regions. Ramaswamier concludes in a tone which reveals his awe of the superhuman Masters:

> And now that I have seen the Mahatma in the flesh, and heard his living voice, let no one dare say to me that the Brothers do not exist. Come now whatever will, death has no fear for me, nor the vengeance of enemies; for what I know, I know![19]

After Ramaswamier's death in 1893, one of his sons published the letters he received from the Masters, intending them as proof that his father had been deceived by HPB. The eloquence of Ramaswamier's report raises the question of how much of it HPB may have written for him. That an elaborate scheme of deception was indeed being engineered is apparent from these letters and those directed to Mohini Chatterji and R. Keshava (Casava) Pillai, which suggest a conspiracy to prove the Masters' existence.

Ramaswamier's first letter from the Master M was a very brief note, consisting of greetings, acceptance as a chela, the information that "Upasika has all the instructions" and the advice that the new chela follow those instructions. This was received in September 1881 in Bombay.[20] The following September, KH wrote to Ramaswamier telling the chela that he could not go to Tibet until earning the right by two or three years of labor. In the meantime:

> You must be prepared to do anything told to you, anything you are ordered through her. If you have faith in us—others have not—are you prepared to do all and everything to prove our existence?[21]

Instructions from M arrived at the end of the month, advising Ramaswamier to dress as an ascetic, stop in every town he passed through *en route* to Allahabad, and preach Theosophy and the Vedanta. Keeping HPB informed of his whereabouts at all times, Ramaswamier was to follow M's orders which would be transmitted through her. Most importantly:

> Every one must know that he is my chela, and that *he has seen me* in Sikkim . . . His whole aspiration and concern must be directed towards one aim—*convince the world of our existence.*[22]

Even Olcott required some convincing, for Morya advises the chela to "Tell him that he too often mistakes Upasika" and that "she has never deceived him—only left him ignorant of many things in accordance with my orders." The Master continues:

> Dress yourself as a pilgrim from to-day, and tell your friends you have received direct orders from me—how or in what way is no one's business. Silence, discretion and courage. Have my blessings upon your head, my good and faithful son and chela.[23]

In the penultimate paragraph Morya provides a clue to Ramaswamier's willingness to carry out such an elaborate scheme:

> I will not say your surmise as to certain Prince's relation is not correct; but the secret is not mine to impart. Use it in a discreet way, and use your own intuitions. There are two men in T. who know the secret, search them out.[24]

In the next letter, received in Bombay on December 1, Morya wrote to say "You have worked unselfishly and with great profit to both your country and the good cause. And we thank you."[25] These two passages indicate that Ramaswamier was willing to do whatever was asked of him by HPB because he suspected the involvement of a certain prince behind the scenes and he saw the TS as a way to serve his country. With this powerful motive it is small wonder that he did and said all that was asked of him.

Ramaswamier was not the only young Indian receiving strange instructions in the fall of 1882. The letters received by Keshava Pillai, a young police inspector from Nellore, appealed to the same motives and gave rather bizarre instructions. The first letter he received was unsigned, and was apparently addressed to the entire Nellore branch TS after its President resigned. It asserts that until each member considers it "a duty to work for his country regardless of any consequences," the branch will not "be looked upon with confidence and respect, by those who—think what you may—still watch over the destinies of India tho' themselves unseen and unsuspected."[26] Again, the Master appeals to patriotic motives. Sometime later, Pillai was told of an opportunity to prove the existence of the Masters.

Koot Hoomi informed him that Babaji had been ordered to go to Darjeeling, where he would receive letters to be delivered to A. P. Sinnett in Simla. The Master requested that Pillai join him, promising that "The task is easy and there will not be much to do for either but be silent, and successfully play their parts," adding "If the mission is accomplished, in return I will permit some of our secrets to be taught to Keshu . . ."[27]

The next letter from KH to Pillai was received "phenomenally" (meaning paranormally) on a train, and advised him to carry out "literally and faithfully" the instructions received from Damodar.[28] This involved a change of name to Chandra Cusho and a change of attire to a Tibetan yellow robe and cap. The Master sternly warned, "From the moment you set foot in Darjeeling you have ceased being K.P. You are Chander. Go direct to D. [Darjeeling] from Mogul S. [Sarai] Do as you are bid. Save your nation—my blessings upon you."[29] Small wonder that such instructions occasioned "unfortunate doubts," as is mentioned in KH's last letter to Pillai, received at Adyar during the 1883 Convention of the TS.

After Emma Coulomb published her denunciation of HPB, which accused Pillai and other chelas of being her accomplices in fraud, he answered her with a very long letter published in the *Indian Mirror* of 3 March 1885. The newspaper's publisher, Norendro Nath Sen, was a devoted Theosophist, which may explain why he was willing to provide space for Pillai's response. The first half of the letter consists of a spiritual autobiography detailing the events which led Pillai to Theosophy. It begins with a vision he experienced at the age of seventeen in 1869. A "majestic figure in very likeness of the Great Mahatma M, whom I have subsequently seen on the other side of the Himalayas,"[30] appeared in Pillai's bedroom as he was falling asleep. The Master handed him an English translation of the Upanishads and warned him against converting to Christianity, which he had been considering. After reporting several less dramatic events of the following years, Pillai explains that it was through a chela in Nellore that he came into contact with Damodar in early 1881. In the following year, the unnamed chela (apparently Babaji), HPB and Olcott visited Nellore to help establish a TS branch. A series of paranormal performances helped strengthen the commitment of the new believers, for example when "Madame Blavatsky was writing at the table, we were seated down, and on her telling us that she felt the presence of the Guru in the room, we all looked up, and then within a minute or two, a letter fell before us from the ceiling in broad daylight at about 3 P.M."[31] During this visit, HPB informed Pillai that he was being watched by the Masters, and that his own guru was Mahatma KH. After several weeks of meditation and prayer directed toward establishing psychic contact with the Master, Pillai received a long-awaited message: "I fervently prayed to him that I might be allowed the happiness of seeing him in his physical body, to which after a moment's consideration, the *Guru Deva* replied that I should have to cross the Himalayas *alone*."[32] Four months later, he visited the TS headquarters in Bombay, and on 15 September left with HPB for North India. Emma Coulomb had commented about this departure that Pillai's change of attire was intended by HPB to be deceptive:

> before he left he had his costume made consisting of a yellow cotton satin blouse, a cap of the same shape as Mr Deb, a pair of top boots, and a pair of very thick cloth trousers . . . they started very quietly, and Madame begged us not to say to anyone that she had left. This was to give the thing a mysterious appearance as usual.[33]

Pillai indignantly rejects the implication that there was anything suspicious in his change of attire; he is, however, silent on the change of name that accompanied it.

The most impressive claim appears at the end of Pillai's letter, after a lengthy accounting of his travels with HPB. Arriving in Darjeeling on 20 September, he met Babaji and they proceeded together on a gruelling northern journey:

> We were both together until the 28th idem. We travelled together, both on horseback and on foot in Bhutan, Sikkim, etc. We visited several "Gonpas" (temples) . . . In the course of these travels, just about Pari or Parchong on the northern frontier of Sikkim, I had the good fortune and happiness to see the blessed feet of the most venerated Master Kut Humi and M. in their physical bodies. The very identical personage whose astral bodies I had seen in dreams, etc., since 1869, and in 1876 in Madras and on the 14th September 1882 in the headquarters at Bombay. Besides, I have also seen a few advanced chelas, among them, the blessed Jwalkul also, who is now a Mahatma.[34]

Juxtaposing these tales with the Mahatma letters received by Pillai indicates that he, like Ramaswamier, lent himself for use in a scheme of disinformation, believing real Masters to be directing it toward a patriotic end. Although Jinarajadasa notes that Pillai eventually lost interest in the TS, as late as 11 March 1898, Olcott saw Pillai in Gooty and had long friendly conversations with him and "the other admirable workers who have been leading this local group so successfully for so many years."[35]

Proving the Masters' Existence

Mohini Chatterji was active in the TS for five years, beginning in 1882. A Bengali Brahmin from Calcutta, Chatterji was a descendant of Ram Mohun Roy, founder of the Brahmo Samaj. He was also related to the Theosophist Debendra Nath Tagore, current leader of the Brahmo Samaj and father of the famed writer Rabindranath. Maharaja Sir Jotendro Mohun Tagore of Calcutta was another friend of Theosophy in Bengal, and welcomed the TS founders as guests in his home. Like Subba Row, Chatterji was a promising lawyer at the time of his affiliation with Theosophy.[36] As a "newly accepted chela" Mohini received a letter from Koot Hoomi which advised him that he was expected to, among other things, "devote all his energies to (a) prove to the unbelievers that we, the heirs of the Risis, are not dead, and that the Fr. of the TS are acting in many things under our direct orders."[37] The Master advised his chela to "never doubt, nor suspect, nor injure our agents by foul thoughts," and gave him a year's probation, until 17 September 1883, to "show what he can do and how much he is worthy of my trust."[38] Two months later, KH wrote a letter advising Mohini to attend the meeting of the TS to be held in Bombay in a few weeks, presumably to testify to an investigation he had allegedly made into tales of Koot Hoomi in Tibet.

This was to be the last conference in Bombay, for on 17 November, a South Indian Theosophist paid the mortgage on Huddlestone's Gardens, which became the new Headquarters. A week later, HPB returned to Bombay with Ramaswamier, who obligingly told of his meeting with Master M to a large gathering on 6 December. Two weeks later, the founders had arrived in Adyar. On 16 January 1883, they were welcomed by the Madras Hindu community in a large public ceremony. Part of the many housekeeping chores involved in setting up the headquarters was the installation of the "Occult Room" which Hodgson later made famous. By February, the Headquarters was ready to receive guests, the first being the Thakur Daji Raja of Wadhwan. In March, the Sinnetts visited Adyar on their way home to England, and the first occult phenomena of the Shrine Room took place during their stay. At the end of the month, the Sinnetts left India forever. Through April and May, Olcott toured Bengal lecturing and healing for the TS. In June, Olcott was in Ceylon while HPB vacationed at Ootycamund. While the President-Founder returned via a healing tour of South India, HPB stayed in the hill country.

Three letters to Olcott from the Masters reveal that a change in the situation of KH during this period required a new author for his letters. On 1 June, an unsigned letter advised:

> Unless you put your shoulder to the wheel yourself Kuthumi Lal Singh will have to disappear off the stage this fall. Easy enough for you.[39]

On the 13th, the Master Hilarion wrote:

> You are asked by Maha Sahib to put your whole soul in answer to A.P.S. from K.H. Upon this letter are hinged the fruits of the future.[40]

Two days later, a letter in Morya's script advised Olcott to attempt to heal the Maharaja of Indore on his upcoming trip to the North West Provinces, for "Indore is a big bird and if you help him in his ailings you will get a name and fame." He concluded with the reminder "Be careful about letter to Sinnett. Must be a really *Adeptic* letter."[41]

The significance of all this may be illuminated by the fact that Thakar Singh Sandhanwalia was planning to go to England in the fall of 1883 to visit his cousin Dalip Singh. Although on 9 November he wrote Dalip that the Lieutenant-Governor of the Punjab had refused him permission, by late 1884 he was, nonetheless, in England. He was therefore still in the Punjab at least through the visit of Olcott and Damodar in November, but apparently his plans and preparations for the trip led him to resign temporarily from his role as correspondent to Sinnett. In anticipation of his departure, he asked M or HPB to find a replacement, and the above letters make it clear that Olcott was selected to fill the gap. Thakar Singh may have renewed his involvement with the KH correspondence once he arrived in England, where Sinnett had relocated several months before.

Hodgson and most other anti-Theosophical writers have concluded that Olcott was an innocent victim manipulated and deceived by HPB, who had invented the Masters. Theosophists have believed both to be entirely honest about their adept sponsors. But these and other letters from June 1883 suggest that both were serving real Masters, and willing to use deceptive methods when necessary. "Pass it off to him someway" sounds like a suggestion to deliver Subba Row's Mahatma letter in a way intended to make it seem paranormal. Since the young man was widely proclaimed as a personal pupil of M, seeing him as a victim of such manipulation is rather disappointing. The passages about getting shares and saving the journal refer tc a failed effort to establish a newspaper, to be called the *Phoenix,* funded by native capital and edited by Sinnett under KH's inspiration. The collapse of this attempt would, HPB warned Sinnett, lead to KH's complete withdrawal from contact with the TS. Yet before the end of 1883, Koot Hoomi was to be involved in some of the most dramatic events in Theosophical history.

In August, an article signed by 201 Hindus, "Gurus and Chelas," protested A. O. Hume's irreverence to the Masters. Hodgson was later to note that several of their names seemed to have been invented for the occasion. Madras newspapers began to insinuate that the Theosophical founders were secret political agents. In September, after returning to Adyar from Ootycamund, HPB wrote to Sinnett that KH had ordered Olcott to "go to a certain pass."[42] On the 27th, Olcott left on a North Indian tour, and two days later William T. Brown arrived at Adyar with Mrs. Sarah Parker. On 10 October, Brown joined Olcott *en route* at Sholapur, and on the following day, Damodar left Adyar to join the party. On the 20th, HPB met Olcott, Damodar, and Brown at Bombay, but two days later she was *en route* to Madras. At the end of the month, "A Protest of Theosophists" appeared, in which five hundred Hindus objected to Dr. George Wyld's irreverence to the Teachers. On the 30th, Swami Dayanand Saraswati died in Ajmer. Olcott's tour with Brown and Damodar continued into November, and the trio arrived at Lahore the evening of the 18th. They were welcomed to the city by a party that included the Singh Sabha leaders Sirdar Dayal Singh Majithia and Bhai Gurmukh Singh. On the second night of their stay, Koot Hoomi made his famous visit to Olcott and Brown in their tents, during which each had a message materialize in his hands. Another KH visit, in the company of Djual Kul, occurred the following evening, when the Master had long talks with Damodar and Olcott. The following day, the group headed to Jammu to visit Ranbir Singh, the Maharaja of Kashmir. On 25 November, Damodar vanished from the house in Jammu where Ranbir had lodged him, but HPB telegraphed that all was well in response to Olcott's worried queries. On the 26th, Brown received another note from the Master, and on the 27th, Damodar returned, greatly altered by the experience of the Master's ashram. In Hodgson's report, Brown, who had seen KH at a distance in Lahore in daylight and received a nocturnal visit from him in his tent, is dismissed as unable to distinguish between the Mahatma and any person who may have slipped into the tent at night.

Brown described his background and his experiences with the Theosophical Masters in a report to the Society for Psychical Research which was never published during his lifetime. Recently published for the first time, it makes claims about his encounters with Koot Hoomi that are so specific as to have possibly raised concerns in the minds of Olcott and HPB. Although Brown's testimony would seem to be of great value to the TS, it remained unpublished for reasons unknown. One might speculate that its details about the Masters were considered too indiscreet for public consumption, especially in the wake of the Coulomb scandal.

The report, entitled "Some Experiences in India," opens with an account of Brown's first encounter with Theosophy through Mary Gebhard, who he met at the home of a homeopathic physician in London in 1883. Upon graduation from the University of Glasgow in April 1882, Brown traveled extensively for several months in North America and Europe, which resulted in a breakdown of his health. After an allopathic doctor's treatment caused him to decline further, he found Dr. Nichols, under whose care he "recovered my pristine vigour, and was quite restored to health."[43]

Mrs. Gebhard, a former pupil of Eliphas Levi, introduced Brown to Theosophical literature, which inspired him with the compulsion to visit the East. After an exchange of letters with Sinnett, he proceeded to Ceylon and India, arriving at Adyar in the fall of 1883. Olcott had already begun a lengthy tour through central and northern India, arranging for Brown to meet him *en route.* Before leaving Adyar, Brown received a Mahatma letter from KH, who suggested that "we may yet become friends."[44] He next received a long letter from Olcott warning of the arduous conditions of travel but promising that "if all these warnings do not repel you, and you have decided to sacrifice yourself, your strength, your talents for our cause, then come and I shall treat you as a son or a younger brother, as the differences in our ages may call for."[45]

After meeting Olcott in Sholapur and being joined by Damodar in Poona, Brown proceeded with them to Bombay, Jabalpur, and Allahabad. In Jabalpur at a TS lecture, he saw mysterious men who seemed majestic and holy in the audience, and was later assured by Damodar that they were Mahatmas in their astral bodies. In Allahabad, he saw one of these figures again, this time in his physical form. Proceeding by an indirect northward route, the group arrived in Lahore on 18 November, and it was here that their real adventures began:

> . . . Lahore has a special interest, because there we saw, in his own physical body, Mahatma Koot Hoomi himself.
>
> On the afternoon of the 19th November, I saw the Master in broad daylight, and recognized him, and on the morning of the 20th he came to my tent, and said "Now you see me before you in the flesh; look and assure yourself that it is I," and left a letter of instructions and silk handkerchief, both of which are now in my possession.
>
> The letter is as usual written seemingly with blue pencil, is in the same handwriting as that in which is written communication received at Madras, and has been identified by about a dozen persons as bearing the caligraphy *[sic]* of Mahatma Koot Hoomi. The letter was to the effect that I had first seen him in visions, then in his astral form, then in body at a distance, and that finally I now saw him in his own physical body, so close to me as to enable me to give to my countrymen the assurance that I was from personal knowledge as sure of the existence of the Mahatmas as I was of my own. The letter is a private one, and I am not enabled to quote from it at length.

On the evening of the 21st, after the lecture was over, Colonel Olcott, Damodar and I were sitting outside the shamiana, when we were visited by Djual Khool (the Master's head Chela, and now an Initiate), who informed us that the Master was about to come. The Master then came near to us, gave instructions to Damodar, and walked away.

On leaving Lahore the next place visited was Jammoo, the winter residence of His Highness the Maharajah of Cashmere. Colonel Olcott had been specially invited, and was received and entertained as a distinguished guest. Here everything presents a novel aspect to the stranger. Being a native state and independent of British rule, one is enabled from it, to form an idea of the pomp and splendor of ancient Aryavarta. "Native" Statesmen Councillors and Judges, "native" Generals and Officers of Court reflect their glory on the Maharajah, who is literally and absolutely "The Monarch of all he surveys."

Our party was kindly provided with elephants and horses for private use, and we enjoyed a most inspiriting holiday in full view of the Himalayan Mountains.

At Jammoo I had another opportunity of seeing Mahatma Koot Hoomi *in propria persona.* One evening I went to the end of the "compound," and there I found the Master awaiting my approach. I saluted in European fashion, and came, hat in hand, to within a few yards of the place on which he was standing . . . After a minute or so he marched away, the noise of his footsteps on the gravel being markedly audible.[46]

During the disappearance of Damodar from Ranbir Singh's palace, Brown received a letter from KH welcoming him to the territory of "our Kashmir prince" and commenting that "in truth my native land is not so far away but that I can assume the character of host."[47] References to Tibet and its wisdom sufficed to serve as "blinds" for the revelations already made, and Brown left Jammu without suspecting that he had been in the presence of Morya as well as Koot Hoomi, or that he had been in the homelands of both. He returned from the journey more devoted than ever to the cause of Theosophy. In January 1885, he left India for America, visiting China and Japan *en route.* While in the United States, he decided to return to India, but changed his mind and spent the rest of 1885 in Europe. In 1886, he returned to America and joined forces with Josephine Cables of the Rochester, New York, branch of the TS. Both he and Cables soon left the society, and Brown subsequently returned to India, adopted Roman Catholicism, and married an older Eurasian woman. The reasons for his defection and his ultimate conclusions about the Theosophical Masters remain unknown.[48]

Another character, too often left unexamined, figures prominently in Hodgson's evaluation of testimony about the Masters:

> The chief persons who testify from personal experience to the actual existence of the Brotherhood in Thibet are (besides Madame Blavatsky) Mr. Damodar and Mr. Babajee Dharbagiri Nath . . . With regard to Babajee D. Nath . . . he has made statements which I cannot but regard as wilfully [*sic*] false concerning matters connected to the Shrine. Again, he stated to me that he had lived with the Brothers only during certain months out of a period of two years which immediately followed his leaving, in 1878, the position of private secretary to a deputy-collector in the Kurnool district, although he had previously stated to Mr. Sinnett that he had been living with Koot Hoomi for ten years.[49]

Babaji is a shadowy character not only from the point of view of his honesty, but also from that of his identity. He arrived at the TS Headquarters as Gwala K. Deb, but later returned under the name Dharbagiri Nath. His real name was S. Krishnaswami (Krishnamachari according to some accounts), and he actually appeared under all three names in a single annual report of the TS. He also signed a protest of two hundred Hindu chelas as both Deb and Nath. With reasonable justification, Hodgson comes to these conclusions about Babaji:

> I think that all will agree that the mere assertion of a person who has made false and contradictory statements, and has appeared under different aliases, is insufficient to prove him "the Chela of Koot Hoomi that he declares himself to be," though it is difficult to avoid the conclusion that he is a false witness, invented to prop up Mme. Blavatsky's vast imposture.[50]

The fact that Babaji was penniless and grateful to HPB for his support rendered him liable to say anything to please her, Hodgson concluded. The other witnesses to the Masters were worse than useless, in Hodgson's eyes, in proving their existence:

> Rama Sourindo Gargya Deva, from whose alleged letter to Madame Blavatsky, asserting his intimacy with the Masters

> (published in *The Theosophist* for December, 1883), an extract was quoted in our first report, cannot be regarded as an independent witness; seeing that his own existence is even more problematical than that of the Mahatmas, the only evidence for it being the statement of Madame Blavatsky, Mr. Babajee, and Mr. Damodar, that they know him. And Mr. Mirza Moorad Alee Beg, whose assertions (published in *the Theosophist* for August, 1881) committed him, as we thought, nearly as fully as Madame Blavatsky and Mr. Damodar are committed, to the existence and powers of the Mahatmas, turns out, according to the statements of various Theosophists, to be altogether untrustworthy and to have shown evident marks of insanity. He is said to have practiced Black Magic [!] before his connection with the Theosophical Society, which he left long ago, and became a Roman Catholic; he is now a Mussulman. I must conclude, then, that the strongest apparent evidence for the existence of the Mahatmas comes to nothing at all.[51]

"Mirza Moorad Ali Beg" was the name adopted by the Englishman Godolphin Mitford after his conversion to Islam. Mitford, whose surname seems almost synonymous with English eccentricity, was without a doubt the most bizarre of the Mahatmas' chelas. Born at Madras, Mitford was Chief Cavalry Officer of the Maharaja of Bhaunagar when he met Olcott and HPB on 20 January 1881. He had already converted to Islam and adopted Indian dress. As Moorad Ali Beg, Mitford wrote two remarkable articles for *The Theosophist.* His "The Elixir of Life" discussed occult methods of attaining longevity and implied the author's acquaintance with the adepts. In *Old Diary Leaves,* Olcott reports that Mitford's eccentricities were so evident that he refused to accept him as a member of the TS. HPB intervened on Mitford's behalf, however, only to be rewarded on a subsequent trip to Wadhwan by his attempt to slay her with a sword while shouting that she and her Mahatmas were devils.[52]

One can propose Damodar Mavalankar as an accomplice in all the activities of HPB and KH without making the latter a nonentity, as did Hodgson. Damodar's encounters with Koot Hoomi in Lahore and Jammu followed a year of frenzied speculation about the Masters. Sinnett's *Occult World* had stimulated European imaginations with its tales of Mahatma letters, and the Masters therein portrayed were much more remote from the geographical and historical truth than those revealed to Russian readers in *Caves and Jungles of Hindustan.* In their first years in India, the TS founders operated mostly on a Bombay-Punjab axis, because these were the strongholds of the Arya Samaj. Through Arya Samaj contacts, Blavatsky and Olcott developed an acquaintance with leaders of the Singh Sabha, which was also temporarily allied with Swami Dayananda's organization. Both the TS and the Singh Sabha eventually fell out with the Aryas due to their Hindu fanaticism. By late 1883, the alliance among the three groups was over, and Sinnett had returned to England, never to return. The Mahatma correspondence was also virtually at an end. Its goal had been to convert the most important newspaper editor in Anglo-India and one of its greatest political leaders to the cause of Indian cultural revival and social reform. This met with limited success in both cases.

Damodar had genuinely met Koot Hoomi outside Lahore and at the palace of Ranbir Singh, and had gone so far as to publish an account of this exploit in *The Theosophist,* naming Jammu and Lahore as the sites of these encounters. This is one of the great true Mahatma stories of Theosophical history; KH and his colleagues Dayal Singh Majithia and Bhai Gurmukh Singh did indeed welcome Olcott, Damodar, and Brown to Lahore. Damodar's article "A Great Riddle Solved" is extremely emphatic about the significance of his encounter:

> *There* [in Lahore] *I was visited by him in body, for three nights consecutively for about three hours every time while I myself retained full consciousness* . . . HIM whom I saw in person at Lahore was the same I had seen in astral form at the Headquarters . . . now at Lahore, Jummu, and elsewhere, the impression was utterly different . . . [in Jammu] I had the good fortune of being sent for, and permitted to visit a Sacred Ashram where I remained for a few days in the blessed company of several of the much doubted MAHATMAS . . . These are all stern facts and no third course is open to the reader. What I assert is either true or false . . . If these few lines will help to stimulate even one of my brother-Fellows in the Society or one right-thinking man outside of it to promote the cause the GREAT MASTERS have imposed upon the devoted heads of the Founders of the Theosophical Society, I shall consider that I have properly performed my duty.[53]

Although it is impossible to know who or what Damodar had seen in his astral visions, the rest of his story is indeed literally true. But his insistence that there is no third course open to the reader is quite misleading. That he had genuinely met the

Theosophical Masters on his journey in no way proves the far-fetched allegations made about them, although he seems not to recognize this. It soon dawned on him that there were some problems involved in reconciling his testimony with previous statements about the Mahatmas. Criticism of Damodar's claims necessitated a response, published in a letter to *The Epiphany* of 16 February 1884: "As regards my 'flying to Tibet and coming back within two days' . . . on my return to Jammoo, I distinctly told enquirers there that I had gone to a place within His Highness' Dominion, but that for certain reasons I could not give its name or exact locality."[54]

Olcott estimates sixty hours as the length of time Damodar was missing from Jammu. The Masters' ashram could thus hardly have been in Tibet, as had been claimed for so long. HPB had written to Mary Hollis-Billings, however, that the home of KH was "in Little Tibet [Ladakh] and belongs now to Kashmir. It is a large wooden building in the Chinese fashion, pagoda-like, between a lake and a beautiful mountain."[55] Morya also frequently stayed there, HPB added. In a letter to William Q. Judge, Damodar had written of an astral journey to KH's house at "the upper end of Kashmir at the foot of the Himalayas," from whence he proceeded to "an open plane in L———k [Ladakh?]" where he saw a "large massive building." He continues:

> This is the Chief Central Place where all those of our Section who are found deserving of Initiation into Mysteries have to go for their final ceremony and stay there for the requisite period. I went up with my Guru to the Great Hall, The grandeur and serenity of the place is enough to strike anyone with awe . . . The splendor of the Chief's Throne is incomparable [and] has about it an indescribably glory, consisting of an effulgence which seemed to radiate from the one who occupied it.[56]

It is not implausible that Damodar's visions were inspired by HPB's descriptions of a place she had seen in Ladakh. But he is no more likely to have journeyed to Ladakh and back from Jammu in sixty hours than to have made it all the way to Tibet. In any event it is most peculiar to find Damodar, Olcott, and Brown proving the reality of the Masters in Punjab and Kashmir just a year after HPB, Ramaswamier, Babaji, and Pillai had proven them to be a thousand miles east, in Sikkim and/or southern Tibet. Indeed, further testimony placing M and KH in the latter region was forthcoming almost simultaneously with the conflicting evidence given by Damodar, Olcott, and Brown.

In December, *The Theosophist* included a letter by the possibly mythical Rama Sourindo Gargya Deva, criticizing HPB on the subject of "supposed desecration of Masters' names." This was dated from Darjeeling. Also in December, Franz Hartmann arrived at Adyar and by the end of the month, the Shrine phenomena were in full bloom, with four KH letters delivered. Alleged proofs of the Masters' existence were plentiful that month. Mohini's article "The Himalayan Brothers—Do They Exist?" is described by Boris de Zirkoff as "one of the most important contributions to the early *Theosophist*."[57] It represents part of a well-orchestrated scheme to shore up faith in the Masters. Mohini reports on two independent proofs of the existence of a Tibetan brotherhood called the Koothoompas or "men of Koot Hoomi." One account is from a Tibetan peddler in Darjeeling, the other from a Brahmacharin at Dehra Dun. The letter from KH directing Mohini to write the article is quite specific:

> I want you, my dear boy, to write an account for the Theosophist, of what the pedlar said, and the Dehra Brahmacharia. Make it as strong as you can, and have all the witnesses at Darjeeling and Dehra. But the name is written Koothumpa (disciples of Kut-hoomi) tho' pronounced Kethoomba. Write and send it to Upasika. Allahabad.[58]

The series of Mahatma letters to Olcott, Ramaswamier and Mohini written from 1881 to 1884 provides support for the hypothesis that KH was a living person, independent of HPB, guiding a scheme from behind the scenes with a clear purpose in view. She arrived in Bombay regarding Swami Dayananda as a great Hindu Mahatma, and expected to work in harmonious partnership with his Arya Samaj. But other sponsors soon supplanted him, most notably several maharajas and the Singh Sabha leadership. Therefore, it was to Lahore and Jammu that Damodar was taken to be rewarded with a genuine encounter with the lodge of HPB's adept sponsors. It seems, however, to have been intended as a publicity stunt, in light of the coverage given in *The Theosophist*. HPB added an editor's note to Mohini's article about the Tibetan Koothoompas:

> Secondary evidence is no longer necessary. On November the 20th at 10 A.M. two telegrams were received by us, dated Lahore, one from Colonel Olcott, who notified us that he had

> been visited in person by Mahatma "K.H." on the preceding night; and the other—from Mr. W. T. Brown, F.T.S. of the "London Lodge," Theosophical Society, in these words: "Visited early this morning by Mahatma K.H. who left me a silk handkerchief as a memorial, etc!" and today 22nd having telegraphed to both those gentlemen for permission to announce the long expected event in *The Theosophist,* we received an answer that not only could "Master's visit be mentioned," but that our President, Mr. Brown, and Mr. Damodar "had another call last night near their tent, the Master being accompanied in flesh and body by Brother Djual Khool." Unless W. T. Brown, to complete the trio, be classed by our Spiritualistic friends also among the "Occidental Humourists," the question as to the real existence of the Mahatma, is pretty well settled now. One witness may be mistaken as to facts, and even a doubt may be cast upon the evidence of two witnesses. But when it comes to the testimony of three or more witnesses speaking to a fact that occurred in their presence doubt would become absurd even in a Court of Justice. We have not yet received the particulars, but since we have been notified that Mahatma K.H. on his way to Siam would most likely pass via Madras in a week or so, we have every reason to suppose that our President and Mr. Brown saw the real, living body, not merely as before—the astral form of the Master.[59]

Damodar was the chela who met real Masters in Lahore and Jammu; Ramaswamier and Mohini were willing tools in a scheme to simultaneously prove the adepts' existence and distort their identities. This explains KH's peculiar emphasis to Mohini: "Make it as strong as you can, and have all the witnesses at Darjeeling and Dehra." Why "have" the witnesses anywhere in particular, except to mislead readers as to the whereabouts of the Mahatmas? Koot Hoomi's astral trips all over India, his supposed impending physical voyage to Siam, and his alleged disciples in regions north of Darjeeling all served to draw attention away from the Sikh reformers in Amritsar or the Theosophical princes of India. Nonetheless, the truth of Damodar's encounter was revealed, although at the same time concealed in a mass of disinformation. Hodgson did not recognize the complexity of his task, so instead of selecting any of the chelas as the real acquaintance of KH, he rejected them all and declared the Masters nonexistent.

The Coulombs and the SPR

The period from May 1882, when the Founders first visited Madras, to December 1885, when HPB received the Hodgson report, forms a single continuous drama. 1882 and 1883 witnessed an elaborate effort to prove the existence of the Masters, while the two following years brought the inevitable consequence, the SPR investigation.

In February 1884, HPB, Mohini, Franz Hartmann, and Emma Coulomb visited the Thakur Daji Raja of Wadhwan and Prince Harisinghji Rupsinghji, before the founders sailed from Bombay to Marseilles, leaving on the 20th. Hartmann's *Report of Observations,* published in October 1884, before Hodgson's arrival, noted the unpleasant events which may have motivated the Coulomb conspiracy against HPB. This is summarized by William Kingsland in "Was she a Charlatan?," reprinted as an appendix to the Arno edition of Hodgson's report:

> In December 1883, during the annual Convention of the T.S. at Adyar, Mme. Coulomb endeavoured to obtain a 'loan' of 2,000 rupees from Prince Harisinghji, who attended that Convention. In this she was unsuccessful. When Mme. Blavatsky left Adyar in February 1884 for Bombay en route for Europe, she visited Prince Harisinghji on the way. Mme. Coulomb had asked and had been granted permission to accompany her to Bombay, and she then made another effort to obtain this 'loan' from the Prince. The Prince complained at last to Mme. Blavatsky, who immediately put a stop to Mme. Coulomb's efforts. Dr. Hartmann, who was present, says: "Her [Mme. Coulomb's] fury knew no bounds, and her passionate outbursts of anger and jealousy were in no way soothed down by Mme. Blavatsky reproaching her for her unjust attempt at extortion." Whether this was an attempt to blackmail is not stated, but Mme. Coulomb evidently thought that she had some hold on the Prince to enable her to ask for such a 'loan.'
>
> Be that as it may, this appears to have been the turning-point in her rupture with the Society, for Dr. Hartmann says that when leaving the boat at Bombay after saying good-bye to Mme. Blavatsky, she turned to Babula, Mme. Blavatsky's servant, and said: "I shall be revenged on your mistress for preventing me from getting my 2,000 rupees."[60]

Mme. Coulomb was later to allege that the TS was engaged in a conspiracy against British rule in India. Her choice of a Rajput prince as a blackmail victim suggests that Harisinghji may have been somehow involved in a compromising situation. Yet there can be little doubt that Harisinghji and Daji Raja were sincere Theosophists and believers in the Mahatmas. In an appendix to the Hodgson report there is testimony from Harisinghji which reveals him to be a correspondent of the Master KH via the Shrine:

> I was at Headquarters very often during my sojourn with my friend H.H., the Thakore Sahib of Wadhwan at Madras, whither we had gone last March for the celebration of his marriage with the daughter of the Hon. Gujpati Row.
>
> One day I asked Mr. D. K. Mavalankar to let me put a letter from me to my revered Master K.H. in the Shrine. It was in a closed envelope, and was regarding private personal matters, which I need not lay before the public. The day after I visited again the Shrine in company with my wife. On opening the Shrine I did find my letter unopened, but addressed to me in blue pencil, while my original superscription, "My revered Master," had a pencil line running through it. This was in the presence of Mr. Mavalankar, Dr. Hartmann and others. The envelope was intact. I opened it, and on the unused portion of my note was an answer from my Master K.H. in his, to me, familiar handwriting. I should very much like to know how others will explain this, when as a fact both founders were thousands of miles away,
>
> Harisinghji Rupsinghji, F.T.S.
> Varel, 9th September, 1884[61]

Others might explain this by the obvious hypothesis of fraud by Damodar. Harisinghji and Daji Raja were among the two princes who showed the greatest support for the TS by publicly espousing belief in the Masters. After the deaths of Daji Raja and Ranbir Singh in 1885, Harisinghji would be the most devoted of the Indian princes to the Theosophical movement. In the third volume of *Old Diary Leaves,* he is described in glowing terms:

> he has always been beloved at Headquarters for his sweet character and loyal friendliness. He has worn as well as any man who has joined us from the beginning. Among Indian princes he is the best as man and friend whom I have met,

and if all were like him, religion would be on a far better footing in India than it is in these degenerate days.[62]

Soon after the failed attempt at blackmail, the Coulombs began to make trouble at Adyar in the absence of the founders. On the 2nd of March, Alexis Coulomb refused to allow the Board of Control into HPB's room for a meeting which had been scheduled there. On the 7th, Emma refused to allow Damodar into the room, and a few days thereafter told him that HPB had ordered Alexis to make trap doors in her room. The Coulombs argued between themselves and with the Headquarters staff. KH wrote a letter to Damodar advising charity toward Emma Coulomb, and on the same day, 11 March, wrote to Emma advising her to go to Ootycamund. On the 12th, the founders reached French soil, and were welcomed on the 15th by Lady Caithness at Nice. William Q. Judge arrived in Paris on the 25th, en route to India, and found Mohini already there. The end of the month found Mme. Coulomb at Ootycamund while HPB and Olcott were arriving in Paris, where Lady Caithness provided lodging for the Theosophical travellers. Around the same time, Mohini received a letter from KH in Paris which directed him to show dramatic obeisance to HPB in order to impress the "Pelings." In April, KH dropped a letter to Olcott in a railroad car, warning him of the dangers emerging at Adyar. Early in the month, HPB made a brief trip to London, where she appeared unexpectedly at a meeting of the London Lodge. This was Mohini's opportunity to follow KH's instructions, which he did by prostrating himself abjectly at HPB's feet. After resolving the Kingsford/Sinnett struggle by advising creation of a second "Hermetic Lodge," HPB returned to France. Within a few weeks, the Hermetic lodge seceded to form a separate society. Back in India, Franz Hartmann was being warned by Morya, in a letter that appeared in Damodar's room, to act immediately against the Coulomb conspiracy.

May was the month in which the events occurred that led ultimately to Hodgson's investigation. The Coulombs were expelled from Headquarters at the order of the Board of Control, after alleging that HPB had ordered Alexis to build trapdoors for secret access to the Occult Room. Sometime that month, HPB met V. S. Solovyov in Paris, where she had been joined by her sister Vera and aunt Nadyezhda. Through July and August, HPB travelled between London, Paris, and Elberfeld, meeting almost all the noted Theosophists of Europe. On 11 September, the *Christian College Magazine* of Madras published letters supplied by the Coulombs, purporting to prove the nonexistence of KH. The fact that more than three hundred students of the college protested this event shows that Indians perceived it as an attack on their country. In late September or early October, the Adyar Shrine was burned in mysterious circumstances. On 10 October, KH wrote to Sinnett about events at Adyar:

> However caused—whether by faults at Adyar, or Allahabad, or by my negligence, or H.P.B.'s viciousness—a crisis is here, and it is a time for the utmost practicable expansion of your moral power. It is not the moment for reproaches or vindictive recriminations, but for united struggle. Whomsoever has sown the seeds of the present tempest, the whirlwind is strong, the whole Society is reaping it and it is rather fanned than weakened from Tchigadze . . . You have too much intelligence not to see clearly, as the Americans would say, the *fix* I am in, and that I, personally, can do very little. The present situation, as you will find from M.'s letter, has been gradually created by all of you as much as by the wretched "Founders."[63]

A few days later, HPB denied the authorship of the Coulomb letters in a pamphlet published by the London Lodge. On the 20th, Olcott sailed from Marseilles for Bombay. HPB followed suit, leaving Liverpool for Adyar on the 31st. Hartmann's *Report of Observations Made during a Nine Months Stay at the Headquarters of The Theosophical Society at Adyar (Madras), India* and Gribble's *Report of an Investigation into the Blavatsky Correspondence . . .* were both published at Madras around this time. Their conclusions on the existence of the Masters and the genuineness of the Shrine phenomena were diametrically opposed. En route back to India, HPB stopped in Egypt to gather damaging information about the Coulombs. In Cairo, she dined with Nubar Pasha, the Prime Minister, and was invited to a reception for the Vice-reine. Leaving Alfred Cooper-Oakley in Cairo to investigate police records, HPB, C. W. Leadbeater, and Isabel Cooper-Oakley departed for Ceylon, where they were met by Hartmann and Olcott on 17 December. On the following day, Richard Hodgson arrived in Madras. Three days later, HPB arrived there with her companions. On the 22nd, Hodgson first visited Adyar and on the 23rd, Mme. Coulomb's pamphlet on her association with HPB was published. The defense of the TS was undertaken by a committee formed by that purpose, which led to a published reply to Gribble by Major-General H. R. Morgan late in the month. Also in December, Hodgson's first SPR Report, generally favorable, was issued in London.

1885 was the year in which the partnership between Damodar, HPB and the Masters came to a sad end. Hodgson interviewed HPB on 2 January, leaving the following day to meet with the Coulombs. During the month, HPB became seriously ill, prompting her to file her Last Will and Testament on the 31st. In February, the TS General Council issued a report defending HPB. Her health improved somewhat early in the month, which she attributed to intervention by her Master Morya. Franz Hartmann and St. George Lane-Fox challenged Olcott's authority, while Damodar and Subba Row became deeply discouraged by the state of affairs. On the 23rd, Damodar left "for Tibet" via Darjeeling, never to be seen again. In March, A. O. Hume attempted to lead a rebel takeover of the TS and displace the founders, but this effort failed. Hume, who had served as an assistant investigator to Hodgson, was never again to be on good terms with HPB. On the 17th, the graphologist F. G. Netherclift issued an opinion that the KH letters were written by HPB, and on the 21st, HPB decided to resign her office of Corresponding Secretary. Four days later, Hodgson called to say goodbye, on the day before his departure for England. On the 29th, HPB handed in her resignation, and on the 31st left India forever. Damodar's last diary entry before his final disappearance was made on 23 April, the day before HPB's arrival in Italy. In May and June, Hodgson reported his findings to the SPR in private meetings, but the final report was not published until the end of the year. HPB received her copy on 31 December, marking the end of the most turbulent period in her life.

Endings and Beginnings

By 1886, the circumstances faced by the Theosophical leadership had changed drastically. Before the arrival of Richard Hodgson, the TS enjoyed a growing prestige and influence among Europeans and educated Indians. HPB was secure in the secret sponsorship of the most powerful maharajas of the native states. Her alliance with the leaders of the Singh Sabha had survived Swami Dayananda's break with the TS founders. Several promising young Indians were wholeheartedly devoted to serving Blavatsky and her Masters. But within a relatively short period, all these encouraging developments came to an end, and HPB was obliged to rebuild her work on a more solid foundation. That the TS was able to survive the staggering reversals of 1885 while continuing to expand its membership is testimony to Blavatsky's incredible resourcefulness and resilience.

The most apparent reversal in the fortunes of the TS was HPB's denunciation as a fraudulent psychic. At the beginning of its existence, the SPR was viewed by the Theosophists as a powerful potential ally. Members were so confident of the phenomena performed by HPB (and allegedly by the Masters) that they welcomed scientific investigation. After Hodgson's report, Theosophy was firmly defined in the public mind as a cult devoted to imaginary Mahatmas. Although membership continued to grow steadily, the loss of legitimacy entailed by the SPR denunciation permanently weakened the society's intellectual respectability.

A much less obvious reversal was the collapse of secret sponsorship by HPB's most important allies in India. The death of Maharaja Ranbir Singh of Kashmir in September 1885 deprived the TS of its most powerful royal supporter. Ranbir's son and successor Pratap Singh was to become an equally ardent supporter of the TS leaders. In 1905, he welcomed Annie Besant to his palace in Srinagar, where she gave a stirring public lecture in the garden. During this visit, Besant began working toward the transformation of the Srinagar Hindu High School into the first western-style college in the kingdom. In August 1906, the maharaja laid the cornerstone for the Sri Pratap Hindu College, operated under the auspices of the TS and its Central Hindu College in Varanasi. Pratap Singh's personal secretary, Raja Daya Kishan Kaul, a Theosophist, was instrumental in bringing this about.[64] But the death of Ranbir created a void that his son could not fill. No other maharaja was perceived by the TS founders as a spiritual mentor in the same sense as he. Whether or not the hypothesis of his being the basis of the Master Morya is correct, he was indubitably a Vedanta scholar and a committed supporter of the TS. Daji Raja of Wadhwan also died in 1885, followed in 1886 by Maharaja Holkar of Indore. These were, unbeknownst to all but a handful of TS members, the "three kings of Orient" upon whose moral support the founders had most relied.

Another royal sponsor of the TS, Maharaja Bikram Singh of Faridkot, was by 1886 embroiled in a dispute which rent asunder the Singh Sabha. Bikram Singh, patron of the organization, was allied with Thakar Singh Sandhanwalia (KH), Baba Khem Singh Bedi (the Chohan), and Dayal Singh Majithia (Djual Kul) in support of a military uprising against the British. Thakar Singh had returned in 1885 from a year in London, where he had succeeded in persuading his cousin Dalip to return to India and the Sikh faith. Although Dalip sailed for Bombay in March 1886, he was detained *en route* in Aden and refused permission to continue. At this point, he proceeded to Paris, and thence to Moscow, where he issued a proclamation calling for an Indian uprising. The far-fetched scheme organized by Dalip's supporters envisioned the dethroned maharaja as the leader of an independent India allied with France and Russia. Although he was joined in Moscow by Jamal ad-Din "al-Afghani" and sponsored by HPB's publisher Mikhail Katkov, their efforts to induce a Russian military invasion of India fell on deaf ears. Even after Thakar Singh and Katkov died in the summer of 1887, Bikram Singh, Baba Khem Singh Bedi, and Dayal Singh Majithia continued to support Dalip's lost cause. The majority of the Singh Sabha members, led by Gurmukh Singh, turned against their founders and rejected Dalip and his supporters. All but three of the branch sabhas endorsed Gurmukh Singh's policy, and HPB's later correspondence indicates that she too was unsympathetic to the schemes involving Dalip. Although cordial relations between the TS and the majority faction of the Singh Sabha continued for many years, by 1886 KH's "lodge" was no longer the same harmonious group with which the TS had been secretly allied in the early part of the decade.

All these behind-the-scenes developments are crucial to understanding the behavior of the patriotic chelas after the Hodgson report. About Damodar, Theosophical and critical writers have reached diametrically opposed conclusions, both of which are probably false. In the wake of the Hodgson report and HPB's disgrace, Damodar vanished, claiming to be *en route* to the Masters in Tibet. Marion Meade comments:

> Sometime in July, Henry Olcott would receive word that Damodar's naked corpse, frozen stiff, had been found in the snow near Chumboi, Sikkim, with his clothing scattered a little distance away. Henry refused to believe that the body was Damodar's.[65]

Meade is confident that the body was indeed Damodar's, assuming Olcott's faith in his survival to be absurd. Theosophical writers, on the other hand, have assumed that he reached Tibet via Darjeeling to be reunited with the Mahatmas—despite the fact that Damodar's meetings with the Mahatmas had been in Punjab and Kashmir, not Sikkim or Tibet. More likely than either of these alternatives is that Damodar disappeared somewhere in India. In February 1886, Olcott wrote HPB, "No news from Damodar. Tell me exactly what you know about him, and how much I may repeat."[66] This is clear evidence that a year after Damodar's disappearance, Olcott was convinced of his survival but unsure of his whereabouts or circumstances.

When HPB left India, she expected Subba Row to assist her in the writing of *The Secret Doctrine.* But in 1886 he severed his connection with her and the TS, apparently under the inspiration of his Brahmin guru, Swami Sankaracharya of Mysore. In January, Olcott wrote enthusiastically to HPB about the creation of an Advaita Society secretly linked with the TS and sponsored by Sankaracharya. She was delighted with this development, as revealed in a letter from Constance Wachtmeister to A. P. Sinnett. But Olcott's letter expressed anxiety "that there should be no new scandals or rows in connection with the TS for fear Sancaracharya (an Initiate) and the whole orthodox party should get frightened and set themselves to break us up."[67] This indeed happened, and when the "orthodox party" of conservative disciples of the Swami decided to abandon the TS, Subba Row followed suit. Calling HPB a "shell deserted and abandoned by the Masters," he believed it his duty as a Brahmin to reject her.[68] Details on the career of this particular Sankaracharya have been elusive, but Paul Brunton's *A Search in Secret India* devotes a chapter to his successor, the 66th consecutive avatara of the original Sankaracharya, founder of Vedanta philosophy. Brunton quotes his Indian friend Venkataramani extolling "His Holiness Shri Shankara Acharya of Kumbakonum . . . the Spiritual Head of South India . . . the Primate of the Southern Hindu world, a true saint and great religious philosopher."[69] He adds that the first Sankara promised to overshadow his successors, and that at the moment of each avatara's death, he names the next Sankaracharya. The sixty-sixth had been named in 1907, when he was twelve years old. Brunton's son, Kenneth Hurst, notes in the introduction that the highlight of his own journey to India was a visit to the same man in the mid-1980s. Although 91 years of age, he still recalled Brunton's visit of 1934.[70]

Mohini Chatterji's career as a Theosophical chela was even more meteoric than those of Subba Row, Damodar, Mitford, and Brown. He had first gone to Europe in 1884, and was an immediate success with Western Theosophists due to his eloquence and charm. Fluent in English and French, strikingly handsome, and knowledgeable about both Indian philosophy and Western science, Mohini was so popular as to become a threat to HPB and Olcott. But the greatest danger posed by his popularity was his sexual attractiveness to female Theosophists. In Paris, a Miss Leonard fell in love with Mohini, who apparently reciprocated her feelings to the extent of writing her a hundred love letters in six months. When things went awry, perhaps because Miss Leonard learned of the wife Mohini had left behind in Calcutta, she went to Madame de Morsier, a leading French Theosophist, for support. HPB rejected the accusation that Mohini had seduced the girl so vehemently as to place herself in legal jeopardy. Calling Miss Leonard a "Potiphar's wife" in a letter to Mme. de Morsier resulted in the threat of a libel suit. Miss Leonard's conditions for peace were a written apology from HPB and Mohini's return to India, both of which were fulfilled. The following year, Mohini withdrew from the TS. From HPB's point of view, this was no great loss, as in early 1886 she complained to Sinnett that Mohini and Babaji had been "ruining and daily undermining my honour, name and fame with their lies."[71] But even though she blamed his misconduct for the destruction of the French TS, and resented his attempts to undermine her and Olcott's authority, HPB continued to love Mohini. His disloyalty, she felt was inspired by Babaji's bad influence.

The most painful and difficult loss was the defection of "Babaji" alias Dharbagiri K. Nath alias Gwala K. Deb. The young man, whose real name was S. Krishnaswami or Krishnamachari, had left India with HPB in the company of Franz Hartmann in March 1885, and remained in Europe for just over a year. Until late 1885, he remained a loyal chela, assuring the European members of the Mahatmas' continued support of HPB and the TS. By early 1886, he had become passionately hostile, as described by Constance Wachtmeister in a letter to Sinnett:

> When she left India, Leadbeater offered to accompany her, and remain with her, but yielded to Babajee's earnest entreaties that he might come to Europe. The January *Theosophist* will shew you what his professions of devotion etc. were. Now he has turned traitor to the Cause, throws stones at the Founders accusing them of fraud, and so naturally leaves undone the duty which he took upon himself and promised to do. Mme. B. thought that Mohini would come to her after my departure as his letters have always professed the warmest attachment to her, but being now under Babajee's influence, his latter epistle has quite a different tone to any of his former letters and he also begins to throw stones at her. If this is the stuff of which chelas are made I hope no more specimens may be sent to Europe.[72]

Babaji's enmity was of unknown origin, but his accusations of fraud were particularly damaging due to his status as a recognized chela. He accused HPB of forging letters from the Masters when they were no longer working in partnership with her, and even charged Olcott and HPB with financially defrauding Prince Harisinghji. He was successful in creating turmoil in the German TS, and inspired Mohini to rebel against Olcott and HPB. There is more documentary evidence in his case than in those of any of the other patriotic chelas, but this evidence illuminates the historical context in which they all became disciples of the Theosophical Masters.

The Tragedy of Babaji

The chela with the most aliases is also in many ways the most accessible to the contemporary researcher. This is due to the extensive correspondence included in the volume entitled *Letters of H. P. Blavatsky to A. P. Sinnett.* S. Krishnaswami or Krishnamachari, alias Gwala K. Deb, had become Dharbagiri K. Nath, nicknamed Babaji or Bowajee, by the time he appears in the letters. HPB's first letter to Sinnett after returning to Europe from India in 1885 extols Babaji: "the only friend I have in life and death is the poor little exiled Bowajee D. Nath in Europe; and poor dear Damodar—in Tibet. D. Nath keeps me at the foot of my bed, awake for whole nights, mesmerising me, as prescribed by his Master."[73] The same letter provides HPB's explanation of what had gone wrong between Hodgson and the chelas:

> I have learned the whole extent of the conspiracy against the belief in the Mahatmas; it was a question of life or death to the Missions in India, and they thought that by killing me they would kill Theosophy. They have very nearly succeeded. At any rate they have succeeded in fooling Hume and the S.P.R. . . . Hodgson came to Adyar; was received as a friend; examined and cross-examined all whom he wanted to, the "Boys" (the Hindus) at Adyar gave him all the information he needed. If he now finds discrepancies and contradictions in their statements, it only shows that feeling as they did, that it was in their sight pure tomfoolery to doubt the phenomena and the Masters, they had not prepared themselves for the scientific cross-examination, may have forgotten many of the circumstances, in short, not feeling guilty and having never

> either been my confederates or my dupes, they had not rehearsed among themselves what to say, and thus, may very well have created suspicions in a prejudiced mind. But the whole trouble is that we have never looked upon Mr. Hodgson at first, as a prejudiced judge. Quite the reverse.[74]

By September, HPB and Babaji had proceeded from Italy to Germany. In a letter from Würzburg written 2 September 1885, Blavatsky expressed praise for Babaji and blame for Hartmann and Olcott:

> Poor Hartmann. He is a bad lot, but he would give his life for the Masters and Occultism, though he would do far more progress with the *dugpas* than with our people. He is like the tortoise—one step forward and two back; with me now he seems very friendly. But I *cannot* trust him. . . . What he says of Olcott and the Society is true enough, but why should he be so spiteful in the opinions expressed! Speaking of O.—I can only say poor, poor Olcott; I can never cease loving him, one who was my devoted friend and defender for ten years, my chum, as he expresses it. But I can only pity one so dull, as not to comprehend instinctively, that if we were theosophical twins during our days of glory, in such a time of universal persecution, of false charges and public accusations the "twins" have to fall together as they have risen together, and that if I am called—at all events half confessed a fraud by him, then must he be one also. Had I not known him still watched by the Masters, and protected to a certain extent by MASTER, I would have sworn he was possessed by Dugpas. Fancy his writing to Miss Arundale, Baron Hoffmann, and many others I could name that I was mad (in the real sense of the word) and had been mad many years; that I may have been guilty of bogus phenomena at times, in my moments of mental aberration and whatnot!—Guilty in one, guilty in all. Ah poor, poor fool, who digs an abyss under the Theosophical Society with his own hands!
>
> Well, au revoir, Give my love to all, who can accept it and to you two foremost. Bowajee is supremely happy, Mohini and he wept for joy. There is peace and quiet, and the Kingdom of Heaven in my long suffering heart since yesterday, seeing round me my poor old aunt, Miss A., Mohini. Best wishes and love.[75]

Within several months, Babaji [Bowajee] was supremely *unhappy,* as reported by Countess Wachtmeister to Sinnett on 26 January 1886:

> When I came here in the beginning of December I found Babaji perfectly miserable, he said he was contemplating running away or committing suicide. I could see that he was wounded and jealous that Mohini was doing so much work in London, while he was comparatively speaking doing nothing and *nobody.* I was delighted with his teachings and as he had a Tamil and some other books which seemed to contain much that to our Western minds was perfectly new I thought it most desirable that he shd. have facilities for teaching what he knew, and so with Mme. B.'s consent, sent him to Elberfeld where they are all so anxious to learn. Personally I had a great sympathy for B. and was delighted to think that we now had a chela here who could teach us high morals and ethics.
>
> Well a few weeks ago B. began by writing most insulting letters to Mme. B. so at last I wrote to him that I refused to hand her such letters any more; then I received from him a letter which was the letter of a madman in which he begged me to come immediately to Elberfeld or he wd. be lost, that the Dweller of the Threshold had come to him, and that I and I alone could save him, that all the Gebhards could do nothing for him, that I on account of my psychic powers could help him, that he called on me as a sister, and that if I refused to come, that the consequences would be dreadful, and that all the Karma wd. fall on my head. Well knowing that Mme. G. is a sensible woman I wired to her "if my presence is really required"; the answer came "Yes." I started at night, had a most anxious journey, wondering which lunatic asylum he cd. be put into etc. amd when I got to Elberfeld my first enquiry was "is he raving, is he violent?" Mme. G. looked at me with astonishment and said no "B. is quite well, he only wanted to force you to come here, because he said Mme. B. wanted to psychologize you." B. received me with scoffs and jeers—and when I said to him "now B. tell me truly your trouble? I have come all this long distance to help you," he said "What do I want of your sympathy! What do I want of your friendship, I only want to get you away from Mme. for I hate her." I had a private interview with him and no words can describe the

> scene. He was no better than a wild beast with the most fiendish look of hatred in his face and finished by foaming at the mouth, he knocked about the furniture to that extent that Mr. G. who was in the drawing room below said he thought the chandelier would come down and every piece of furniture was being smashed upstairs; the upshot of all this row was his intense hatred to Mme. B. He said he would draw her life's blood out of her, he wd. kick her out of the Society, that he wd. tear her to pieces, that he wd. write articles against her, that he wd. send to the public papers in London, that he wd. destroy the T.S. and wd. form out of its remnants a Society for himself where he wd. preach only ethics. On asking why he was possessed of such a violent feeling against Mme. B. he said firstly because she had desecrated the Masters by connecting them with phenomena, and 2nd because she had insulted himself several times, *(and I say wounded his vanity)* . . . I asked him to state the charges he brought against Mme. B. and which he wd. publish they are as follows:—that Mme. B. had written to some Indian that Col. O. had never really seen the Masters, that she had herself psychologized him to see them and that later on when the Col. was shown this letter, for 3 days he was on the verge of suicide; that Mme. B. and the Col. wanting money they had written a letter in the Master's name to some Indian, asking for money and promising that if he gave it his sick child would recover—the child died, and the Indian was furious;—that Mme. B. wrote you a letter about Mohini and women in which there were a few words from the Master M. and that naturally such a thing was a desecration . . . B. told me that he *wd. never return* to Mme. B.—that he *would prevent* M. from doing so and that he had written to 100 Hindus about Mme. B. and that he had written expressly to prevent any chela from coming to replace me when I am gone; that he wished she wd. go to Russia and throw the S.D. to the dogs and then he could preach his philosophy in peace.[76]

On the same day, Babaji wrote to HPB, addressing her as "Respected and dear Upasika," assuring her that he was as devoted to the Masters as any Theosophist, and that "my only justification for all that I have done and said was *that Masters' names and philosophy have been so desecrated that* in my opinion all I did was not strong enough." Yet "now that you have at last condescended to reform the existing state of affairs, no one could worship you more and honor your nobleness of heart and self-sacrifice more, than my humble self! Master would have pointed out the least mistake I might have wilfully *[sic]* committed, if any. *They* only know all that tore my heart of late."[77]

The next day, 27 January, Babaji responded to a telegram from HPB, repenting of the wild statements he had made to the Countess:

> I assure you—swear to you *by all that is sacred to me and to you*—that I had been so excited and perfectly mad with rage against the desecration of Masters' names that I spoke to the Countess as though I would ruin the T.S. which so much desecrated Them. Before I wrote that unfortunate and strong letter to the good Countess I groaned all night after 12 P.M. and raved madly, thought even of committing suicide because I could not stop the ever growing desecration of Masters' names. Few, among the Gebhards none at all knew that beneath my apparent laughing there went a torrent of rage that tore my heart. But believe me dearest Mother that as you have condescended to guarantee against further desecration, no one is more devoted to you and to the T.S., again and again I repeat to you, than my humble self. I never really meant nor even believed that I had the ability to form a new Society. I shall always work hard to defend you, Theosophy, T.S. and Colonel Olcott. If I have told Countess or anyone else in a moment of rage that I would ruin the Society it was merely because the Masters' names were desecrated.[78]

By 31 January, Babaji was thanking HPB for her "kindest letter of absolute forgiveness" and encouraging her to blame his rebellion on the bad influence of his sorceress grandmother. In her next letter to Sinnett, Wachtmeister reports HPB's explanation for Babaji's frenzy, which is his use of a Tamil manuscript on black magic, leading to something like demonic possession. Rituals performed for seven days and nights were noted in a diary of Babaji's found by HPB, and she attributed to these practices his transformation into a case of Dr. Jekyll and Mr. Hyde.[79]

After reading Hodgson's report, Sinnett became suspicious of Babaji's changes of name, and wrote demanding an explanation. On 1 February, Babaji replied from Elberfeld admitting that Dharbagiri Nath was not his given name. However, he added, it was his initiation name:

> I never made a secret of the fact that I belonged to the ascetic order and to one small South Indian Fraternity of Occultists besides my connection with Mahatma K.H. . . . the name D.N. is purely Sanscrit and has been given to me by the exoteric Ascetics of a particular order of Adwaitees and followers of Sankaracharya while by "birth" I belonged to what you call in your "Esoteric Buddhism" as Vishishthadwaitees who are apparently opposed to the teachings of Sankaracharya."[80]

On 16 February, HPB explained to Sinnett her own view of the transformation undergone by Babaji. She lamented that "all the Gebhards" and Mohini had fallen victim "to Tamil mantras and psychology." Babaji had poisoned all these Theosophists against her by lies and black magic, and this left her no choice by "to fight alone, and single handed a POWER—that acts through him; and which, if I do not conquer, will conquer (ruin) the whole Society, yourself, and ALL through me."[81] Earlier she had called him "the copy of Moorad Ali [Mitford]—who died *raving mad,*" and his charges "infamous lies."[82]

In April, an event occurred which destroyed forever any rapprochement between Babaji and HPB. She wrote to tell him of it from Würzburg, where she remained, to London, where Babaji was now living:

> On Saturday—April the 10th, Walter Gebhard was found dead in his bed, having *shot* himself without *any reason* and *no cause.* The fiends of rage, of vindictiveness, malice and hatred let loose by you in their home have fastened on the poor boy you boasted to influence so forcibly, and *have done their work* . . . He is the first victim of your wicked father's son, and your grandmother's worthy grand-son . . . he is killed through you . . . May your karma bear fruit.
>
> Mr. Sinnett writes in despair: "Mohini used to attract all the theosophists [to] Elgin Crecent—and now they have nearly dropped off from doing this; I think he and Babajee together *are ruining* the Theosophic movement here." . . . The German Society died owing to what you said to Hubbe Schleiden about the two notes received by him. The fools who listen to *a chela* of Mahatma K.H., and were made to believe that the Master had turned away from me—will reap the fruit of their credulity—or [be] made to choose between yourself and me. They will *shake us off both*—most likely when they learn the *whole* truth. However, they may open their eyes and see it in the light of the

> *proofs I have.* I will play my last card if you please—you were offered friendship and *alliance,* you preferred reigning alone—it is your own choice and since you are against Mr. Sinnett there's an end of it. I will be in London before you expect me.[83]

On 20 April, the Countess wrote to Sinnett that HPB "says she is quite willing to come to London and use all her influence with Babajee and Mohini to try and bring them round to a better state of mind."[84] This proved unnecessary, however, as Babaji wrote to HPB on the 28th that "Ill-health and other considerations have decided me to return to India as quickly as I can. I am writing to Colonel Olcott for money to pay my passage back. I have lost all interest in the politics of the Theosophical Society."[85] After his return to India, Babaji vanished from Theosophical history.

What was responsible for the collapse in Babaji's mental health, and his nefarious influence over the Gebhard family? In a letter of 2 March, Olcott offered Wachtmeister his explanation:

> The terrible scene you witnessed at Elberfeld with Babajee was the outbreak of an epileptomania that had been developing in him since even before he left for Europe. His nervous excitable temperament was terribly strained by the excitements of 1884, and his most unwise departure with H.P.B. inevitably resulted in the maniacal scene in question.[86]

Olcott assured the Countess that Babaji's charge of financial fraud had been refuted in a statement by the alleged victim, Prince Harisinghji Rupsinghji. The prince remained a loyal and devoted Theosophist until his death in 1903.

The most compelling clue to Babaji's breakdown is his repeated reference to "desecration of the Masters' names" by HPB. Juxtaposing this with successful persuasion of Wilhelm Hubbe-Schleiden that HPB was forging messages from the Masters, and Babaji's allusions to some secret tearing his heart, provides an explanation which applies equally well to the collapse of Mohini's enthuasiasm.

In May 1883, a supplement to *The Theosophist* described a visit by the Aryan Patriotic Association to Jammu, where they met the Maharaja Ranbir Singh:

> His Highness took so much interest in the deputation that he was pleased to invite all the members at once to a private interview which lasted for an hour and a half, among those

> present being the Heir Apparent and all the princes . . . His Highness, in order to signify the pleasure he felt in meeting the deputation—especially D. Nath Bawaji—offered the latter gentleman a seat higher than his own on account of his proficiency in the occult sciences. His Highness promised to cooperate heartily with all patriotic schemes tending toward the re-establishment of Aryavarta's ancient glory.[87]

Babaji's special treatment by the maharaja, in context of the frequent allusions to patriotism in letters to chelas, suggests why he had a breakdown and loss of faith in HPB in the fall of 1885. In June of that year, Ranbir Singh died. Although Babaji was content to support HPB as agent of the Masters while Ranbir was alive, after his death the chela's behavior suggests a frenzy of grief. When HPB continued to produce messages from M as if he were alive, and from KH as if he were still involved in her work, something in Babaji snapped and he became obsessed with destroying her and the society. His destructive rage continued for months, but when Walter Gebhard's suicide was attributed to his influence, the young Indian's will to fight collapsed, and he quickly returned to India and Theosophical oblivion. Perhaps his greatest influence on Theosophical history was the change of course adopted by HPB in the aftermath of his rebellion. Her promise to end the "desecration of Masters' names" may well have been a commitment to cease referring to them publicly, as she seems to have become much less verbose on the subject after 1886.

Chelas and the Raj

The ambivalence revealed by the words and behavior of the Theosophical chelas is symptomatic of more than the specific circumstances described above. The evolution of the ideal of the Mahatma in 19th century India was conditioned by the general cultural environment created by British imperialism. Hinduism had been severely demoralized by several centuries of Mogul rule prior to the arrival of the British. By the time of Theosophy's emergence on the scene, several religious movements were attempting to adapt to a new set of challenges. The material superiority of European civilization was undeniable; as young Hindus were increasingly educated according to Western standards, a crisis of faith developed. Christian missionaries had plentiful justification for condemning Hindu superstition and the horrors of the caste system. Brahmin corruption was rampant, and belief in traditional Hinduism became increasingly rare among the best and brightest young Indians.

The inroads of Western scientific materialism on one hand, and Christian missionary success on the other, made Hindu intellectuals seek to reformulate their tradition to withstand these challenges. Peter Berger, in *The Heretical Imperative,* provides a model for interpreting the responses of religious traditions to the challenges of modernity. Although derived from the experience of Christianity in the late twentieth century, his perspective is equally applicable to the Hindu Theosophists portrayed in this chapter. Berger describes the modern situation as one in which no religious identity can be taken as given and fated for the individual who has never conceived of alternatives. The plurality of worldviews available to the modern individual makes all religious affiliation a matter of choice rather than fate. Since the etymology of the word *heresy* derives from the Greek *hairein* "to choose," Berger concludes that modernity is the universalization of heresy. Religious traditions, based on experience but mediated by interpretation and historical accident, face three options in adapting to the modern situation, in which science rather than religion or philosophy is the dominant paradigm for truthseeking. The deductive possibility entails the reaffirmation of tradition in the face of the challenges of modernity. It is exemplified by fundamentalism of every sort. The reductive possibility reinterprets religion in terms of the modern scientific/secular worldview. A third, inductive possibility is implicitly endorsed by Berger. This returns to the experiential roots of the tradition and rebuilds in accord with contemporary circumstances.[88]

Theosophy was the last of the major new religious movements to emerge in nineteenth-century India. Its evolution was intertwined with that of each of its predecessors. Comparing and contrasting these movements and their historical impact may be helpful in providing a context in which to understand the ambivalence of the patriotic chelas.

The first modern Hindu movement was the Brahmo Samaj, with which Mohini Chatterji was affiliated. Founded in Calcutta in 1828 by Ram Mohun Roy, the Brahmo Samaj attempted to Westernize Hinduism by purifying it of all polytheistic elements, priestly authority, and temple ritual.[89] Allying himself with Unitarians in Europe and America, Roy created a movement which was strongly appealing to Bengalis of the emergent middle class. By the time of Theosophy's arrival in India, the Brahmo Samaj was the leading reformist religious movement in the country. Yet by the death of its second leader, Keshub Chunder Sen (1884), the Brahmo Samaj had expended most of its vitality. Sen's successor, Debendranath Tagore, was a Theosophist, and his son Rabindranath became twentieth-century India's most celebrated writer and only Nobel laureate. Thomas J. Hopkins writes:

> By the time Sen died, the Brahmo Samaj had largely completed its mission, having met the initial impact of Christianity and Western culture and having shown how they could be used to strengthen Hinduism instead of destroying it. In the process, the movement created a new and lasting religious model that could release the creative energies of a class of people who had formerly been patrons rather than leaders in the Hindu system. Although the Brahmo Samaj survived as an independent organization, the energies of that class after 1884 were largely expressed in other movements of religious, social, and political reform.[90]

The Brahmo Samaj, in redefining Hinduism according to Western standards, conforms to Berger's "reductive" option. When HPB and Olcott arrived in India, there was a strong hunger for a movement that would affirm more emphatically the roots of Indian spirituality. Their alliance with Swami Dayananda's Arya Samaj, based on inadequate information, was a misguided attempt at a coalition that would satisfy this hunger. Dayananda was far more vigorous in his assertion of Hindu identity than the Brahmo leaders, and was successful in attracting many members of the Brahmo Samaj to his own organization. Indeed, it was only after coming into contact with Brahmo leaders in Calcutta that Dayananda abandoned the loincloth and the life of a rural preacher and established the Arya Samaj. Because the Brahmo Samaj was so closely linked with Bengali middle class intellectuals, Dayananda's Indian nationalism exerted a stronger attraction to many non-Bengalis.

The essence of Dayananda's appeal was to an imagined golden age of Hindu greatness, after which all Indian history was degenerate. The Vedas were proclaimed by the Arya Samaj as the sole authority for Hindu faith and practice. By affirming the authority of scripture and rejecting all subsequent history, Dayananda conforms to Berger's definition of the deductive option. Theosophy's eclecticism and relativism were profoundly incompatible with Dayananda's fundamentalism, so rapid mutual disenchantment was inevitable. One keynote of Dayananda's message was rejection of gurus; Theosophy's proclamations about Mahatmas were therefore offensive to Arya doctrine. Dayananda himself was Mahatma enough for the Arya Samaj, and the TS founders' alliances with Sikhs, Buddhists and Vedantists placed them beyond the pale of his favor.

The most successful new religious movement of nineteenth-century India has striking resemblances to Theosophy, but equally noticeable differences. The Radhasoami faith honors Swami Shiv Dayal Singh (1818–1878) as its founder. Building on the medieval sant tradition exemplified by Kabir, Swami Shiv Dayal promulgated a teaching focused on Surat Shabd yoga. This is defined as "the spiritual exercise by which the current of consciousness is applied to the hearing of the sound within; joining the mind and the attention to the sound current."[91]

The name of Radhasoami was popularized by Shiv Dayal's successor Rai Saligram. It refers to the highest spiritual region attainable through the practice of Surat Shabd yoga. Initiation into Radhasoami provides the believer with instruction in these techniques as well as mantras which invoke the sacred names of divinity. The latter practice is related to Sikh tradition, and the largest Radhasoami sect is headquartered in the Punjab and has been led exclusively by Sikh gurus. Shiv Dayal and Rai Saligram, however, were Hindus by birth and lived in Agra. Rai Saligram entered Theosophical history through his acquaintance with A. P. Sinnett during his tenure as postmaster in Allahabad. Mark Juergensmeyer's *Radhasoami Reality* notes that Saligram was a subscriber to *The Theosophist* and is mentioned in the Mahatma letters. These connections, first recognized by Daniel Caldwell, provide a basis for considering the significance of Radhasoami links to early Theosophy. As Juergensmeyer comments, "In *Voice of the Silence,* Blavatsky describes the sounds that are linked with the higher spiritual region, and her description is strikingly similar to the one given Swami Shiv Dayal."[92] *The Voice of the Silence* presents other striking parallels to Radhasoami meditation. It recommends concentration at the brow chakra as a means of reaching the inner Master, and mentions other details of Radhasoami practice like blocking the ears and closing the eyes during meditation. Thus the evidence for a link to Radhasoami is compelling, although this may result from common sources in the Sant tradition rather than from any direct influence.

There are substantial correspondences between the teachings of Radhasoami and Theosophy, particularly in the construction of models for the involution of spirit into matter through a series of increasingly dense stages of materiality. Such models imply a pathway back to the source for those able to transcend the limits imposed by the material world. In both traditions, the Mahatma is revered as one enabled through long practice and study to attain the spiritual regions. The introduction to the basic Radhasoami scripture, the *Sar Bachan,* describes the search of one disciple for his guru:

> When he [Baba Jaimal Singh] was only a child of seven years, he read Gurmukhi with Baba Khem Das, who was a Vedantist and a Mahatma . . . While still a boy, he travelled about seeking light on this problem from different Mahatmas . . . [at age sixteen] At Rishi Kesh he attended the satsang of every Mahatma there, constantly in search of the one truth . . . finally he overheard two men who were bathing in the Jumna river talking of the satsang of the great Mahatma, and after enquiring of them where this Mahatma lived, he found him. His long search was ended.[93]

This passage provides a striking example of the prodigal use of the term Mahatma in North India to refer to spiritual teachers. In the *Mahatma Letters to A. P. Sinnett,* Morya was dismissive of Radhasoami claims, but not entirely unsympathetic to their aspirations:

> Salig Ram—a truly good man—yet a devotee of another error. Not his guru's voice—*his own.* The voice of a pure, unselfish, earnest soul, absorbed in misguided, misdirected mysticism. Add to it a chronic disorder in that portion of the brain which corresponds to clear vision and the secret is soon told: that disorder was developed by *forced* visions; by *hatha* yog and prolonged asceticism. S. Ram is the chief *medium* and at same time *[sic]* the principal magnetic factor, who spreads his disease by infection—unconsciously to himself; who innoculates *[sic]* with his vision all the other disciples . . . no self-tutored seer or clairaudient ever saw or heard *quite* correctly.
>
> No harm and much instruction may come to you by joining his Society. Go on *until he demands what you will be obliged to refuse.* Learn and study. You are right: they say and affirm that *the one* and only God of the Universe was incarnated in their guru, and were such an individual to exist he would certain be higher than any "planetary." But they are idolators, my friend. Their guru was no initiate only a man of extraordinary purity of life and powers of endurance. He had never consented to give up his notions of a personal god and even gods though offered more than once. He was born an orthodox Hindu and

> died a *self-reformed* Hindu, something like Kechub-Ch-Sen but higher purer and with no ambition to taint his bright soul. Many of us have regretted his self-delusion but he was too good to be forcibly interfered with. Join them and learn—but remember your sacred promise to K.H. . . . [94]

The demand that Sinnett would be obliged to refuse might have been any of these standard Radhasoami obligations listed by David Christopher Lane: "1. The practice of surat shabd yoga (between two and three hours of meditation daily). 2. Obedience to the living master who initiates the disciple into the path. 3. A pure moral life which includes abstinence from meat, fish, eggs, alcohol, drugs, and sex outside of marriage."[95] Obedience to Saligram would presumably have conflicted with the "sacred promise to K.H." mentioned by Morya.

What is perhaps most instructive in this passage is the implication that Morya and his fellow Mahatmas are watching the entire range of contemporary spiritual movements with interest and are attempting to guide developments without visible interference. This corresponds intriguingly to the secret sponsorship of various movements by interested maharajas. The recently deceased Brahmo Samaj leader Keshub Chunder Sen is regarded with slightly less indulgence than Saligram in the above passage, while Swami Dayananda was unsparingly condemned in a letter to Sinnett from KH:

> Note the bare-faced lies of India's "great Reformer." Remember what was admitted to you and then denied. And if *my* word of honour has any weight with you, then know that D. Swami *was* an initiated yogi, a very high chela at Badrinath, endowed some years back with great powers and a knowledge he has since forfeited, and that H.P.B. told you but the truth, as also that H.C. [Hurrychund Chintamon] was a chela of his, who preferred to follow the "left path." And now see what has become of this truly great man, whom we all knew and placed our hopes in him *[sic]*. There he is—a moral wreck, ruined by his ambition and panting for breath in his last struggle for supremacy, which, *he knows* we will *not* leave in his hands.[96]

It would be premature to draw firm conclusions from letters whose authorship still remains mysterious. But both the above letters suggest that M and KH were men with considerable power in India. Morya's description of Shiv Dayal Singh as "too good to be forcibly interfered with" implies that he had the means to forcibly interfere with religious leaders who were *not* too good for such treatment. KH's defiant statement that "we will *not* leave in his [Dayananda's] hands" the supremacy craved by the Swami has equally threatening implications. The above passages are helpful in providing a context for the turbulent feelings of the Theosophical chelas. Behind the scenes of nineteenth-century Indian religious movements, there were secret sponsors whose motives were both nationalistic and spiritually idealistic. The Theosophical movement was allied with such sponsors, but their interest also extended to the Arya Samaj, Brahmo Samaj, and Radhasoami movements.

Theosophy and Radhasoami were parallel in their choice of Berger's inductive option; they preserved a core of Indian spirituality based on experience, but deemphasized outmoded traditions like caste and ritual. The two movements were quite divergent, however, in their subsequent development. Radhasoami shattered into many competing sects based on adherence to rival claimants to guru status. Theosophy's fragmentation was derived from the more modest claim that competing sect leaders were in contact with the original sponsors of the movement. Theosophy was far more successful than Radhasoami or the Brahmo Samaj in affecting India's development as a nation. Mohandas Gandhi was first awakened to an appreciation of Hindu spirituality after meeting HPB in London and reading a Theosophical translation of the *Bhagavad Gita.*[97] Jawaharlal Nehru joined the TS in his teens, after being tutored by F. T. Brooks, an English Theosophist employed by his father Motilal, a long-standing member of the society. Although Nehru later lost interest in Theosophy, his daughter Indira Gandhi was interested in both the TS and Jiddu Krishnamurti. In her later years she was especially respectful of Krishnamurti, who had by that time emerged as one of India's most renowned living spiritual teachers.[98] Rabindranath Tagore, Krishnamurti, Mohandas Gandhi, and Sri Aurobindo were among the most influential thinkers of twentieth-century India; all were linked indirectly with the TS although none was a member for very long. Annie Besant's leadership of the society included periods of deep involvement in Indian political movements, culminating in her presidency of the Indian National Congress in 1917.[99] But since Besant's death, TS membership in India has been stagnant or declining. The Arya Samaj supplied the freedom movement with a more extremist radical cadre of recruits. While Theosophy permeated upper class Indian society, the Arya Samaj succeeded in promoting independence at the grassroots level.

Radhasoami, on the other hand, was never significantly involved in the freedom movement, educational reform, or feminism, as Theosophy had been. Social idealism in the Radhasoami tradition was focused on building new communities as showcases for progressive reform. These survive to the present in the Agra area as well as the Punjab. By the late twentieth century, Radhasoami's membership exceeded one million while the TS stagnated at less than forty thousand worldwide.

Although its interaction with Theosophy has been minimal, mention should be made here of the Ramakrishna Mission, devoted to the teachings of the illiterate Bengali saint Ramakrishna (d. 1875). The foremost missionary of Vedanta to the West was Ramakrishna's disciple Vivekananda, whose visit to the Parliament of Religions in Chicago in 1893 was a resounding success. But the Ramakrishna Mission and its Western successor the Vedanta Society have been indifferent to social reform in comparison to the other groups under consideration. Still, the widespread veneration for Ramakrishna as nineteenth-century India's greatest saint is yet another indication of the general Hindu revival of the period. Juergensmeyer compares the roles of the TS, the Vedanta Society, and the Radhasoami movement as bridges between Indian spirituality and the West:

> One of the reasons people gave for switching from Theosophy to Radhasoami was their desire to join a movement that seemed to them more authentically Hindu. Even though the leaders of Theosophy borrowed their ideas from Hinduism, and perhaps even from Radhasoami, their movement was essentially Western in form and interests. The Vedanta Societies also had a strong Western impetus; although their teachings had Hindu roots, they were presented in such a way as to answer to Western philosophic concerns, and a Christian style of worship was adopted. Radhasoami was different: it maintained the same ideas and practices throughout all its outposts, whether in India or the United States. And it was open to all. In fact, Radhasoami was the first religious movement of Hindu ancestry where foreigners had direct and easy access to an original, un-Westernized form of religion.[100]

What, then, can be concluded about the historical dilemma of the Hindu Theosophical chelas? All were proud sons of India, alarmed at the degradation of Hindu spirituality and the inroads of Western modes of thought and belief. Although they were disenchanted with orthodox Brahminism, they were still filled with respect for the ideal of the guru. The Mahatmas they sought, however, were required to be more than authorities on Hindu philosophy. Because the chelas had been exposed to the Western scientific mode of thought, as well as to foreign religions, they sought a source of authority that was universal. Their Mahatmas had to be able to answer a far wider range of questions than those posed by chelas of the past. The Brahmo Samaj offered this in a watered-down Hinduism which was nearly identical to Western Unitarianism. But this was ultimately unsatisfying to young Indians in search of a teaching which could affirm Hindu identity in a more vital and compelling fashion. The Arya Samaj provided a persuasive alternative for those willing to submit to Dayananda's Vedic fundamentalism. This tended to attract the most passionate but repel the more reflective of the young seekers. Radhasoami promised a simple, direct, and effective path to liberation, which required only total obedience to the authority of the Satguru. It would ultimately prove more satisfying to a greater number of seekers for a reformed Hinduism than any of its competitors.

Theosophy was simultaneously the most and least successful of the movements attempting to articulate a nineteenth-century reformulation of Hinduism. It was the most successful in mobilizing Western-educated intellectuals to productive efforts at social and political reform. Furthermore, its success at gaining support from a wide range of maharajas, although little recognized, was remarkably swift and effective. Even in present-day India, the Theosophical Society enjoys near-universal name recognition, and is honored for its role in the freedom movement. At the same time, its membership has stagnated as its role in the vanguard of social and cultural change has been relegated to the history books.

The patriotic chelas were drawn to Theosophy by its paradoxical combination of universalism and Hindu revivalism. But with the deaths of several of HPB's Mahatmas and her departure for Europe, the patriotic appeal of Theosophy diminished so drastically that the most celebrated chelas rapidly abandoned the movement. In succession, most of the alleged chelas of the Theosophical Masters were lost to the movement between 1885 and 1887. First Damodar vanished, and within two years Babaji, Mohini, Subba Row, and Brown all "lost interest" in Theosophy, and Mitford died insane.

Because patriotic motives were deeply involved in the chelas' allegiance to the Theosophical Masters, it was inevitable that the events of the mid-eighties would reduce their enthusiasm for the cause. The death of several royal sponsors of the society and the breakup of the Singh Sabha created a void in Mahatmic sponsorship. In the wake of Hodgson's report, the promise of support from Swami Sankaracharya was lost, and with it that of his Vedanta disciples. The foundation of the chelas' loyalty to HPB and her TS was thus weakened by 1886, and Indian disciples were no longer to play a major role in Theosophical propaganda in the West. Wrenched from their homes and families to serve as missionaries in Europe, Mohini and Babaji came to regret ever having become entangled with Theosophy. In this they foreshadowed the experience of J. Krishnamurti years later.

The failures of this period, although largely hidden, determined a great deal of future development of the Theosophical movement. After 1886, the Masters, whose allure had always been intricately connected with their remoteness, moved completely out of the realm of current history and into that of myth. After the end of the chelas' careers as Theosophical missionaries, initiations of the Masters' disciples were portrayed as happening almost exclusively at a distance through clairvoyant and telepathic means. The element of normal contact and conversation with corporeal teachers, which had been so large a part of HPB's spiritual life, disappeared into the shadows of occultism. As shown in the prologue, the Masters of Theosophical belief grew increasingly remote from historical reality in the century after HPB's death.

This does not mean, however, that the work of the Masters came to a dead end. Outside the ranks of Theosophy, their initiatory lineages continue to the present day. In Parts Two, Three, and Four, several initiates of HPB's Masters are revealed as historical figures whose contributions are a remarkable testimony to the influence wielded by those men and women who had been supplanted in the minds of Theosophists by imaginary Mahatmas.

Jamal ad-Din "al-Afghani" (by Ray M. Hershberger)

Part Two.

The Secret World of Jamal ad-Din

Jamal ad-Din "al-Afghani" exerted unparalled influence throughout the nineteenth-century Islamic world. Born in Asadabad, Iran in 1839, he studied Shiʿa theology in the Iraqi holy city of Najaf as an adolescent. In his early twenties, Jamal ad-Din spent several years wandering, mainly in India, where he sought to learn about all religions. This period coincides with HPB's first trip to India, and is one of many such coincidences. In the early 1860s, his wanderings took him to Central Asia and the Caucasus. HPB was living in Tbilisi during this period. Jamal ad-Din's first appearance in government records is found in the late 1860s, when he was advisor to a pro-Russian ruler in Afghanistan. When a British-sponsored rival displaced the ruler, Jamal ad-Din was expelled from the country and returned to India. In 1870, he surfaced in Istanbul, where he was allied with educational reformers in the establishment of a new university. It was at this point that he began to use the name "Afghani," falsely implying Afghan nationality. He was expelled from Istanbul in 1871 after giving a lecture comparing prophecy to philosophy, which was condemned as heretical. At this point he proceeded to Cairo, where he was to remain throughout the decade. There, he gathered a circle of disciples whose allegiance to him was both spiritual and political. HPB seems to have been among his acquaintances during this period, if not before. At the end of the 1870s, he was expelled from Cairo, after supporting the replacement of the ruling Khedive Ismaʿil by his son Tawfiq. Afghani's disciples had followed him into Freemasonry in the mid-seventies, just as HPB was establishing the TS with Masonic support in New York. Her claims of adept sponsorship at the time referred more to Egypt than to India, and Afghani's circle in Cairo has marked similarities to her "Brotherhood of Luxor." But around the time that Blavatsky and Olcott decided to relocate in India, Afghani and most of his disciples were forced to leave

Egypt. Jamal ad-Din settled in Hyderabad, India, in 1879, the year the TS founders arrived in Bombay.

Afghani's next change of address occurred in response to political upheaval in Egypt in 1882. He left India, spent a short time in Egypt, and then proceeded to Paris where he remained throughout 1884. The following year, he proceeded to London, and then on to Russia, where he was allied with HPB's publisher Mikhail Katkov. After Katkov's death, Afghani was invited to return to his homeland by Nasir ad-Din Shah. After he established subversive secret societies, the shah decided to expel him in 1891. The violence with which the orders were carried out nearly ended Afghani's life, and he conceived a lifelong hatred for Nasir ad-Din. From 1892 through his death in 1897, Afghani lived in Istanbul as a guest of the Sultan ʿAbduʾl-Hamid. Almost from the moment of his arrival in Cairo, Jamal ad-Din functioned as a guru to devoted followers, which role he continued to fulfill in ever-changing circumstances until death. A survey of the careers of Afghani's most significant disciples yields insight into the nature of his influence.

What is the evidence for Jamal ad-Din's connections with Blavatsky? Their travels coincided repeatedly over a twenty-five year period: India in the late 1850s, the Caucasus in the early sixties, Cairo in the early seventies, India again from 1879 through the early eighties, and Paris in 1884. On 1 April 1884, HPB wrote to Alexis Coulomb from Paris that "if you compromise me before Lane-Fox, Hartmann and the others—ah well, I shall never return to Adyar, but will remain here or in London where I will prove by phenomena more marvellous still that they are true and that our Mahatmas exist, *for there is one here at Paris and there will be also in London.*[1] This was written in the middle of Jamal ad-Din's stay in Paris and a few months before Thakar Singh's arrival in London. In another letter, HPB referred to one of the "highest Mahachohans [who] lived in Egypt and went to Tibet only a year before we did (in 1878) and he is neither a Tibetan nor a Hindu."[2] HPB and Olcott went to India, not Tibet, and arrived there in 1879, not 1878. But despite the vagueness of this passage, it does correspond to some relevant facts about Jamal ad-Din. In a letter to Sinnett written in the summer of 1882, KH stated that "The Egyptian consequences of your blessed countrymen involve such local consequences to the body of occultists there and to what they are guarding, that two of our adepts are already there, having joined some Druze brethren and three more on their way."[3] This refers to the British occupation of Egypt, completed in the fall of 1882, which seems to have precipitated Afghani's departure for that country *en route* to Europe. Two other crucial bits of evidence relating Jamal ad-Din to HPB involve their mutual acquaintances, and will be discussed below.

Afghani's historical significance is assessed by Wilfred Cantwell Smith in *Islam in Modern History*. Smith calls him "supremely comprehensive, the complete Muslim of his time," a man who united "Islamic scholarship, a familiarity with Europe, and an acquaintance with its modern thought," who was "active in both internal reform and external defence," who "inspired political revolutionaries and venerable scholars" and "advocated both local nationalisms and pan-Islam."[4] His role was that of an agitator, who recognized the threat posed by Europe to the entire Islamic world and was the first to use the terms "Islam" and "the West" as "connoting correlative—and of course antagonistic—historical phenomena."[5] The first explicit nostalgia for Islam's lost glories appeared in Afghani's work. He evoked this feeling in Muslim countries around the world where it continues to resonate today. Smith regards Afghani as important for his appreciation of Western science and philosophy, but more so for his energy in arousing his fellow Muslims to work for an Islamic renaissance. He concludes, "It was his vision and his determination (as it has become the aspiration providing the clue to most subsequent Muslim 'modernism') that Islamic history shall once again march forward in full truth and full splendor."[6]

Muhammad ᶜAbduh

Among Jamal ad-Din's disciples, Muhammad ᶜAbduh has clearly had the greatest influence on Islamic history. The *Encyclopedia of Religion* recognizes him as "the architect of Islamic modernism."[7] When he met Jamal ad-Din, he was a student at al-Azhar, Cairo's first university, where he studied philosophy and religion. After Afghani's departure from Egypt, ᶜAbduh was involved in the anti-British revolt led by General ᶜUrabi. This led to six years of exile in Lebanon and France. While in Beirut he worked toward the creation of a system of Islamic schools. In Paris, ᶜAbduh was reunited with his Master Jamal ad-Din, with whom he published the radical paper *al-Urwa al-wuthqa* (The Firmest Bond).

Like Afghani, ᶜAbduh is a subject of controversy in the contemporary Islamic world. *The Reformers of Egypt* by M. A. Zaki Badawi takes a conservative view of both figures, whom the author defends against charges of heresy. Still, Badawi is forced to admit some difficulty in explaining away a letter to Afghani from ᶜAbduh.

In it, he expresses relief that a French publication in which Afghani had taken a frankly anti-religious stance was not to be translated into Arabic for distribution in the Islamic world. ʿAbduh continues:

> We are at present following your straight path (the head of religion is cut off only with the sword of religion) if you therefore saw us you would see ascetics continuously worshipping, bending and prostrating, never disobeying God in what He orders them and doing what they ordered. "Without hope, life would be unbearable."[8]

Such a double standard for European and home consumption need not imply that Afghani and ʿAbduh were charlatans, Badawi argues. They both sincerely believed in the superiority of Islamic culture, which they stressed over theology. Afghani's writings continue to be published in Arabic, and his reputation as an Islamic hero continues to expand.

Elie Kedourie's *Afghani and ʿAbduh* portrays both men as secret heretics, as seen in the subtitle *An essay on religious unbelief and political activism in modern Islam.* Kedourie makes it clear from the start of this brief study that his goal is to induce a thorough revisionism in scholarly approaches to Afghani. He regards with a critical eye the extent to which Afghani's own version of his life has attained official recognition in the Islamic world. Kedourie cites Western scholars whose discoveries imply that Afghani used Islam for political purposes and in fact believed that all religions were equally bad. The hagiographical studies by disciples, notably Rashid Rida and ʿAbduh himself, are only recently being reexamined in light of new documentary discoveries.

ʿAbduh appears to have been just as truly Afghani's spiritual disciple as his political associate. When the two met, ʿAbduh was a twenty-two year old student, consumed by a spiritual quest. Kedourie concludes that "Afghani must have had a powerful magnetic personality to have exercised over ʿAbduh then and for many years afterwards so strange and tenacious an influence. The link between them is very much that of the master and disciple in some secret, esoteric cult."[9] This hyperbolic paean to Afghani by ʿAbduh reveals the spiritual relationship between them:

> You have made us with your hands, invested our matter with its perfect form, and created us in the best shape . . . Through you have we known the whole universe; . . . I have been endowed by you with a wisdom which enables me to change

> inclinations, impart rationality to reason, overcome great obstacles, and control the innermost thoughts of men . . . I have been given by you a will so powerful as to move the immovable, deal blows to the greatest of obstacles, and remain firm in the right (haqq) until truth (haqq) is satisfied.[10]

What excited such enthusiasm in the disciples of Afghani? His philosophy was apparently laced with Indian pantheistic notions and Western freethought ideals. The channel for the latter was the Masonic lodges with which Afghani was affiliated in the middle and late seventies. Jamal ad-Din joined first an English lodge led by British vice-consul Raphael Borg, after which he defected to a French Grand Orient lodge. Borg was a behind-the-scenes sponsor of HPB and the TS as early as 1878 and until at least 1886. When Afghani and his leading disciples were exiled in 1879, this was the end of his Masonic involvement, except for a brief period in Paris in 1884 when he and ᶜAbduh renewed their membership.

In an obituary published upon ᶜAbduh's death, Rashid Rida, his disciple, recalled this explanation of the role of Masonry in his relationship with Afghani:

> I asked him once what masonry really was, and he said that its role—now ended—in the countries in which it is found was to resist the authority of kings and popes who were fighting against knowledge and freedom, and that this was a great achievement and one of the pillars of European progress . . . He also told me that his membership and the Sayyid's (Afghani) was for a political and social purpose.[11]

In 1889, ᶜAbduh returned to Cairo, where he was appointed judge, and ten years later became Mufti of Egypt, the chief interpreter of Islamic law.[12] By the time of his death in 1905 he had attained recognition as the leading writer on Muslim law and theology. His primary works balance mysticism and orthodoxy.[13] He opposed *taqlid* or blind adherence, and emphasized the need for individualism and freedom of thought. Believing true Islam "tolerant of all rational inquiry and science," he sought a full acceptance of modern educational reforms.[14] His accommodation to British imperialism recognized that in some ways Islamic society could benefit from its enforced contact with Western culture. Although ᶜAbduh adjusted in later life to the very international forces which Afghani had strenuously resisted, in his religious views he remained a true disciple of his Master.

Heretics and Infidels

Among the disciples of Jamal ad-Din, few other than ᶜAbduh even claimed to be orthodox Muslims. The range of heretics and infidels found in Afghani's company suggests the unorthodox nature of his private convictions. In Paris, he was associated with Mirza Baqir, whose religious eclecticism led him through Shiᶜa and Sunni Islam, Sufism, Christianity, Judaism and ultimately his own "Islamo-Christianity."[15] In Paris, Afghani became involved in a debate with French Orientalist Joseph-Ernest Renan, rebutting the latter's lecture "l'Islamisme et la science" with the assertions that all revealed religions are guilty of obscurantism, and that Islam is no more guilty than others. In Hyderabad, Jamal ad-Din was regarded as a "free-thinker of the French type." Kedourie calls his Egyptian disciples "a group of intellectual malcontents and religious rebels, to whom he purveyed secret and subversive philosophical doctrines."[16] Among the leading characters of Afghani's circle in Cairo were the journalist ᶜAbdullah al-Nadim, the Syrian Christian writer Adib Ishaq, and the Reverend Louis Sabunji, a Catholic priest who was driven out of Beirut in the 1870s following a religious altercation, and who was described by Afghani's British sponsor Sir Wilfred Blunt as "more in sympathy with Islam than his own faith."[17]

A strong Western influence on this circle of associates is seen in their links to Masonry. Kedourie cites a report that Afghani was expelled from a lodge in Cairo for atheism, which coincides with the crisis that provoked the separation of the Grand Orient from the Grand Lodge in 1877.[18] The police later confiscated papers belonging to ᶜAbduh, which included, according to his letter to Afghani, "the book of masons by the hand of my exalted lord."[19] Such confiscations made it impossible to determine the history of Afghani's Masonic affiliation, until major documentary research published by Juan R. I. Cole in 1993. In *Colonialism and Revolution in the Middle East,* Cole reports, "I was fortunate in being able to use a dossier in the Egyptian National Archives, of private papers confiscated from the Iranian activist Sayyid Jamaluᵓd-Din, that gives great insight into the world of secret organizations in the Egypt of the 1870s."[20]

Afghani's most energetic disciple in Egypt was Yaᶜqub Sannuᵓ, known as James Sanua to his Western friends. Born of Italian-Jewish parents in Cairo, Sanua was educated in Livorno at the expense of the pasha, a family friend. He was drawn into Carbonari subversive circles during his education, but was obliged to return to Egypt to earn a living. He served as a language tutor, but gradually developed an Arabic theatre. Having fled to Paris after alienating the Khedive Isma^cil, his former patron, Sanua became "Abou Naddara" (Blue Glasses), editor of a satirical journal of that name.

Sanua introduced secret societies in the salon he founded in Cairo in the early 1870s. His Circle of Progress taught modern French and Italian literature and history at four meetings per week. After this was disbanded by the police, he formed a Society of the Lovers of Knowledge, which was also soon closed down. Henceforth, Sanua's interest in secret societies would focus on Freemasonry.[21]

Rivalries among Masonic factions in 1870s Egypt were politically inspired. Raphael Borg, a Maltese British diplomat, established an Eastern Star lodge which enrolled Afghani and his disciples, including Sanua. Although all Cairo's Masons agreed that Khedive Ismaᶜil should be replaced immediately, they differed on the proposed replacement. Afghani and ᶜAbduh supported Ismaiᶜl's son Tawfiq, who was duly named Khedive. But he almost immediately expelled them from his domain. Sanua, already exiled, joined Borg and Ishaq in supporting Tawfiq's rival and uncle ᶜAbduʾl-Halim.

Adib Ishaq is identified by Cole as an "anti-imperialist Syrian Christian" who "deserves much greater credit than he has generally received as an advocate of liberal ideals and democratic government."[22] Born in Damascus in 1856, he moved with his father to Beirut around 1871. Working as a customs clerk, he devoted his spare time to literary salons. Cole summarizes his early years as a writer:

> at age 17 he managed to hire on as a writer for the newspaper *at-Taqaddum* (Progress). In the early 1870s he anonymously published two translations from the French, one on ethics and the other on health, following these with a book of his own. He became the president of a local literary society, and in 1875 at age 19 he translated Racine's *Andromaque*. With his friend Salim an-Naqqash, he became active in authoring and translating stage plays for a troupe in Syria.[23]

The two moved to Alexandria together in 1876, and there Jamal ad-Din entered Ishaq's life immediately. Afghani arranged through a royal patron for Ishaq to obtain a license to publish a newspaper *Misr* (Egypt) which led to rapid financial success. Ishaq was more involved with the Masonry of Alexandria than of Cairo, and was more an Ottoman loyalist than an Egyptian nationalist.

The 1877–78 war with Russia aroused his patriotism and evoked an outpouring of political journalism which is a crucial element in reconstructing the world of Afghani's disciples. Ishaq, a "romantic liberal, sees liberty as an almost mystical force shaping modern history," and "views the Young Ottomans and Ottoman constitutionalism as a link in the great chain of intellectual movements for liberty" according to Cole.[24] Ishaq's faith in constitutional monarchy as practiced by the Ottoman sultan was somewhat misplaced, but he had valid reasons for suspecting the intentions of the rival imperial powers. Cole concludes of the interests binding Ishaq and fellow Christian Syrian Masons:

> The freemasons of Syrian Christian background appear to have widely supported a constitutional, parliamentary regime patterned on the Ottoman experiment of 1876–78. They had been strongly socialized to these values, and not only by reading French progressive literature. They had after all had strong links to Ottoman Syria, which sent elected delegates to the first Ottoman parliament, and they regularly voted for their own lodge officers within masonry. I can think of no one in Egypt who wrote publicly in support of democracy more strongly, or earlier, than Adib Ishaq.[25]

The crime for which Afghani was expelled by Tawfiq was forming a secret society of "young thugs" aimed at "the ruin of religion and rule."[26] Underlying this may have been the discovery of his involvement in a plan to assassinate Isma^cil, sponsored by French interests. Later, he was apparently indebted to French support; *al-Urwa,* which Jamal ad-Din published in Paris, was financed by someone other than the penniless Sayyid. The French government may have supported it financially as it had such previous anti-British publications as *al-Basir,* which welcomed Afghani to Paris as "the man of action and science . . . the perfect philosopher."[27] *Al-Basir* was controlled by the Maronite Khalil Ghanim, former Dragoman for the Vali of Syria. After serving as Dragoman for the Grand Vizierate in Istanbul, he became a Syrian representative to the first Ottoman parliament. In 1879, ʿAbduʾl Hamid dissolved the assembly and Ghanim went to Paris. Employed by the French government, he was given citizenship and awarded the *Legion d'honneur.* His aim was clearly to promote pro-French sentiment among the Arabs. Khalil Ghanim introduced Afghani to Joseph-Ernest Renan, who described him as "an Afghan entirely liberated from the prejudices of Islam."[28]

By the 1880s, Renan had completed his multi-volume study of Christian origins, of which the *Life of Jesus* is best known. His scholarship had dealt a severe blow to the Church, powerfully affecting public opinion in a liberal direction. His extensive travels in the Near East may have brought him into contact with some members of HPB's network of adept acquaintances. In a letter to her sister written in the summer of 1884, Blavatsky mentioned Renan among those who regularly attended meetings of the *Société Théosophique d'Orient et d'Occident* at the home of Lady Caithness: "You shall see there the elite of Parisian society and intelligentsia. Renan, Flammarion, Madame Adam, and lots of the aristocracy from the Faubourg St. Germain."[29] Another reference to Renan is found in Felix K. Gaboriau's bitter farewell to readers of *le Lotus* written upon his resignation as editor in March 1889:

> I like to believe that the Adepts of Tibet exist nowhere other than in the *Philosophical Dialogues* of M. Renan who had invented before Mme. Blavatsky and Col. Olcott a fabric of Mahatmas at the center of Asia under the name of Asgaard, and presented interviews with them in the style of Koot Hoomi before the latter's manifestation.[30]

Renan went so far as to call Afghani "a great unbeliever" and Kedourie comments of their debate that "Afghani makes no secret here of his belief that religion has been on the whole a force for evil in human history."[31] This recalls KH's comment that "the chief cause of nearly two thirds of the evils that pursue humanity ever since that cause became a power" is "religion under whatever form and in whatsoever nation."[32]

In his debate with Renan, Afghani emphasized the superiority of philosophy to religion, yet within the next two years, he became the public champion of an extreme example of religious fanaticism, the Sudanese Mahdi. He made apparently false claims about his intimacy with the Mahdi and even inspired a French journalist, Olivier Pain, to penetrate into Mahdist territory, where he died of illness and hunger. Kedourie defines Afghani's vision of the Mahdi as "a secular apocalypse" and his creed as "political messianism."[33] The death of the Mahdi claimant Muhammad Ali in 1885 deprived Afghani of the rallying point of his magazine, *al-Urwa,* which was published from May through December 1884. Afghani told his British friend Wilfrid Scawen Blunt that he wanted the Mahdi or his successor to replace the Sultan as Caliph, which he later expressed in print:

> Does she [England] think herself able to stifle the voice before making itself heard in all the East from Mount Himalaya to Dawlaghir, from north to south, speaking to the Muslims of Afghanistan, of Sind and India, proudly proclaiming the coming of the Saviour whom every son of Islam awaits with such impatience. El-Mahdi, El-Mahdi, El-Mahdi![34]

This was not the first case in which Afghani was to support a rival claimant to the caliphate, as is seen in the memoirs of his confidant Blunt.

Wilfrid Scawen Blunt's life intersects with the world of the Theosophical Masters in a striking variety of historical circumstances. Born in 1840 to a Sussex landowning family, he was educated at public schools and entered the foreign service at eighteen. After serving as legation secretary in several European capitals and Buenos Aires, he married in 1869, and ended his diplomatic career. His wife, Lady Anne Isabella Noel, was the granddaughter of the poet Byron, and became a full partner in Blunt's life of travel and political intrigue. The death of his elder brother in 1872 left Blunt independently wealthy and owner of Crabbet, a Sussex estate. For the next dozen years, the Blunts devoted their lives to travel in the Middle East and India.[35]

In the spring of 1873, just as HPB was ending her veiled years of travel and preparing to emigrate to America, the Blunts began their peregrinations through the same regions she had visited. After spending several months exploring Turkey, they returned to England, only to set out for North Africa the following winter. In Algeria, they first tasted the Arab hospitality which was to become a keynote of their future lives. Blunt's biographer Elizabeth Longford remarks of this visit that Anne "was 'worn out' before she had reached the cous-cous and then had to taste four kinds of pastry and dates and listen to ballads about Abd-el-Kader, the great Algerian patriot now exiled to Damascus."[36] This trip ended in spring 1874, followed in the next few years with three more journeys through Arab lands. In 1876–77, the Blunts explored Egypt and the Sinai. During the winter of 1877–78, they journeyed down the Euphrates from Aleppo to Baghdad. In 1878–79, they explored the little-known Nejd region of Arabia. During the latter trip, recorded in their book *A Pilgrimage to Nejd,* the Blunts first met Lady Jane Digby and her Bedouin husband Medjuel el-Mezrab. Six years before, HPB had made the acquaintance of Lady Jane during a visit to Damascus. Another figure of Theosophical interest whom the Blunts met on this journey was the Algerian shaykh Abdelkader, whose praises they had heard in Algeria four years earlier.[37] They were so entranced by Arabia that when they returned in late 1880, in his diary Wilfrid noted that it was "perhaps for ever."[38]

Although they were to spend most of their lives in England, the changes wrought by this period were indeed permanent. During this second visit to Egypt, Blunt began to be interested in Jamal ad-Din. Lady Anne had been studying Arabic in London under Louis Sabunji, the former Christian clergyman who had become Afghani's disciple in Cairo and been exiled along with most of his entourage in 1878–79. Muhammad ᶜAbduh, however, remained in Cairo, and in 1880, he began a lifelong friendship with Blunt. The Englishman gradually became a Muslim convert under the influence of Afghani and ᶜAbduh, and shared their hopes for the establishment of an Arab caliphate based in Mecca to replace the Ottoman Sultan as spiritual leader of Islam. During an 1881 excursion to Syria, the Blunts again visited Damascus, where they spent a week in a house next door to Lady Jane and her husband. While there, they resumed their acquaintance with Abdelkader, and Blunt decided that he was the most promising candidate for the Arab caliph, an opinion shared by Afghani and ᶜAbduh.[39] After Abdelkader's death in 1883, other candidates were sought, including, briefly, the Sudanese Mahdi Muhammad Ahmad.

It is at this point that Blunt's career intersects most strikingly with that of HPB. During her visit to Damascus eight years before, she had been acquainted with Lady Jane and apparently with Abdelkader as well. ᶜAbduh was the sole remaining leader of the circle around Afghani with which she had likely been associated when she lived in Cairo. Another source of striking parallels is the relationship between Blunt and Sir Richard Burton. When HPB had visited Damascus, Burton was British consul there, and his closest friend was Abdelkader. His wife Isabel was equally friendly with Lady Jane Digby. Burton's later membership in the TS suggests a secret link with HPB, although its exact nature remains mysterious. Like Blunt, Burton was a convert to Islam who nevertheless retained links to Catholicism. Both were renowned as travelers, poets, and womanizers. The two had met in Buenos Aires in the seventies, where they spent many evenings together, in Blunt's words, "talking all things in Heaven and Earth, or rather listening while he talked till he grew dangerous in his cups, and revolver in hand would stagger home to bed."[40] Although both had careers in British diplomatic service, the parallels break down when one compares their political views. While Burton was in many ways an agent of British imperialism, Blunt opposed it almost continually for most of the late nineteenth century. His interest in Egypt was especially strong after he purchased an estate outside Cairo in 1881, to which he returned frequently thereafter.

After their Nejd pilgrimage ended in 1879, the Blunts proceeded to India, where their friend Robert Lytton was serving as Viceroy. Arriving within months of the TS founders' relocation there, the Blunts spent most of their time in Simla but explored much of the subcontinent. Their next trip to India, in 1883–84, occurred after Blunt met Jamal ad-Din, who strongly influenced his itinerary. Edward G. Browne's *The Persian Revolution of 1905–09* includes Blunt's "memorandum on Sayyid Jamaluʾd-Din" which gives many details of the relationship between them:

> I knew Sayyid Jamaluʾd-Din well, and saw much of him in the years 1883, 1884, and 1885. The first time I met him was in London in the spring of 1883. He had just landed from America, where he had sojourned for some months after his expulsion from India, with a view to obtaining American naturalisation. Later, in the month of September in the same year, we met again at Paris. He was living then in the company of certain Egyptian refugees of my acquaintance, and I was anxious to see him in order to consult him about a visit I intended making to India, as I wished to obtain introductions from him to some of the principal Indian Muslims, the object of my visit being to ascertain their condition as a community, and their relations with the rest of Islam and with the Reform Movement. I find the following note regarding him in my diary of the time:
>
> Sept. 3, 1883. Sabunji [my private secretary] came in with Shaykh Jamaluʾd-Din. When I saw him in London in the spring he wore his Shaykh's dress. Now he has clothes of the Stambouli cut, which sit, however, not badly upon him. He has learned a few words of French, but is otherwise unchanged. Our talk was of India, and of my being able to get the real confidence of the Muslims there. He said that my being an Englishman would make this very difficult, for all who had anything to lose were in terror of the Government, which had its spies everywhere. He himself had been kept almost a prisoner in his house, and had left India through fear of worse. Any Shaykh who gained notoriety in India was tracked and bullied, and, if he persisted in an independent course, was sent on some charge or other to the Andaman Islands. People, he said, would not understand that I wished them well, and would be too prudent to talk. The

poorer people might [do so, but] not the Shaykhs or the Princes. He thought Haydarabad would be my best point, as there were refugees there from every province in India, and they were less afraid of the English Government. He said he would write me some private letters to explain my position, and [would also write] to the editors of some Muhammadan newspapers. I told him what the political position (in England) was, and how necessary it seemed to me to be that the Muslims should shew that they joined with the Hindoos in supporting the Ripon policy. All depended on the Indians shewing a united front. He said that they might have courage if it could be proved to them that there were people in England who sympathized with them; but they only saw the officials "who never smiled when they spoke to them" . . .

The letters which the Shaykh gave me proved of the greatest possible use to me. I found him held everywhere in India in the highest esteem, and I was received as few Englishmen have been for his sake. At Calcutta there were a number of young Muslim students who were entirely devoted to his Pan-Islamic doctrines of liberal reform, and the same was the case in others of the chief cities of Northern India. He was a whole-hearted opponent of English rule, but at the same time without the smallest fanatical prejudice, and would have welcomed honest terms of accommodation with England, had he believed such to be obtainable. This was proved to me on my return to Europe in 1884.

I found him again at Paris that spring, living with my friend Shaykh Muhammad ʿAbduh in a little room some eight feet square at the top of a house in the Rue de Seize, which served them as the office of the Arabic newspaper they were editing . . . He was delighted at the success of my Indian journey, and urged me to further exertions in the cause of Islam.[41]

Blunt attempted to use Jamal ad-Din's connections to establish peace with the Sudanese Mahdi, but was rebuffed by the British Foreign Office. In 1885, after a change of government, Blunt invited Jamal ad-Din to return to England, where he spent three months as a guest, alternating between Blunt's London town house and his Sussex estate:

I got Jamaluʾd-Din to come over to England to see him, in order to discuss the terms of a possible accord between England

> and Islam. He remained with me as a guest for over three months, partly at Crabbet, party in London, when I came to know him very intimately. I introduced him to several of my political friends, notably [Randolph] Churchill and Drummond Wolff . . . it was arranged that he should accompany Wolff to Constantinople on his special mission to the Sultan, with a view to his exercising his influence with the Pan-Islamic entourage of ᶜAbduᵓl-Hamid in favour of a settlement which should include the evacuation of Egypt, and an English alliance against Russia with Turkey, Persia and Afghanistan. Unfortunately Wolff at the last moment suffered himself to be dissuaded from taking the Sayyid with him, and I attribute (in part at least) to this change of mind the difficulties he met with in his mission, and its ultimate failure. The Sayyid was greatly offended at being thus thrown over, for his ticket to Constantinople had been already taken; and, after lingering on for some weeks in London, he ultimately left in dudgeon for Moscow, where he made acquaintance with Katkoff and threw himself into the opposite camp, that of the advocates of a Russo-Turkish alliance against England.[42]

Blunt makes no mention here of another precipitating factor in Afghani's departure. After three months as Blunt's guest in his London house, Jamal ad-Din was asked to leave due to the tumult caused by some of Afghani's associates in the house. One of them was ᶜAbduᵓl Rasul, the Kashmiri who later served the cause of Dalip Singh in intrigues in Istanbul and Cairo. Although he did not see Afghani for many years, Blunt maintained a sympathetic interest in Indian, Irish, and Egyptian struggles against the British empire, and twice stood for Parliament, where he hoped to oppose imperialism from within. In 1887, he was imprisoned for two months as a result of inflammatory remarks he had made in Galway.

Jamal ad-Din next surfaced in Russia, having arrived by October 1886, perhaps "invited by the order of the Russian government" according to an Indian informant of her majesty's spies.[43] Afghani was in Russia for most of 1887, 1888 and 1889. Whether or not these events were linked with the French government, there seems no doubt that he was a sympathizer and subsequently an agent of Russian interests. Afghani apparently went to Moscow at the invitation of HPB's editor Mikhail Katkov, who was interested in organizing anti-British agitation in Central Asia and India.[44] In a note, Browne comments that a Persian source identifies Madame Olga Novikov as another of Afghani's contacts in Russia. This is noteworthy from the Theosophical point of view in that Novikov was on very friendly terms with HPB later in London.

Homa Pakdaman's *Djamal ad-Din Assad Abadi dit Afghani,* adapted from a Sorbonne doctoral dissertation, identifies several influential Western supporters of Jamal ad-Din. Henri Rochefort's leftist politics and journalistic career place him at the center of the milieu in which important early French TS leaders moved. Louis Dramard and Arthur Arnould were both, like Rochefort, exiled communards who became involved in Socialist journalism after their return to France.[45] A letter by HPB refers to "M. de Rochefort, whom I highly esteem, but who is not a Theosophist and laughs at us."[46]

Georges Clemenceau, born in 1841, entered politics as mayor of Montmartre. From 1876 to 1885 he served as a deputy for Paris. Representing the extreme left, he wielded great influence, overturning three cabinets in 1882, 1885 and 1886. In 1887, he obliged the president to resign. During Jamal ad-Din's stay in Paris, Clemenceau was director of *La Justice,* where he published articles by Afghani. Later he was publisher of *l'Aurore,* which was to become a leading voice of the Dreyfusards. In 1906 and again during the World War he was President of the Conseil (the Third Republic's most powerful post), but failed in his effort to become president of the Republic after the war.

Pakdaman's study exposed several facts about Jamal ad-Din previously unknown in the West. He was in Bombay for a month in the spring of 1869 before he went to Cairo, which coincides with a brief trip by HPB to India.[47] In Alexandria, his disciples published a journal in Arabic and French entitled *Jeune Egypte,* which suggests a Mazzinian inspiration.[48] James Sanua had been educated in Livorno and become a disciple of Mazzini there; he presumably helped inspire the Alexandrian group.

Afghani's sojourn in France is particularly well documented by Pakdaman. The first journal to welcome Jamal ad-Din to Paris was Sanua's *Abou Naddara,* which on 19 January 1883 proclaimed him as "the beauty 'Jamal' of religion 'Din' and science, our master al-'Afghani.' "[49] The following week, Khalil Ghanim's *Basir* announced his arrival, calling him an "eminent savant and perfect philosopher."[50] It is to these two colleagues that Pakdaman attributes Afghani's rapid success in establishing himself among the Paris intelligentsia. Ghanim introduced him to Ernest Renan, who commented of Afghani that "few persons have produced in me such a vivid impression."[51] Parisian police reports underscore the importance of Sanua in Afghani's life at the time.[52] They also mention that Ghanim had known Jamal ad-Din in Istanbul, which the Syrian left in 1877 after having incurred the wrath of the Sultan.[53]

Another French journalist with a strong interest in Afghani was Ernest Vauquelin, described by Pakdaman as "a free-thinker, fiercely anti-clerical" who had been expelled from Egypt for his hostility to the English and his close connections with nationalist Egyptians.[54] Vauquelin, who introduced Jamal ad-Din to Henri Rochefort, described him in an article on Egypt published in the *Intransigeant* 13 August 1882. Vauquelin reports that Jamal ad-Din had been involved with a Mazzinian group in Istanbul called *Jeune Turquie*, and that his first contact with Freemasonry was there rather than in Egypt. His diverse intellectual background is described: "Having learned in India the language of the conquerors, he had studied Greek philosophy in English texts, and from a blending of the doctrines of Plato with the books of the Far East has resulted in the eclectic philosophy which he teaches to his disciples."[55] Vauquelin, who appears to have met Afghani in Cairo, describes his relations with his pupils there: "He taught, or rather he preached wherever chance brought together several listeners: at his home, or that of a friend, or in a corner of the mosque, at times in a public plaza . . . His philosophical discourses ended almost always in political harangues, and he never began to speak of free will except to conclude in speaking of self-government."[56]

This description of Jamal ad-Din is taken directly from Rochefort's memoirs:

> I was introduced to an exile, celebrated throughout Islam as a reformer and revolutionary, the Sheikh Jamal ad-Din, a man with the head of an apostle. His beautiful black eyes, full of sweetness and fire, and his dark brown beard which flowed to his belly, gave him a singular majesty. He represented the type of the dominator of crowds. He barely understood French which he spoke with difficulty, but his intelligence which was always awake made up easily enough for his ignorance of our language. Under his appearance of serene repose, his activity was all-consuming.[57]

Mirza Reza Kirmani first entered Jamal ad-Din's life during his visit to Amin-ez-Zarb's home in Shah-Abdol-Azim. Amin-ez-Zarb, who was a member of the Shah's court, gave Mirza Reza to Afghani as his personal servant.[58] Kirmani was imprisoned with several Babis some time after Jamal ad-Din's final departure from Iran.

The Shah had decided to release him in November 1892, but the pardon was cancelled when Kirmani announced that he immediately would seek out Afghani upon release. It was not until three years later that Kirmani, desperately ill and partially paralyzed, was finally freed. Once he had arrived in Istanbul, Afghani arranged for his hospitalization. After three months there, he went to live with another Iranian from Kirman who was a disciple of Jamal ad-Din. But in January 1896, Kirmani returned to his homeland where later that year he assassinated the Shah.

The Iranian government demanded Jamal ad-Din's extradition, but Ottoman authorities were ambivalent in their response. One source suggests that they were willing to evacuate him to another location to avoid his being assassinated by an Iranian agent, while another indicates that the extradition was prevented only by Afghani's illness and death.

In *l'Intransigeant,* the only journal to uphold his innocence, this testament was published:

> At the moment I write this letter I am in prison and unable to meet my friends. Without hope of succor, without hope of survival. I do not suffer from being a prisoner, nor do I fear my approaching death . . . But what desolation in knowing that I have not yet reaped the fruit of the seed I have sown, and that the ideal I cherished has been only partly realized. For the sword of tyranny forbids me to contemplate the reawakening of the social conscience of the peoples of the Orient, and the forces of obscurantism prevent me from hearing the cry for liberty exhaling from the bellies of the same peoples. Would it have been better had I planted my seeds in the fertile soil of the people instead of the arid soil of royal courts? All grows and flourishes in the former and all rots in the latter . . .
>
> You who are the ripe fruits of Persia, having the will to awaken the social conscience of the Persian people: Fear neither prison nor death. Never retreat before the tyranny of monarchs. Work rapidly and ably. The currents of civilization advance into non-being. It is necessary that you strive, as you are able, to destroy the foundations of the system.
>
> Accentuate your efforts to make disappear above all those customs which separate the Persian people from happiness, rather than destroy the persons who maintain them. You lose your time in occupying yourselves with the latter, for he who respects traditions and customs, if he loses one will adopt

another. Try to overcome the obstacles placed between you and the other peoples. Do not be the dupes of demagoguery.[59]

Blunt's memorandum resumes with an account of these final years:

I lost sight of Sayyid Jamaluʾd-Din for several years, but in 1893 I found him established at Constantinople as a prime favourite with Sultan ʿAbduʾl-Hamid, one of his pensioners at the Musafir-khana [guest house] at Nishan-Tash, just outside the Yildiz garden-wall. Only a few days before my arrival he had brought himself into prominent notice at one of the Court ceremonies connected with the Bayram festival. A court official had sought to turn him back, but, with the independence which had always been his characteristic, he had insisted that he had a right as an ʿalim [doctor of theology] and a sayyid [descendant of the prophet] to a place of equality with anyone there, and had forced his way forward. This had attracted the attention of the Sultan, who had called him up and made him stand next him behind the imperial chair, 'nearer even then the chief Eunuch.' This, I say, was very characteristic of him, for he had a democratic contempt of official pretensions, and had asserted himself in much the same way many years before with the then Shaykuʾl-Islam, on the occasion of his first visit to Constantinople, and with much the same result. Nevertheless, though in high favour in 1893, he was under that close surveillance to which ʿAbduʾl-Hamid subjected all his guests.

I was glad to have seen him then, for later he fell upon less fortunate days, and through the intrigues of Shaykh Abuʾl-Huda [the late Sultan's astrologer], who regarded him with jealousy, the Sultan's favour was withdrawn. Nevertheless he continued to reside at Nishan-Tash to the end. I have little doubt in my own mind that he was privy to the assassination of the Shah (I mean that his violent words led to its being undertaken by one of his Persian disciples), for Jamaluʾd-Din was no milk-and-water revolutionist. Also I am not disinclined to believe the story of his fatal illness having been the result of poison. He had many enemies, and had become an encumbrance to ʿAbduʾl-Hamid. Be that as it may, his last days were sad ones. According to Shaykh Muhammad ʿAbduh, who told me of it at the time, his fall from favour with the Sultan had caused his former friends to avoid him, and he found himself gradually deserted by his fellow-residents in the Musafir-khana, and died in the arms of a single devoted servant, and that servant a Christian.[60]

Enemies of the Shah

Kedourie summarizes Afghani's message to his countrymen as "the same gospel of esoteric infidelity and political activism" that he had preached in Cairo.[61] Jamal ad-Din's last years were marked by association with Babis and other dissident Iranians. One of the more eminent was Malkam Khan, an Armenian convert to Shiᶜism who fell out with the Shah in 1889, after having been his ambassador in London. Afghani joined Khan in publishing newspapers denouncing Nasir ad-Din Shah. Khan, a freethinker, envisaged a "religion of humanity," which would be the means of introducing Western thought in the Islamic world.[62] When resident in Iran, especially in 1886–88, Afghani had continued his pattern of using secret societies to further his political agenda. But his authority rested as much on perceptions of his spiritual status as on his political acumen. During his stay at his home, Amin ez-Zarb wrote a letter to his brother describing Jamal ad-Din:

> By the grace of the Imam of the Age . . . God has today made my lot better than that of any Sultan. His Excellency the mujtahid of the Age and the unique one of his time, Hajji Sayyid Jamal ad-Din, known as Afghani . . . is staying in the house. All spiritual and bodily perfections are united in this great person and he pays special attention to Aqa Husain . . . [63]

The search for the Imam has been a recurring motif in Iranian political history, most recently in the case of Khomeini. Although Jamal ad-Din's decision to return to Iran from Russia in 1889 seems doomed from the start, at the time he had nowhere else to go. Katkov's death left Afghani frustrated in his effort to influence Russian policy. He was eager to promote a war between Britain and Russia, but their recent Ottoman experience had weakened the Russian will for war. His efforts to meet with the Czar having failed, Afghani was ready for a new challenge when Nasir ad-Din Shah appeared in St. Petersburg in 1889 *en route* to Paris for the centennial of the French republic.[64] He accepted the Shah's invitation to return to Iran with him. But two years later, in the midst of the successful struggle to overturn Nasir ad-Din's tobacco agreement with Britain, Jamal ad-Din was violently expelled.

The assassination of the shah is thoroughly documented in Keddie's biography of Jamal ad-Din. His rage against the ruler burned fiercely from his expulsion in 1891 until the assassination, which occurred in 1896. Although the assassin, Mirza Reza Kirmani, visited him in Istanbul before committing his crime, Jamal ad-Din denied direct responsibility in an interview with a French newspaper:

> They accuse me of being involved in a conspiracy against the life of the Shah. Surely it was a good deed to kill this bloodthirsty tyrant, this Nero on the Persian throne who destroyed more than 5,000 people during his reign . . . thus for a tyrant to receive the just recompense for his deeds. As far as I personally am concerned, however, I have no part in this deed, and I do not know whether a conspiracy of several people existed to this end. . . . I desire nothing but the truth and my sole aim is to spread its light, to bring about reforms, and to have toleration prevail.[65]

This interview so impressed the reporter that he described Jamal ad-Din as "a most interesting and attractive man, both prophet and warrior, inspired by noble humanitarian ideas, and having astounding knowledge and learning."[66] This evaluation echoes the words of ʿAbduh and other disciples, whose testimony provides evidence of their Master's power to inspire ardent devotion. The attraction of former Babis to his entourage suggests that they may have been motivated in part by a religious quest as well as by political ideals.

In Iran as well as Syria and Lebanon, the years between 1810 and 1840 had marked an increasing hope for the coming of the Imam Mahdi. Two theologians, Shaykh Ahmad Ahsaʾi and his successor Sayyid Kazim Rashti, brought to a fever pitch the anticipation of their followers, known as the Shaykhis. Before his death, Sayyid Kazim predicted the appearance of the Mahdi in 1260 A.H., a thousand lunar years after the Imam's disappearance. One of the leading disciples of Kazim, Mulla Husayn, was among many who were actively seeking the Imam, and on 23 May 1844, his search was rewarded. In Shiraz, the young Sayyid Ali Muhammad proclaimed to him that he was the Promised One so long awaited. Taking the title "the Bab," meaning "the gate," Ali Muhammad asserted that a new revelation was at hand. This aroused great enthusiasm among seekers, while the ᶜulama and government officials quickly labeled the new prophet a heretic, a threat to the nation, and an enemy of Islam. By 1847, thousands of Iranians had become Babis, followers of the Bab, who was imprisoned at the fortress of Mah-Ku, in Azerbaijan on the Russian border. Even the primitive Kurdish tribesmen of the region were affected by the charisma of the young prophet, prompting the government to move the Bab once more, now to Chihriq, another fortress in Kurdistan. In 1848, the Bab was taken to Tabriz where he was tried for his crimes and sentenced to the bastinado. The only Westerner to meet the Bab was the English physician who treated him after his torture. He described the Bab as a "very mild and delicate-looking man, rather small in stature and very fair for a Persian, with a melodious soft voice, which struck me much," and commented that the Bab's teachings were less fanatical and more sympathetic to women and Christianity than those of Islam.[67] Indeed, among the Bab's followers was Tahirih, who abandoned the veil as an expression of her adherence to the new revelation. Executed for her alleged involvement in Babi assassination plots, Tahirih became a symbol of the liberation of Iranian women.[68] The Islamic mullas instigated mob violence against the Babis, who in self-defense took refuge in various fortresses, where they were exterminated by the troops of 16-year-old Nasir ad-Din Shah.[69] The Prime Minister, Mirza Taqi Khan, ordered the public execution of the Bab on a charge of heresy. On 9 July 1850, the sentence was carried out in Tabriz. Since most of the Babi leaders had been killed by this time, the government regarded the problem as having been brought under control. However, when in 1852 two Babi youths attempted to assassinate the Shah, a new reign of terror was unleashed, involving ghastly tortures and murders which led Prince Dolgorukov, the Russian ambassador, to condemn them to the Shah as "barbarous practices" which "did not even exist among the most savage nations."[70] The prince was a distant relative of HPB.

In their 1984 study *The Bahaᵓi Faith,* Bahaᵓi historians William Hatcher and Douglas Martin portray the Bab's teachings as being almost impenetrable to the Western mind due to their emphasis on obscure points of Shiᶜa doctrine. His major work, the *Bayan,* in separate Persian and Arabic volumes, provided a completely new shariᶜa, or code of laws, which retained many aspects of that of Islam. An important feature of the Bab's teaching was the coming of another prophet, "He Whom God will make Manifest."[71] The Bab promised that "A thousand perusals of the *Bayan* cannot equal the perusal of a single verse to be revealed by 'Him Whom God shall make manifest.' "[72] There is considerable uncertainty about the immediacy of the succession expected by the Bab. Baha'is insist that the new Manifestation was to come within nine or nineteen years of the Bab's declaration of his mission. While a few Babis rejected the claims of the self-proclaimed new manifestation, Mirza Husayn Ali, the great majority became his followers, known as Baha'is. Baha'u'llah was one of the few Babi leaders who escaped the massacres of 1848–1853. A nobleman whose family holdings included extensive tracts in the province of Mazandaran, Mirza Husayn Ali was among the earliest of the Bab's disciples. His social status seems to have preserved his life, and with the loss of many talented Babi leaders, Baha'u'llah became a key figure in the survival of the Babi community. Imprisoned for four months in the Siyah-Chal [Black Pit], a grim underground dungeon in Teheran, Baha'u'llah awaited daily word of his fate. His survival appears to be partly due to the Russian ambassador, who personally intervened on his behalf. Dolgorukov asked that Baha'u'llah not be executed without a trial. He presumably knew that a trial would almost certainly have led to acquittal, since "The would-be assassin of the Shah had confessed at his own arraignment, in the presence of a representative sent by the Russian government, and had completely exonerated the Babi leaders, including Baha'u'llah, of complicity in his act."[73]

While imprisoned in the Siyah Chal, Baha'u'llah was overwhelmed with the conviction that he was the promised Manifestation of God. His description of his illumination opens with the words, "One night in a dream, these exalted words were heard on every side: 'Verily, We shall render Thee victorious by Thyself and by Thy pen.' "[74] Upon his release from prison, Baha'u'llah was exiled. Russia offered him refuge (perhaps again at Dolgorukov's instigation), but he chose Baghdad as his place of exile, and here he was joined by a colony of the faithful. Mirza Yahya, Baha'u'llah's younger half-brother, also known as Subh-i-Azal, "Morn of Eternity," had been appointed head of the Babi community by the Bab himself. His resistance to Baha'u'llah's claims to prophethood initiated a period of tension which was resolved by Baha'u'llah's removal to the wilderness of Sulaymaniyyih in Kurdistan. Completely out of contact with the Babis, Baha'u'llah devoted his time to prayer, meditation and writing in the company of Sufi mystics.[75] As the Babi community in Baghdad fell victim to power struggles and theological disputes, Baha'u'llah was summoned to return to help restore unity to the infant faith. There he wrote the *Kitab-i-Iqan,* which treats of the theme of progressive revelation through infallible prophets called Manifestations of God. In 1863,

Baha᾿u᾿llah was exiled once more, this time to Istanbul. Just before his departure from Baghdad, he declared his mission openly to the Babis in the Garden of Ridvan (Paradise) outside Baghdad. After a brief stay in Istanbul, the Babis were exiled further to Edirne (Adrianople) in European Turkey. Due to increasing political pressures from the Iranian government, exacerbated by rumors of political conspiracies among the Babis, the community as a whole was transferred to Acre, (Akka) Palestine, at the order of the Sultan in 1868. Here he wrote a series of prophetic letters to the rulers of the leading nations of the world. Mirza Yahya was sent to Cyprus, where he stayed until his death in 1912. By this time he was asserting his own claims to prophethood and not merely denying those of his half-brother. Baha᾿u᾿llah remained in the vicinity of Acre for the remainder of his life, but the severity of his imprisonment was gradually relaxed until by the end of his life he was allowed to inhabit a beautiful mansion known as Bahji [Delight]. His writings continued during the Acre period, where most of his letters to sovereigns were written. These included outright warnings of disaster to most of the recipients, which were generally proven accurate within the following few years. In his *Lawh-i Maqsud* (1884), Baha᾿u᾿llah predicted the creation of the United Nations:

> The time must come when the imperative necessity for the holding of a vast, an all-embracing assemblage of men will be universally realized. The rulers and kings of the earth must needs attend it, and, participating in its deliberations, must consider such ways and means as will lay the foundation of the world's great peace amongst men . . . It is not for him to pride himself who loveth his country, but rather for him who loveth the whole world. The earth is one country, and mankind its citizens.[76]

In Acre, Baha᾿u᾿llah's writing occupied an increasing share of his time, as did receiving pilgrims from abroad. Although the Baha᾿i Faith had spread from Iran into Russia, India and the Ottoman Empire, it was the destiny of his oldest son, ᶜAbdu᾿l Baha, to introduce it to the West.

Edward Granville Browne

Among Jamal ad-Din's Western admirers, none recorded his impressions of the Master at greater length or with more enthusiasm than Edward Granville Browne. This is an uncanny link with the

Baha᾽i movement, since Browne performed the same function as eyewitness and scholar of its history. In his introduction to ᶜAbdu᾽l Baha's history of the Babi movement, *A Traveller's Narrative,* Browne writes of the first of his four 1890 interviews with Baha᾽u᾽llah:

> The face of him on whom I gazed I can never forget, through I cannot describe it. Those piercing eyes seemed to read one's very soul; power and authority sat on that ample brow . . . No need to ask in whose presence I stood, as I bowed myself before one who is the object of a devotion and love which kings might envy and emperors sigh for in vain![77]

Among Baha᾽u᾽llah's remarks to Browne were some passages found in his writings as well, which convey the essential Baha᾽i message: "These strifes and this bloodshed and discord must cease, and all men be as one kindred and one family . . . Let not a man glory in this, that he loves his country; let him rather glory in this, that he loves his kind."[78]

Browne was the eldest son of a wealthy Gloucestershire family. While a student at Eton during the Russo-Turkish war of 1877, he became interested in the Turkish language. From his sixteenth year onward he was ever more absorbed by Oriental studies. Although he prepared for a medical career, he simultaneously pursued Asian languages. When he completed his medical degree in 1887, his only travels to the East had been to Istanbul. But in late 1887, at the age of twenty-five, Browne discovered his life's purpose when he made a year-long visit to Iran.[79]

During that fateful year, Browne traveled to all parts of the country, living apart from Europeans and entering into unprecedented intimacy with the Iranian people. Having learned of the Babis just before his departure, he set out to document as thoroughly as possible their history subsequent to the Bab's martyrdom. Although he was passionately sympathetic to the Babi cause, admiring their heroic devotion to their prophet, Browne never adopted the Babi or Baha᾽i faiths. After his return to England, however, he began to publish a series of books which have been invaluable to the study of Babi/Baha᾽i history. In 1891, he translated ᶜAbdu᾽l Baha's *A Traveller's Narrative,* a history of the Babis, followed two years later by publication of his own *A Year Among the Persians.*

From 1888 until his death in 1926, Browne taught Persian and Arabic at Cambridge University, where in 1902 he became a full professor. His most important literary study is the multivolume *Literary History of Persia.*[80] But his interest in Iran was not merely an academic pursuit. For many years he was the West's leading spokesman for the Iranian revolutionaries, and the greatest influence on this aspect of his life was Jamal ad-Din. They met only once, at the home of Malkam Khan in London, but Browne remarked ten years later, "I have still a vivid recollection of that commanding personality."[81] He continued:

> We talked a good deal about the Babis, as to whom he was very well informed . . . though he had no great opinion of them. In the course of conversation I asked him about the state of Persia, and he answered, so far as I can recollect, that no reform was to be hoped for until six or seven heads had been cut off; "the first," he added, "must be Nasiruʾd-Din Shah's, and the second the Aminu's-Sultan's." It is curious to note that both of these were assassinated, though Sayyid Jamaluʾd-Din survived the Shah less than ten months, and was survived by the Aminu's-Sultan for ten years.[82]

Browne was the most influential Western observer of the Iranian political scene during the tumultuous first decade of the twentieth century. His history of the period, *The Persian Revolution of 1905–1909,* begins with a chapter entitled "Sayyid Jamaluʾd-Din, the Protagonist of Pan-Islamism." He explains his reasons for opening his book with an account of Afghani:

> It is a matter still open to discussion whether great men give rise to great movements, or great movements to great men, but at least the two are inseparable, and in this movement towards the unity and freedom of the Muslim peoples none played so conspicuous a role as Sayyid Jamaluʾd-Din, a man of enormous force of character, prodigious learning, untiring activity, dauntless courage, extraordinary eloquence both in speech and writing, and an appearance equally striking and majestic. He was at once philosopher, writer, orator and journalist, but above all politician, and was regarded by his admirers as a great patriot and by his antagonists as a dangerous agitator. He visited, at one time or another, most of the lands of Islam and a great many European capitals, and came into close relations, sometimes friendly, more often hostile, with many of the leading men of his time, both in the East and the West.[83]

Calling ᶜAbduh "one of the greatest Muhammadan thinkers and teachers of our time," Browne notes that he was "proud to call Sayyid Jamaluʾd-Din his master."[84] In his summary of Jamal ad-Din's life, Browne acknowledges that he was widely known in Persia to have been born in Asadabad, despite his claims to Afghan nationality. After a reasonably thorough account of Afghani's career, Browne concludes that "to write his history in full would be to write a history of the whole Eastern Question in recent times, including in this survey Afghanistan and India, and, in a much greater degree, Turkey, Egypt, and Persia, in which latter countries his influence is still, in different ways, a living force."[85] Browne's meeting with Afghani in late 1891 had a profound impact on the young scholar, further galvanizing his support for the Iranian revolutionaries whose cause he would later chronicle. Hatcher and Martin note that Browne "raised money for the movement in Europe, spoke widely on its behalf, and made his home at Cambridge a way-station for Persian exiles."[86]

The enigma of Jamal ad-Din's relationship with the Babis, and its influence on his feelings toward the Shah, is clarified somewhat by H. M. Balyuzi's *Edward Granville Browne and the Bahaʾi Faith.* Browne's most important language tutor was Muhammad Baqir, Jamal ad-Din's London associate who preached his own Islamo-Christianity.[87] In 1889, Browne entered into correspondence with Mirza Yahya (Subh-i-Azal), then in Cyprus, and was even more closely associated with Shaykh Ahmad Ruhi, Azal's chief disciple and advisor. Balyuzi's account of Jamal ad-Din expands understanding of his connections with the Babis. Shaykh Ahmad Ruhi and Mirza Aqa Khan became disciples of Jamal ad-Din despite his skepticism about the Babi faith. Balyuzi concludes that this was because "It served their purposes to support and aid and abet Sayyid Jamaluʾd-Din against the reigning monarch of Iran, because the partisans of Subh-i-Azal were dedicated to the violent overthrow of the existent order in that land [while] Bahaʾuʾllah, on the other hand, had laid an injunction upon his followers to eschew political action, and shun every manner of violence and rebellion."[88] The entry on the Babis written by Afghani for Bustrus al-Bustani's Arabic Encyclopedia was called "astonishing" in Bahaʾuʾllah's *Tablet of the World.* Yet Afghani sent copies of *al-Urwa* to Bahaʾuʾllah from Paris "to atone for his past" according to the recipient in Acre, who commented "We kept silent regarding him."[89] These passages suggest that the hostility and denigration were partly in the eyes of Bahaʾi observers, and that Jamal ad-Din was actually attempting to be friendly with both Bahaʾuʾllah and Subh-i-Azal. This was an unlikely prospect given their antipathy, but Edward Browne later succeeded for a time in being friendly with both. It was to the Azalis that Jamal ad-Din turned for allies in his struggle against the bloodthirsty Nasir ad-Din. Browne's *The Persian Revolution* (1910) gives the reported statement of the Azali assassin:

> You know how, when Sayyid Jamaluʾd-Din came to this city, all the people, of every class and kind, alike in Tihran and in Shah Abduʾl-Azim, came to see him and wait on him, and how they listened to his discourses. And since all that he said was said for God and for the public good, everyone profited and was charmed by his words. Thus did he sow the seed of these high ideas in the fallow ground of men's hearts, and the people awoke and came to their senses. Now everyone holds the same views that I do; but I swear by God Most High and Almighty, who is the Creator of Sayyid Jamaluʾd-Din and of all mankind, that no one, save myself and the Sayyid, was aware of this idea of mine or of my intention to kill the Shah.[90]

Because he was more sympathetic to the Azalis than the Bahaʾis, Browne was a disappointment to the disciples of Bahaʾuʾllah. Yet he continued to be on cordial terms with ʿAbduʾl Baha after writing the introduction to his *Traveller's Narrative;* the two corresponded for years and met in London and Paris during the Bahaʾi leader's 1911 tour of Europe. In Browne's 1922 obituary of ʿAbduʾl Baha, he acclaimed him as the man "who has probably exercised a greater influence not only in the Orient but in the Occident, than any Asiatic thinker and teacher in recent times."[91]

ʿAbduʾl Baha and Theosophy

The Bahaʾi Faith first reached the West during the period of ʿAbduʾl Baha's leadership, and began a dramatic expansion which lasted throughout the twentieth century. The year after Bahaʾuʾllah's death marked the emergence of the faith in America. The 1893 Parliament of Religions is a remarkable event in American history from a number of points of view. For Theosophists, it brought a breakthrough into public acceptance and awareness which had hardly seemed possible a few years before. For Bahaʾis, the Parliament of Religions is equally important, for it marks the first public exposure of their religion in the United States. In a paper by Henry Jessup, a Presbyterian missionary in Syria, it was announced that Baha᾿u᾿llah had recently died in Acre. Jessup quoted Browne's interview with Baha᾿u᾿llah in his closing words.[92] Within a year of the Parliament, a Syrian Baha᾿i, Dr. Ibrahim Khayru᾿llah, resident in Chicago, began to proselytize in that city. The growth of the Baha᾿i Community in America and elsewhere in the West was warmly encouraged by ᶜAbdu᾿l Baha. When political upheavals in the Ottoman Empire freed ᶜAbdu᾿l Baha from incarceration in 1909, he was able to plan a series of travels that would catapult him and the Baha᾿i Faith into public prominence throughout the Western world. Prior to this, his only contact with Western Baha᾿is had been through their pilgrimages to Palestine. The Western travels of ᶜAbdu᾿l Baha began on 4 September 1911, when he sailed from Cairo for Marseilles. He spent most of the fall of 1911 in London and Paris, returning to Egypt for the winter of 1911–12. On 25 March 1912, he departed for New York, which was the beginning of an eight-month tour of America. During this visit, he traveled to thirty-eight cities from coast to coast. On his return trip, he visited Europe again, this time including Scotland, Germany, Austria, and Hungary in his travels, as well as England and France. He returned to Haifa on 5 December 1913. During this time, ᶜAbdu᾿l Baha captured the imagination of thousands with his flowing white beard, his turban and robes, his gentle humor, and his eloquence in proclaiming the Baha᾿i beliefs. His endurance and stamina were the marvel of his hosts, yet the most remarkable feature of his presence in the West was, as described by Shoghi Effendi, "the genuineness and warmth of His sympathy and loving-kindness shown to friend and stranger alike, believer and unbeliever, rich and poor . . ."[93] A constant stream of visitors filled his days, described by his hostess in London as "ministers and missionaries, oriental scholars and occult students, practical men of affairs and mystics, Anglicans, Catholics, and Non-conformists, Theosophists and Hindus, Christian Scientists and doctors of medicine, Muslims, Buddhists and Zoroastrians."[94] The Baha᾿i message of world brotherhood found a capable and inspiring spokesman in ᶜAbdu᾿l Baha, and Theosophists figured among the most frequent hosts of his appearances. Annie Besant visited the Baha᾿i leader during his stay in London, as did A. P. Sinnett on numerous occasions. Each invited him to address the TS at its London headquarters.[95] ᶜAbdu᾿l Baha continued his addresses to Theosophical audiences in New York, where on 30 May 1912 he gave his strongest endorsement of the TS, opening his talk with the comment that "Tonight I am very happy in the realization that our aims and purposes are the same, our desires and longings are one . . . the certainty of unity and concord between Baha᾿is and Theosophists is most hopeful."[96] Theosophists appear just as prominently in the record of his Paris visit. His English hostess, Lady Blomfield, remembered of those who came every morning to hear ᶜAbdu᾿l Baha in London:

> They were of all nationalities and creeds, from the East and from the West, including Theosophists, agnostics, materialists, spiritualists, Christian Scientists, social reformers, Hindus, Sufis, Muslims, Buddhists, Zoroastrians and many others.[97]

It seems unlikely to be a mere coincidence that Theosophists appear first in the above list, for in a visit to Vienna of only a few days, ᶜAbdu᾿l Baha addressed a TS meeting in the only public appearance there recorded by Shoghi Effendi. In a somewhat more extended visit to Budapest he again addressed the TS, and was visited by "Professor Robert A. Nadler, the famous Budapest painter, and leader of the Hungarian Theosophical Society."[98]

Although these associations are an interesting footnote to Theosophical history, in themselves they do not substantiate any important relationship between Theosophy and the Baha᾿i Faith. If the hospitality extended to ᶜAbdu᾿l Baha by Theosophists were the only evidence of a connection, the strongest case one could make would be that Theosophy helped create the atmosphere of *ex oriente lux,* which enabled him to be so successful in his travels in the West. However, further evidence of a connection between Theosophy and Baha᾿i history is to be found in ᶜAbdu᾿l Baha's expression of Baha᾿i doctrines. Balyuzi refers to ᶜAbdu᾿l Baha's last public address in London, made to the TS, as "the first time ᶜAbdu᾿l Baha made a systematic presentation of the basic principles of the Faith of his Father."[99] (Interestingly, ᶜAbdu᾿l Baha's last public address in New York had also been made to the TS, although his final talk was to well-wishers on board the *Cedric.*)

At the time of ᶜAbdu᾿l Baha's death in November 1921, the London TS officials sent this message: "For the Holy Family Theosophical Society sent affectionate thoughts."[100] That this was a reciprocal affection is seen in his blessing, written in the TS guest book in London: "He is God! O Lord! Cast a ray from the Sun of Truth upon this Society that it may be illumined."[101]

Life in Cairo after the Young Turks revolution had provided provided ᶜAbdu᾿l Baha an atmosphere of relative tolerance and cosmopolitanism which prepared him for his Western travels. The reform elements in the Ottoman Empire with which HPB and Jamal ad-Din had been involved were responsible for freeing ʿAbduʾl Baha from imprisonment, thereby setting the stage for the expansion of the Bahaʾi Faith to the status of a world religion. There is irony in the fact that the TS was later successful in promoting ʿAbduʾl Baha as an Asian messenger to the West during the same period that it was beginning its ill-fated promotion of Krishnamurti. In 1906, according to Wilson, there were 1280 Bahaʾis in America and 2336 Theosophists.[102] In 1994, there are approximately one hundred twenty thousand Bahaʾis and five thousand Theosophists in the United States; worldwide figures of five and a half million and thirty-five thousand, respectively, give an even clearer indication of the relative success of the two movements.[103] That Theosophy has contributed to the success of Bahaʾi expansion is indubitable. A partnership between the Bahaʾis and Theosophists continued throughout the twentieth century, according to Peter Smith's *The Babi and Bahaʾi Religions.* In discussing Bahaʾi propaganda in Europe, he comments:

> Contacts with 'other liberal groups' became a particularly characteristic feature of Bahaʾi activity in Europe between the wars . . . Everywhere the Theosophical Society provided a convivial home from home.[104]

In his description of Bahaʾi efforts to expand into the Third World, Smith again discusses the TS. He portrays a crucial shift in emphasis in Bahaʾi propaganda during the 1950s. Up until that time, Bahaʾi groups were found mainly in what Smith calls "cultural outliers" of the Iranian homeland, such as Parsis in Bombay. He adds that "during the period in which Bahaʾi expansion was confined to such outliers, Bahaʾi teaching techniques were almost entirely addressed to establishing contact with liberal and educated religious and social groups, often with meetings sponsored by the local Theosophists or Esperantists, or, on occasion, by a sympathetic university professor."[105] In his discussion of Indian teaching efforts, Smith comments that emphasis was placed on "public lecture tours, with talks being given in universities and business association meetings and under the auspices of fellow 'liberal' organizations such as the Theosophical Society . . . "[106] Unlike Theosophy, however, Bahaʾi has been able to expand vastly in numbers during the last thirty years due to its adoption of "mass teaching" techniques adapted to illiterate audiences in the Third World.

In his introduction to a series of histories of Bahaʾi communities, Richard Hollinger describes a period (1917–18) in which

Theosophical interest in Baha'i led to open conflict in the Chicago community. A Theosophically oriented group dominated the affairs of the Baha'i Reading Room in Chicago, and was opposed by another group of more orthodox Baha'is. An investigating committee decided to expel the Reading Room faction from the faith and order that they be shunned by members as "Covenant-breakers." The writings of W. W. Harmon, a Theosophist, precipitated the crisis, as explained by Hollinger:

> He published books and circulated lessons within the Baha'i community that offered esoteric interpretations of the Baha'i scriptures and explanations of the stations of Baha'u'llah and ʿAbdu'l Baha that were influenced by the teachings of Theosophy . . . If there was the possibility that Theosophy could absorb the Baha'i Faith theologically, there was a fear that the Baha'i community could be dominated by persons sympathetic to Theosophy. In this context, the "Harmonites" came to be seen as conspirators who sought to usurp or infiltrate the legitimate leadership of the Baha'i community so that they could contaminate the Baha'i movement with Theosophical doctrines.[107]

Thus, even within a few years of ʿAbdu'l Baha's visit to America, the Theosophical alliance he had promoted was producing conflict. Nonetheless, continued cooperation between the two groups appears to have been the rule rather than the exception, judging from Smith's findings.

The history of contacts between Baha'is and Theosophists merits further investigation. Any objective inquiry into Baha'i history faces obstacles similar to those presented by the study of Theosophical history. Neither subject has received much attention from impartial outsiders. In both cases, most publications are hagiographic in approach, while critical studies tend to be hostile. The two leading non-Baha'i works on Baha'i were written by Christian missionaries. Baha'i scholars must submit their work to prior censorship by a review committee of the National Spiritual Assembly of the country of publication, even for works published independently. In the United States, this process produced considerable tension in the late 1980s as a series of articles written for the liberal Baha'i journal *Dialogue* were rejected by the review committee. Some contributing authors were subsequently sanctioned by the Baha'i administration, and the journal went out of existence after a few years of publication.

Progress in translating primary source materials (the sacred scriptures of the Baha᾿is) has been steady but slow, with the *Kitab-i-Aqdas*, designated the "Most Holy Book," being published in English translation by Baha᾿is only in 1993. (A 1961 translation by Christian missionaries was virtually ignored within the Baha᾿i community.) The most consistent disparity between opposing viewpoints on Baha᾿i history is in the perception of discontinuities. Baha᾿is, believing their religion to have evolved according to a divine plan, tend to minimize or explain away the apparent contradictions between successive phases of the movement's evolution. Hostile critics emphasize discontinuities in order to invalidate the Baha᾿i faith, rather than to understand it. Any effort to explore Baha᾿i history impartially is unlikely to please either side.

There are nevertheless signs of hope for the future of Baha᾿i scholarship. The appointment of a professional historian, Robert H. Stockman, as head of the Research Office of the National Center brings scholarly standards to bear on matters involving Baha᾿i history. A number of other Baha᾿i scholars are producing work of academic quality which is gradually illuminating several long-obscure points.

The research of Juan R. I. Cole provides many heretofore missing pieces to the puzzle of Jamal ad-Din. In his "Iranian Millenarianism and Democratic Thought in the 19th Century," Cole explains the evolution of Baha᾿i political attitudes during the lifetime of Afghani. During the period 1876–82, there is evidence "of a convergence of Young Ottomanist ideas with those of the Bahai movement."[108] Although Azalis have been more frequently linked with such liberal ideals, Cole argues that Baha᾿is have been overlooked in this context. Later professions of neutrality have confused understanding of early Baha᾿i history. For example, ῾Abdu᾿l Baha supported the Persian constitutional movement from 1905 through 1907, before becoming disenchanted, and remained "convinced that his father, Bahaullah, had prophecied the revolution and constitution."[109]

In his letters to the rulers of the world, Baha᾿u᾿llah promoted parliamentary government after his exile to Acre in 1868. Cole notes that during this period, Malkam Khan, an Iranian exile in Istanbul, was involved in dissident journalism. He adds that "Malkum had once sought refuge with Bahaullah in Baghdad from the wrath of the Shah, and probably knew Baha᾿is in Istanbul."[110] Malkam Khan was later a close associate of Jamal ad-Din in Europe, and may have been a link between him and the Baha᾿is of Istanbul during Afghani's period there in 1870–71. Jamal ad-Din had also sought refuge from the shah in Baghdad, possibly with Baha᾽u᾽llah, during his youth.

A most intriguing document produced by Cole is this letter from ᶜAbdu᾽l Baha to Jamal ad-Din, written around 1877:

> I read your splendid article printed in the newspaper *Misr,* which refuted some English newspapers. I found your replies in accord with prevailing reality, and your eloquence aided by brilliant proof. Then I came across a treatise by Midhat Pasa, the contents of which support your correct and magnificent article. So, I wanted to send it along to you.[111]

ᶜAbdu᾽l Baha emerges from this letter as "a widely read intellectual with a brief against Western imperialism."[112] Within the next few years, the Egyptian reformers were scattered by these very forces of imperialism. As late as 1884, Jamal ad-Din was still attempting to preserve good relations with the Baha᾽i community, sending *al-Urwa* from Paris. But near the end of his life, Baha᾽u᾽llah condemned Afghani and his disciples for "scapegoating of the Bahais and his manipulative approach to politics."[113] As seen above, by the time of his own death, Afghani himself had come to regret the flawed methods he had adopted to influence royal courts.

Despite Baha᾽u᾽llah's condemnation of Afghani, ᶜAbdu᾽l Baha was on friendly terms with ᶜAbduh during the latter's exile in Beirut. Rashid Rida claimed that ᶜAbdu᾽l Baha attended ᶜAbduh's study sessions more than once during visits to Beirut in the late 1880s, and the two corresponded after ᶜAbduh's return to Cairo.[114]

The Shaykhi Legacy

The relationship between Theosophy and the Babi/Baha᾽i movement is made more comprehensible by the research of Abbas Amanat, whose *Resurrection and Renewal* is the definitive history of the early years of the Babis. Based on years of intensive study of primary sources, Amanat's book places Babi doctrine and activity in the context of centuries of Shiᶜite history. This is helpful in evaluating the multiple roles of Jamal ad-Din as well.

Although some of his later disciples in Iran may have regarded Jamal ad-Din himself as the Mahdi, in France he had supported the claims of Muhammad Ahmad of the Sudan to that position. In Afghanistan, Egypt, India, France, England, and Russia,

Jamal ad-Din had successfully preserved the illusion that he was a Sunni by birth. Like Blunt, Burton, and Borg, he had wished for an Arab Caliphate that would remove religious legitimacy from the Ottoman Empire. This concern is relevant only from a Sunni perspective, and Jamal ad-Din will be remembered more for his influence on Sunni than Shiᶜa disciples; he spent his final years "under the protection" of ᶜAbduʾl-Hamid, at the very heart of the Sunni world.

Despite the impressive accomplishments of his Sunni Afghan disguise, Jamal ad-Din remained profoundly influenced by Shiᶜa theology. During the tobacco boycott, he allied himself with the conservative ᶜulama against Nasir ad-Din Shah, and ultimately Azali Babism provided the disciples whose devotion brightened his life in Istanbul.

The central dogma of Twelver Shiᶜism, the dominant sect in Iran, is that a son had secretly been born to the eleventh Imam, who died in 847 apparently childless. The son had been deliberately hidden, but became the Twelfth Imam and continued to live in concealment. Until 941, he was alleged to be "in regular contact with four successive agents . . . who represented him among the community of his followers, communicating their questions and requests to him and his answers and instructions to them."[115] After a century of the lesser *ghaybah* or absence, the fourth agent of the Imam died without a successor, inaugurating the greater absence. Although "during this *ghaybah* no one can claim to be in regular contact with the Hidden Imam," he in fact "continues to live unrecognized on earth," and may "occasionally identify himself to one of his followers or otherwise intervene in the fortunes of his community."[116] He will return as the Qaᶜim and the Mahdi, "expected to reappear in glory to rule the world and make the cause of the Shiᶜah triumphant."[117]

Amanat distinguishes between two types of Mahdi claimants, neither of which accounts entirely for Afghani. Mahdis who defined their role as reviving the *shariᶜa* were not necessarily confronted with eschatological questions. But, Amanat points out, "when a claimant went so far as to proclaim the abrogration of the accepted shariᶜa, he would be compelled to provide a symbolic interpretation for the occurrence, or the near occurrence, of the Qiyama [resurrection]—without which the previous shariᶜa could not be nullified."[118]

Through his influence on Muhammad ᶜAbduh, Afghani decisively affected the liberalization of the Islamic legal system. ᶜAbduh could be seen as a liberal consolidator of the *shariᶜa,* of which he was the highest exponent in Egypt. This alone is evidence of Jamal ad-Din's powerful influence on Sunni history. Nonetheless, Jamal ad-Din's deepest motivations may well be connected to the fundamental dilemma of Shiʿism, the simultaneous presence and absence of the Imam. Amanat writes:

> The consecutive phases of Occultation and Advent, once they were infused into the gnostic themes of sacred knowledge and the prophetic light, were likely to promote a dynamic view of history, for the emergence of the Imam would begin a new age essentially different from the old. On the other hand, the fact that he was the same Imam now returning for the seclusion of Occultation strongly implied the recurrence of an age modeled on the primordial paradigm of prophethood.[119]

This expectancy is fundamental to the evolution of the Bab and Bahaʾuʾllah as well as Jamal ad-Din. Although Jamal ad-Din never became a Babi, he was to some degree a disciple of the Shaykhis, who "discovered" the Bab. Nikki Keddie points out that among Afghani's documents was a treatise on gnosticism by Ahmad Ahsaʿi, founder of Shaykhism. This was a copy made in Afghani's writing, which includes an annotation: "I wrote this in the abode of peace, Baghdad, and I am a stranger in the lands and banished from the homeland, Jamal ad-Din al-Husaini al-Istanbuli."[120] The Iranians banished to Baghdad included Bahaʾuʾllah and Subh-i-Azal, but it is unclear to what extent Jamal ad-Din was exiled as a Shaykhi or Babi, and how much interaction with the Babi exiles he had during this period. Later he felt he had reason to hide the details; Keddie notes that "after his trip to Afghanistan Jamal ad-Din not only wrote 'Kabuli' over 'Istanbuli' in red ink, but tried to obliterate the word 'Baghdad' with the same ink by writing another word over it."[121]

A theosophical element in Bahaʾi thought may well relate to its Shaykhi sources, as seen in Amanat's review of Shaykhi doctrines. There had been a theosophical current in Persian Shiʾite thought for hundreds of years, most recently exemplified by the eighteenth-century Isfahan school, described by Amanat:

> The immortality of the soul, the nature of the life hereafter, and, most troubling of all, the doctrine of the corporeal resurrection came to occupy a substantial part of the theosophists' discourse . . . [which] entailed a dynamic view of history that was decidedly at odds with the conventional notion of ultimate salvation.[122]

The religious establishment was threatened by any such dynamic view, which implied a possible end to its dominance. A further eroding influence was the theology of the Akhbaris, a declining school recently revived by Mirza Muhammad Nishapur, a full-fledged occultist. Reputed to have supernatural powers, Nishapuri was author of several books on esotericism. Rather than being accessible only to the clergy as general deputy, according to Akhbari doctrine the Imam was available to all through a human mediator. This mediator, or "gate," was a necessary part of the Imami doctrine, according to Nishapuri:

> [T]he pole of the progeny [of the Prophet] is the pole of poles who is also called the greatest aid. In his own time, he is the Riser [Qaᶜim] and the Lord of the Age and the pole of the time and the heralder. Without his manifestation [Zuhur], the Occultation of the Imam will not take place . . . [123]

The description of the permanent role for a living Qaᶜim in Nishapuri's writings helped define the expectations affecting the mission of the Bab. But it was only with the rise of Shaykh Ahmad Ahsaʾi (1756–1825) that there emerged a recognizable common ground for both Afghani and the Babi/Bahaʾi revelation. Both the doctrines and the disciples of Babism were found mainly among the Shaykhis. Ahsaʾis teachings are defined by Amanat as:

> the final outcome of a fusion of three major trends in post-Safavid Shiᶜism: (1) the Sadraʾi theosophical school of Isfahan, which itself benefited from the theoretical Sufism of Ibn ᶜArabi, as well as the illuminist theosophy of Suhravardi; (2) the Akhbari Traditionalist school of Bahrain, which traced its chain of transmission to the early narrators of hadith and (3) the diffuse Gnosticism that was strongly influenced by crypto-Ismaᶜili ideas as well as other heterodoxies of southern and southwestern Iran.[124]

Diffuse Gnostic and Crypto-Ismaiᶜli ideas are central characteristics of HPB's mysterious *Chaldean Book of Numbers* (see Part Three) which combines Neoplatonism, Kabbalah, and Sufism with other, more elusive elements. An equally diverse synthesis was created by Shaykh Ahmad Ahsaʾi:

> Ahsaʾi employed dreams, asceticism, and occult sciences as symbolic devices in a complex eschatological system . . . In

> his theory of the hereafter, in a cyclic process, a divine substance accompanies man's spirit in its descent from the realm of the eternal truth to earth, and after passing through earthly life, eventually reascends to its origin. In this journey, man's being also passes through an intermediary realm that belongs neither to elemental existence nor to the realm of eternal truth.[125]

The resurrection promised by the Shaykhis was the "last stage in the process of reunion between spirit and celestial body."[126] This is an elaborately detailed meditative experience in which the awakening passes through the intellect, the pneuma (spirit or breath), the soul, and subtle material vehicle, at last to the "Image, or archetypal form in the first dwelling," at which point "the 'I' spirit finds again its composition and structure, its consciousness and capacity to feel."[127] After all the vehicles are awakened, a series of ecstasies is experienced sequentially in the occult centers of the body.

Ahsaʾi provides a whole new dimension to the Imam doctrine, by postulating an intermediary world in which the soul can encounter the Imam. "It is only in this visionary world of meditation that the existence of the Imam and his eternal presence can be experienced, and it is from this liminal world that the Imam will reappear," explains Amanat.[128]

Once a substantial number of Shaykhis began to have visionary encounters with the Imam, a wide variety of omens was divined from their accounts. The most influential was Sayyid Kazim Rashti, appointed by Ahsaʾi around 1824 to propagate Shaykhism in Karbala, where Jamal ad-Din would study twenty years later.[129] Rashti's disciples were the first to recognize the Bab.

The claims of Sayyid Ali Muhammad began with his status as the Bab or gate to the Imam, but ended with a proclamation that he was in fact the Mahdi and the Qaʿim. Therefore, his prophethood necessitated the Qiyama or resurrection. This in turn required an allegorization of the process depicted in the Quran. Babism was far more revolutionary than its predecessors in sweeping away the legitimacy of the religious establishment:

> [T]he Babi effort was not to reform or rationalize Islam to the new needs of the time. It was a search for renewal of the divine covenant, which could be achieved only if the existing religious order were replaced and loyalties to religious and secular institutions were shaken.[130]

This view placed the Babis on a collision course with government and religious authority. According to Wilson, political subversion was an inevitable implication of the Bab's claims:

> In accordance with this principle the Babis looked upon Mohammed Shah and Nasr-ud-Din as no longer the rightful rulers. They were, *ipso facto,* supplanted by the Bab, the Sahib-i-Zalman or Lord of the Age. The Kajars were called by them "unlawful kings." . . . Disloyalty was an essential corollary of Babism and not a consequence of the repression and persecution which it met.[131]

In a 1979 doctoral dissertation, Denis M. MacEoin clarifies the emergence of the Babi movement from its Shaykhi roots. In 1839 and 1840, the Bab remained in Karbala, the headquarters of the Shaykhis, for about a year. MacEoin cites an Arabic source which reports that the Bab "remained at the ᶜatabat for eleven months, eight in Karbala and three at other shrines; when in Karbala, he would attend the classes of Rashti every two or three days."[132] Another source reports that he "attended the general class of Rashti every day."[133]

In his discussion of the Bab's early writings, MacEoin documents the gradual separation of Babi doctrine from Shaykhism, orthodox Twelver Shiᶜism and eventually Islam itself. In his first major work the *Qayyum al-asma* the Bab proclaims his doctrine to be true Islam, and presents himself as the representative of the Imam.[134] Moreover, in this initial phase the Bab saw himself as leader of an apocalyptic religious war: "Since the laws of Muhammad and the decrees of the Imams were to remain binding 'until the day of resurrection,' there was no question but that the primary means of bringing men to the true faith was to be *jihad.*"[135] In order to prepare for the resurrection, Babis were exhorted: "leave not a single one of the unbelievers (al-kafirin) alive upon the earth, so that the earth and all that are on it may be purified for the remnant of God (baqiyyat Allah), the expected one (i.e. the twelfth Imam in his persona as al-Mahdi)."[136] By the end of his career the Bab had long since abandoned the Islamic shariᶜa and with it his early conception of *jihad,* allowing his disciples violence only in self-defense.

After the Babis were ruthlessly suppressed, there was a division between those who wished to accommodate themselves to the situation and those who preferred continued defiance of authority. Bahaʾuʾllah was the leader of the former camp; Subh-i-Azal (Mirza

Yahya) headed the more radical group. Baha'i doctrine was more pacifist than the militant Babi faith. Azalis remained wedded to the original doctrines, but failed to put the Babi *shari'a* into effect in any consistent manner. Highly secretive, the Azalis "survived within a network of family loyalties and with occasional outbursts of clandestine antigovernment activism."[137] Subh-i-Azal's sons-in-law, Mirza Aqa Khan Kirmani and Shaykh Ahmad Ruhi Kirmani, were both radical reformers and disciples of Jamal ad-Din. According to Amanat, their "later modernist critiques of religion and society" were influenced "more by nineteenth-century European trends than by Babi thought."[138] During the period of the Constitutional Revolution, many key reformers were allegedly secret adherents of the Azalis. But this adherence was more a "nostalgic reverence for the memory of the Bab than adherence to the teachings of that religion."[139]

In his summary of the divergences between Babism and orthodox Islam, Amanat isolates three doctrinal elements:

> The three themes of progressive revelation, conditional recognition of temporal authority, and the this-worldliness of human salvation were in contrast to the Islamic precepts of the finality of Islam, the totality of the prophetic authority, and the other-worldliness of the Qiyama.[140]

In all three respects, Jamal ad-Din's belief was clearly closer to that of the Bab, despite their areas of disagreement, than to Shi'ite orthodoxy.

If common roots in Shaykhism explain something of Jamal ad-Din's ambiguous connections with the Babis, they also imply a new understanding of Baha'i history. The Babi movement originated in the relatively flexible and occult-oriented synthesis of Ahsa'i, but evolved into a militant, intolerant sect with grandiose political goals. Therefore, when its initial "heroic" phase ended in defeat, Babi disciples were ready for a more accommodationist, moderate direction.

Baha'u'llah's solution to the need for moderation was to transform the Qiyama from an imminent social revolution to the future golden age of a Baha'i world guided by his precepts. But in the meantime, Baha'u'llah's disciples could experience a personal Qiyama through their recognition and acceptance of his teachings. His writings balance a mystic appeal to the individual with social idealism for the human race. The more mystical works bear witness to Baha'u'llah's "acquaintance with Sufi dignitaries in

Muhammad Shah's court and his attraction to wandering dervishes," according to Amanat.[141] After his conflict with the Azalis became divisive, Baha᾿u᾿llah retired to Kurdistan, where from 1854 to 1856 he remained "in the refuge of Khalidi-Naqshbandi convents."[142] The works inspired by this period reveal "a mystical outlook pivotal to later messianic claims and his sociomoral reforms [and] . . . in harmony with the growing popularity of Shiᶜite Sufi orders, particularly Niᶜmatullahis, among the notables of Muhammad Shah's time."[143]

This suggests that ᶜAbdu᾿l Baha's liberalization of Baha᾿i teachings was a continuation of the trend established by his father. Baha᾿u᾿llah had tried to liberate his followers from the political claims inherent in Babism. Although Sufis were not prominent among the Bab's disciples, there had been "a few Nimatullahis, theosophists (hikami), and wandering dervishes" among them.[144] These may well have encouraged Baha᾿u᾿llah's universalistic outlook. Amanat discerns in Baha᾿u᾿llah a "greater reconciliation with the needs of the modern secular world" than was true of the Bab.[145] This trend, once established by Baha᾿u᾿llah, was continued by ᶜAbdu᾿l Baha, who found the Theosophical Society a helpful model for advancing this reconciliation.

Amanat sees in the defeat of the Babis a crucial turning point in Iran's history. Conservative religious forces benefited by the suppression of Babism, which despite its flaws was "an effort to find a timely answer to the most fundamental problem of Shiᶜism, and in a broader sense that of Islam."[146] This fundamental dilemma of the Imam's absence remains an unconscious conflict in Shiᶜite thought, which continues to be affected by the backlash against the Babi solution to the problem. In this lies part of the reason that "Iranian society is now experiencing the imposition of a tragically anachronistic solution to problems as old as Shiᶜism itself."[147]

The fundamental problem of Shiᶜism has intriguing correspondences to the present situation of the Theosophical movement. With the occultation of the Imam, the source of Shiᶜite authority was moved to an inaccessible realm, creating a strong desire for his return. Subsequent Shiᶜite history is a record of various attempts to cope with the effects of the occultation. Similarly, when Ranbir Singh and Thakar Singh died, Morya and Koot Hoomi lived on, since neither HPB nor Olcott was willing to admit what had happened. Soon thereafter, the occultation of the two primary Masters of the TS created an exodus among the chelas who had been promoted as their closest disciples. Ever since that time, the Theosophical movement has been affected by the sense of occultation due to the ambiguous withdrawal of the highest spiritual authority. Especially after HPB's death, reestablishing contact with the Masters has been a recurring feature of new charismatic leaders like Leadbeater, the Ballards, and Elizabeth Clare Prophet. HPB's promise that a new messenger would be sent after 1975 but before 2000 has inflamed Theosophical imaginations for much of the twentieth century; thus far no claimant has appeared.

The relationship between the Theosophical and Baha'i movements remains ambiguous and murky. Edward Granville Browne's acquaintance with Jamal ad-Din and Baha'u'llah makes him equally relevant to both traditions, although he adhered to neither. Theosophical Master was only one among many roles played by Jamal ad-Din in his career, and not the role in which Browne came to know him. Afghani and most of the disciples discussed in Part Two have only a peripheral connection to mainstream Theosophy. But they are relevant to the present investigation as examples of the multiplicity and complexity of initiatory connections among spiritual groups. The initiates depicted in Part One were open disciples of the Theosophical Masters, self-acknowledged as such. Those featured in Part Two were connected to Theosophy only indirectly and ambiguously. In Parts Three and Four, a synthesis between these alternatives is found in the careers of a series of initiates whose links to Theosophy were both direct and indirect, acknowledged and concealed, central and peripheral, at different times in their lives.

Prince Esper Uktomskii

PART THREE.

Dharma Heirs

A remarkable feature of Theosophy's history is the disparity between its miniscule membership and its vast and varied cultural influence. Blavatsky's ideas inspired leading figures in the development of modern art, most notably Wassily Kandinsky and Piet Mondrian. Theosophical influence in literature affected the Irish Literary Renaissance, in which William Butler Yeats and AE (George Russell) were prominent. Political activism in colonial India and Ceylon owed an immense debt to Theosophical influence. In the West, many social movements such as educational reform, women's suffrage, and abolition of capital punishment were advanced by the efforts of early Theosophists. But in no field of endeavor has Theosophy's influence been as great as in introducing Eastern religious ideas to the Western public. Although scores of spiritual organizations have emerged from the Theosophical impetus, they are less significant than the indirect influence exerted through Theosophy's sponsorship and encouragement of Eastern spiritual teachings. It can be justly credited with opening the door through which myriad Asian religious traditions have entered the Western world. Within the Theosophical movement and its derivatives, initiatic succession has been seen as linear and unique. Each sect has claimed exclusive status as the true heir of HPB and her Masters, based on the initiatory status of the group leaders. But a review of Theosophy's historical influence shows that HPB's successors are multiple and divergent. The definition of successorship which emerges from the present investigation focuses on objective criteria rather than unverifiable claims.

A few figures of particular interest are examined in Part Three. They are similar in their role as intermediaries between Buddhism and Western culture. Their extensive travels and international perspective made them cultural seed-bearers whose influence continues to be felt around the world.

Anagarika Dharmapala

The history of Buddhism has been powerfully affected by Theosophists. In *How the Swans Came to the Lake,* Rick Fields explains the impact of HPB on Buddhism, which is particularly clear in her relationship with the young man who came to be known as Anagarika Dharmapala. Blavatsky and Olcott felt drawn by destiny to Asia following the 1877 publication of *Isis Unveiled* in New York. They initiated correspondence with leaders of the Arya Samaj in India, and also with two Sinhalese Buddhist monks: Sumangala, the High Priest of Adam's Peak, and Meggittuwatte, celebrated for his skills in debating Christian missionaries. After successfully establishing the society in India among both the native Hindus and the British ruling class in 1879, HPB and Olcott went in 1880 to Ceylon (Sri Lanka). There they were eagerly awaited by a Buddhist population living under a colonial administration that denied legitimacy and educational opportunity to non-Christian children. On 25 May 1880, Blavatsky and Olcott "took pansil" (the five lay precepts) before a Buddhist priest in Galle. Repeating the vows in Pali, they then took the "three refuges" (in Buddha, Dharma, and Sangha) before a large crowd. According to Fields, this marked "the first time the Sinhalese had seen one of the ruling white race treat Buddhism with anything like respect, and . . . the first time that Americans had become Buddhists in a formal sense—that is, in a manner recognized by other Buddhists."[1] (HPB had become an American citizen prior to her departure for India.)

Although the Theosophical acceptance of Buddhism was, in Olcott's words, "not as a creed but as a philosophy"—one regarded as universal—the Sinhalese welcomed the Theosophists as allies.[2] Although HPB was to spend her most creative years in Europe, writing *The Secret Doctrine* and other works, Olcott resided in India until his death in 1907. He was instrumental in establishing an extensive Buddhist educational network in Ceylon. Through the writing of his *Buddhist Catechism,* and through diplomatic visits to Japanese and Burmese Buddhist leaders, Olcott established cooperation among long-separated schools of Buddhism. He is regarded as a national hero in Sri Lanka, and his photograph hangs in the Sinhalese- and Thai-sponsored Buddhist Vihara Society in Washington, D.C.[3]

David Hewivatarne, known to the world as Anagarika Dharmapala, was fourteen years old when he met Blavatsky and Olcott in his native Colombo, Ceylon.[4] Already regarded as a firebrand due to his rebellious refusal to be intimidated by his

Christian schoolmasters, David belonged to a devoutly religious Buddhist family. He enjoyed learning the Bible by heart in order to refute the logical inconsistencies of Christianity, but after a Catholic mob attacked a Buddhist religious procession in 1883, he withdrew from his school and continued his education in the local library. His wide reading emphasized Western philosophy and history, but he retained a fascination with Buddhism. Fields observes that David "did his best to track down bhikkhus and yogis who might have attained arhatship, or who had gained abhijna, psychic powers that sometimes resulted from yogic training, but never found anything more than rumors and stories . . . In 1883 he found what he was looking for in A. P. Sinnett's *Occult World,* the book which introduced the Theosophical Masters to the reading public."[5]

This inspired him to write to TS Headquarters asking to be enrolled in the "Himalayan School of Adepts." When HPB and Olcott returned to Ceylon in 1884, a brief but crucial transition took place in David's life. HPB took a strong interest in him, spending hours telling him about the Masters and their concern for the revival of Buddhism. During her stay, she proclaimed that the Master KH had directed her to bring David back to Adyar with her. David's father gave permission for his departure, but changed his mind after having a dream that he took as a bad omen. This led to a dispute between HPB and the father, supported by Olcott and the High Priest Sumangala, resolved when HPB insisted that David would die if not allowed to return to Adyar with her. Although her initial plan was to take David as a personal chela, a few weeks later she had a sudden change of heart:

> The two had an intimate little chat during which she discouraged his interest in psychic powers and the occult. There was no need to study Occultism, after all, she said, since all that was necessary could be found through the study of the Pali Scriptures. She gave him her blessing and instructed him to devote his life to the good of humanity.[6]

Theosophy's effect in Ceylon was to increase the resistance of the Sinhalese Buddhists to the British colonial government, and to help unite them against Christian dominance. Belatedly concluding that David's future role should emphasize Buddhism rather than Theosophy, HPB directed him into his lifelong vocation.

David stayed in India again in 1890, joining the Esoteric Section at the annual convention in Adyar. His greatest accomplishments began within weeks of HPB's death. On 31 May 1891, he founded the Bodh Gaya Maha-Bodhi Society, devoted to acquiring and preserving a long-neglected Buddhist temple at the site of Gautama's enlightenment, held by Hindus for over three hundred years.[7] By 1893, he was known by the title Anagarika Dharmapala as he represented the Sinhalese Buddhist community at the Parliament of Religions in Chicago. Theosophists figured prominently among the promoters of this remarkable Parliament, held as part of the Columbian Exposition. William Q. Judge in particular was highly visible in the proceedings. Among the Buddhists represented were the Zen, Jodo Shinsu, Nichiren, Tendai, and Shingon sects of Japan, as well as the Theravadins of Siam. A few days after the end of the Parliament, at a meeting on "Theosophy and Buddhism" sponsored by the Theosophical Society, Dharmapala received the vows of Charles T. Strauss of New York City, the first person to be admitted to the Buddhist fold on American soil.[8]

On 10 October 1893, Dharmapala sailed for India from San Francisco. Among the Theosophists who greeted him in Hawaii was Mrs. Mary E. Foster, a wealthy woman who became Dharmapala's philanthropic angel. More than a million rupees were eventually donated to his cause by Mrs. Foster, who claimed Hawaiian royal descent. Dharmapala continued to Japan and China, where he failed to win financial support for his Bodh Gaya plans. He did return with a gift statue from the Japanese, which the Hindus refused to allow on the premises.[9] In 1896, Dharmapala made another American lecture tour, continuing into 1897. A third visit to America came in 1902–1904, in which he visited technical schools, including Tuskegee Institute. He went to a William James lecture at Harvard, and was held up to the students as the avant garde of psychology by the gallant professor, who had invited him to speak to the class. In 1925, he went to London, where he established a *vihara.* In his last visit to San Francisco the same year, he spoke at a meeting of a Japanese Zen master, Nyogen Senzaki. Just before his death on 16 January 1933, Anagarika Dharmapala was ordained as a full Buddhist monk. The end of his life symbolized his faithfulness to the commission HPB had given him:

> Dharmapala vowed, just before his death, that he would be reborn in a Brahmin's family in Benares to continue the fight for Bodh-Gaya. "Let me die, let me be born again; I can no longer prolong my agony," he said in the months he was dying. "I would like to be reborn twenty-five times to spread Lord Buddha's Dharma." In 1949, sixty years after Dharmapala had first seen Bodh-Gaya, the new government of an inde-

pendent India returned the site of Bodh-Gaya to Buddhist possession.[10]

Dharmapala's first major accomplishment after the death of HPB was his emergence as the apostle of Pan-Buddhism, which occurred even before the Parliament of Religions. Dharmapala was sent as the representative of Sinhalese Buddhism to a ceremony in Darjeeling in July 1892. This united Tibetan, Indian, Sikkimese, and Sinhalese Buddhists in a procession through the streets of Darjeeling, with the boy-king of Sikkim in attendance. Dharmapala presented relics of southern Buddhism to the Tibetans. All was under the auspices of the Maha-Bodhi Society. Henrietta Muller, in the *Theosophist* of August 1892, described the events:

> Mr. Dharmapala had been commissioned by the chief Buddhist monks of Ceylon to convey to the Lamas of Tibet some relics of Buddha and a few leaves from the sacred Bo-Tree (Ficus religiosa), now growing at Buddha-Gaya—the place sacred to millions of Buddhists—and also a Buddhist flag . . .
>
> It was arranged that a procession bearing these relics should pass through the town, starting from Lhasa-Villa, the residence of Pandit Sarat Chandra Das, C.I.E., the renowned Tibetan traveller and scholar, to the residence of Rajah Tondub Paljor.
>
> The procession, in starting, was headed by the Tibetan band, which was playing the Tibetan air 'Gya-gar-Dor-je-dan' ('Flourish Buddha Gaya'). It was followed by the flag-bearer on horseback, in the Sikkim military uniform, bearing the above-mentioned sacred flag. Next came the Venerable Lama, Sherab-gya-techo (the Ocean of Learning), head of the Goom Monastery, carrying the casket of relics; after him came Mr. H. Dharmapala, riding on a dark bay horse, dressed in the orange-colored garment of the order of Upasakas. After him came Pandit Sarat Chandra Das, also riding; he was followed by a number of Lamas on horseback and dressed in their characteristic robes—the loose cloth coat with wide sleeves, silken sash, and the remarkable high-pointed 'red cap' of their school.
>
> In front of the low table, and occupying the chief position in the room as head of the meeting, sat the young Prince, son of the Rajah of Sikkim. He was a healthy-looking boy of 13 years of age, with features of marked Mongolian type, and of sallow complexion; his expression and his manner throughout

the meeting was solemn, grave, and dignified. He is being especially educated by Lamas brought from Tibet for the purpose, and prepared by them for the high position he is to fill as the Hierarch of Sikkim of the Red Cap Order . . . the proceedings of the meeting were conducted by Lama Ugyen Gya-tcho, Secretary of the Society, a man of great intelligence and frank, open countenance, with a commanding figure and genial, pleasant manners. He was the companion of Sarat Chandra Das during both his expeditions into Tibet . . . Some introductory remarks were then made by Pandit Sarat Chandra, whose formal address to the meeting, written in Tibetan, was read by the Secretary; speeches were made, too, in the Tibetan language, by Lama Sherab Gya-tcho . . . He was followed by the Lama of Pemayangtche . . . Mr. Dharmapala then followed.

Pandit Sarat Chandra Das then spoke, and described the three schools of Buddhism prevailing in Tibet and Ceylon.

At this stage of the proceedings the young Prince, taking the casket of relics in his hands, raised it to his forehead in a reverential manner; at the same moment the assembled Lamas commenced chanting in very deep bass tones an invocation to the higher influences, consisting of a prayer for their presence and for their aid in the cause. The Lamas were all seated in the position of meditation during this chant, and their hands were folded or inter-locked in front of them in the form of a *mudra*. During the chant the Secretary placed in the hands of each Lama a small quantity of rice, the purpose of which was to purify, in the same way as, and in the place of, water. Every now and then each Lama would unlock his hands and sprinkle some of the rice over the room. When the chant was finished, the Secretary took the open casket and handed it to every one in the room who desired its benediction.

The ceremony concluded, Mr. Dharmapala presented one of the relics and a Bo-tree leaf to the Principal of the Sikkim State Monastery, the other three being destined for Tibet. These were to be carried by messenger from Darjeeling all the way to Lhasa, and delivered into the hands of the Grand Lama of Tibet.[11]

The initiatory character of this journey for the young Dharmapala is suggested by his position in the procession. He rode behind the head of the monastery where HPB had taken refuge on her 1882 trip to Darjeeling. Following Dharmapala was the scholar and translator whose generosity to Olcott may have enriched Theosophical literature. The destination was the residence of the Raja of Sikkim, where they were awaited by the prince, a young man who later would be a patron of the French Theosophist and explorer Alexandra David-Neel.

An eventual falling-out between Olcott and Dharmapala is revealed in the final volume of *Old Diary Leaves*. In the spring of 1896, Olcott visited the home of Dharmapala's father in Colombo. On May 20th of that year, he dissolved his attachment to the Maha Bodhi Society:

> . . . I attended a meeting of the Maha-Bodhi Society, at which I read a paper on the situation of affairs and offered my resignation of the position of Honorary General Adviser, for the reason that, as I explained, Mr. Dharmapala did not seem disposed to take any advice when given. Since that time I have had no responsibility whatever for the management of that Society, nor done anything to secure the considerable success which Dharmapala has achieved with the help of his friends.[12]

Olcott briefly refers to Dharmapala in a list of speakers at the Parliament of Religions and as being present with him on 4 June 1898 in Adyar. The occasion was a meeting to discuss formation of a Dravidian Buddhist Society, aided by the Sinhalese Buddhists.[13] Dharmapala is last seen through Olcott's eyes in a July 1898 meeting in Colombo. Sumangala, the High Priest, spoke first, followed by Olcott and Dharmapala. The latter took Olcott to the site of a failed attempt to create an agricultural college. He then made a proposal which was bitterly rejected by the President:

> Our young friend has a marked tendency to fly kites, the strings of which persist in getting broken; he lets them go and they are out of sight. Dharmapala could not see the absurdity of the proposal he made me after the scheme had hopelessly failed, viz., that as I was growing old and had placed the Buddhists under enormous obligations, I should now retire from the management of the Theosophical Society, settle down at Raja Giri and pass my remaining days in dignified retirement. Stript of all covering of fine talk, the idea was simply that I should pull his chestnuts out of the fire—so illogically and impulsively does his mind work.[14]

This passage may illuminate a generational aspect of the question of Olcott's desertion by the Masters after the death of HPB. From his relationship with Dharmapala, it appears that Olcott would have been contemptuous of any advice which did not suit his preferences, and unlikely to see a younger man as a spiritual mentor. At 65, Olcott was not ready to be put out to pasture, and seems to have mistrusted Dharmapala, who may have hoped to succeed Olcott as President of the TS. Later, as will be seen in Part Four, Dharmapala was harshly critical of early twentieth-century Theosophy.

In 1991, the centenary of the Maha Bodhi Society led to renewed collaboration with the TS. Dr. C. V. Agarwal, General Secretary of the Indian Section of the TS, was a principal speaker at the centenary observation in Sarnath. The Theosophists reciprocated in 1992 by honoring L. Ariyawansa Mahathero, President of the Maha Bodhi Society of India, at the Foundation Day celebration of the TS in Varanasi. As a result of renewed contact, a booklet entitled *The Buddhist and the Theosophical Movements* was published by the Maha Bodhi Society in 1993, authored by Dr. Agarwal and summarizing the historical links between Theosophy and Buddhism.

Agarwal sketches the origins of cooperation, from the Panadura debate of 1874 through the arrival of the TS founders in Ceylon, culminating in efforts to establish Buddhist schools in that country. From 1880 through his death in 1907, the career of Olcott is presented as an unending series of labors for Buddhist revival, beginning in Ceylon but extending into Burma, Japan, and ultimately to the West.

Agarwal provides a thorough account of the emergence of the Maha Bodhi Society, of which the original president was Sumangala. Olcott served as Director and Chief Advisor, while Dharmapala bore the title of General Secretary. Its initial object was defined as "the establishment of a Buddhist monastery and founding a Buddhist College and maintaining a staff of Buddhist Bhikkus at Buddha Gaya representing the Buddhist countries of China, Japan, Siam, Cambodia, Burma, Ceylon, Chittagong, Nepal, Tibet, and Arakan . . . [and] the publication of Buddhist Literature in English and Indian vernaculars."[15] Branches were soon formed in many of these countries, and in October 1891, an International Buddhist Conference was held at Bodh Gaya. Within the society's first year of existence, a high level of initial optimism met with frustration, as the British government rejected Japanese offers to purchase the site as a symptom of emerging imperialist designs.

With the death of a sympathetic Mahant of the site and the appointment of a hostile successor, attacks on Buddhist monks began to occur. After Dharmapala returned from the Parliament, he lived at Bodh Gaya for seventeen years, and succeeded in building a guest house for pilgrims. But in 1912, the government forced him to leave, and the society headquarters was relocated to Calcutta, where it remains today.[16] The TS in Calcutta shares quarters in the same building.

One of the more striking incidents of collaboration between Olcott and Dharmapala occurred in Darjeeling in October 1892, and is described in *Old Diary Leaves:*

> On 17th October [1892] he and I left for Darjeeling for a meeting between the Ambassador of the Dalai Lama of Lhasa and myself, which had been arranged. Reaching there on the following day [from Calcutta], I was received as a guest by my friend Babu Chhatra Dhar Ghose. I found at his cottage, hard at work with a learned Tibetan lama, Babu Sarat Chandra Das, C.I.E., the intrepid and successful Indian traveller to Lhasa and Tashi Lhunpo, the seats of the Dalai and Tashi Lamas respectively. He gave us some of the Tibetan buttered tea, of which we have all read so much . . .
>
> The next morning . . . was passed by us with Sarat Babu, whose conversation about his Tibetan experiences was most interesting and instructive. At 4 P.M. the audience with the Ambassador came off, Sarat Babu and his old colleague and travelling companion Lama Ugyen Gyatso kindly serving as interpreters. His Excellency was a handsome young man, of the distinct Mongolian ethnic type, with fair complexion, a gentle expression of face, small well-shaped hands, and a bearing of the personal dignity which usually marks aristocratic birth. . . . His bearing was dignified, his motions graceful, his voice refined . . . With that instinctive regard for age which is characteristic of the Oriental peoples, he saluted me most respectfully, gave me a seat of honor, and expressed his pleasure in meeting one who had done so much for Buddhism. His reception of Dharmapala was equally friendly.
>
> In the course of our long talk of nearly four hours, he asked me many questions about the state of our religion outside Tibet and China, and how the teachings of the Buddha were appreciated in the countries of the West. He assured me that if it should ever be my fortune to visit Lhasa I should receive an affectionate welcome; it was not within his power

> to arrange for such a journey, but he would report to his Government all that had been said, and it would give the Tibetans great pleasure. As an interlude, buttered tea was served to us. The plans and work of the Maha-Bodhi Society greatly interested him, and he congratulated Dharmapala on the usefulness of his labors; the Dalai Lama would be delighted to hear all he should tell him . . . he gave me a very fine gilt bronze statuette of a sitting Bodhisattva, made at Lhasa, and containing in its interior a folded strip of paper on which the Dalai Lama had himself written a *mantram* invoking the protection of the gods for the ambassador, from all evil influences, and stamped it with his own seal. This unique present is, of course, in the Adyar Library, together with his Excellency's signed portrait. At the close of our interview he accompanied us to the garden gate, shook hands with us in Western fashion, and expressed his deep regret that my engagements elsewhere would prevent our meeting again.[17]

This foreshadowed later cooperation, for example when the present Dalai Lama visited TS headquarters at Adyar, accompanied by the Panchen Lama, in 1957. They donated several palm leaf manuscripts to the library. Since his exile, the Dalai Lama has visited the TS Indian section headquarters several times, and has returned to Adyar occasionally.[18]

Agarwal interprets the later conflicts between Olcott and Dharmapala as a divergence of priorities, with Olcott emphasizing worldwide propaganda and Dharmapala focusing on the temple site. An attempt at reconciliation in 1906 ended in a heated argument, and Olcott died without making peace with his former protege.

A particularly striking indication of Olcott's unrecognized influence on Indian history is his role in championing conversion to Buddhism among the Untouchables. In 1898, he went to Colombo with Dharmapala and two representatives of the Southern Indian Sakya Muni Society. This organization promoted Buddhism among the "scheduled castes," and Sumangala warmly welcomed its delegates in a public ceremony:

> He presented the delegates to the High Priest who was delighted to see them and on the same evening there was a very big gathering to witness their admission to the Buddhist faith. The remarks of the High Priest were very dignified and noble. After explaining the opportunities offered by Buddhism he

admonished them never to lower the dignity of their new condition. Then they took Pancasila.[19]

A half-century later, the leader of the "Untouchables," Dr. Ambedkar, converted to Buddhism, bringing many followers with him.

Dharmapala's legacy to history has been measured in the West by his contributions to international Buddhism, which have been acclaimed by Theosophists. Unfortunately, his historical legacy also includes a virulent nationalism in Sri Lanka, compellingly portrayed in William McGowan's *Only Man is Vile* (1992).

McGowan identifies Dharmapala in Sinhalese context as "part messiah and part Malcolm X."[20] His high caste family were "wealthy entrepreneurs who had made a great deal of money making and selling furniture in Columbo."[21] Like most high-caste Sinhalese parents, Dharmapala's sent him to Christian schools but taught him Buddhism at home. He was expelled from one, where "he learned the Bible by heart," when he "drew a picture of a monkey and labeled it 'Christ.' "[22] His next school, St. Thomas College, punished him for spending the Sinhalese New Year at home, which was against the rules. Violence between Buddhists and Catholics in Colombo led to the end of Dharmapala's schooling. When he met HPB and Olcott at fourteen, he was already a clerk in Colombo's Education Department.[23]

McGowan portrays Dharmapala as the most influential contributor to the Sinhalese nationalist myth which has led to violence in Sri Lanka:

> In Dharmapala's demonology, both Christianity and the British were threats. Christians were "slaves of passion," he wrote, controlled by baser instincts. The British, similarly, were still living in a state of savagery, little different from the days before they were conquered by the Romans . . . "The sweet, tender, gentle Aryan children of an ancient historical race are sacrificed at the altar of the whiskey-drinking, beef-eating, belly-god of heathenism. How long, oh how long, will unrighteousness last in Ceylon?"[24]

The salvation of Ceylon was a return to Buddhism, but a particularly nationalistic version, elaborated in a series of folk tales. The *Mahavamsa* was recommended as a guide by Dharmapala, who derived from this collection of tales a myth of a Sinhalese Golden Age governed by benevolent Buddhist kings. McGowan concludes:

> The resuscitation of ancient Sinhalese myth may have encouraged Sinhalese national pride and raised consciousnesses for the struggle against British colonialism, but for the ethnically mixed society that Ceylon had become it was divisive, racist, and aggressive . . . Dharmapala's resurrected mythology presupposed a Sinhalese national identity based on a common Sinhala language, a common Buddhist religion, and a common Aryan racial stock. In fact, such an identity was really the recent creation of a nationalistic imagination, devoid of anthropological and historical validity.[25]

Fallacious ideas about history and race were so interwomen into Dharmapala's religious thinking that his writings today can be seen as crucial steps in the wrong direction for his country. But his influence on an international scale has been undoubtedly more benevolent. The combination of spiritual idealism and nationalist bigotry makes Dharmapala, like several other Theosophical initiates, complex and hard to evaluate. No character in this book illumines this complexity more than a fellow Buddhist-Theosophist, Prince Esper Ukhtomskii.

Ukhtomskii and Dorzhiev

Prince Esper Ukhtomskii and Agvan Dorzhiev may provide a missing link between Theosophy, Tibetan Buddhism, and the Fourth Way tradition. A 1988 article by Joscelyn Godwin, "HPB, Dorjeff, and the Mongolian Connection," introduced the intriguing figure of Dorzhiev to the field of Theosophical history. Dorzhiev and his fellow Buryat Mongol Buddhists were the liaison between the Russian government and the Tibetan religious hierarchy. Godwin recounts the tale in Volume 10 of the *Notebooks* of Paul Brunton (1898–1981), which was told to P.B. (as he wished to be called) by a "Mongolian philosopher" at Angkor Wat in 1939. The story tells of HPB's encounter with a party of Russian Buddhist Kalmyks *en route* to Lhasa on pilgrimage in 1849. Fleeing from her husband, HPB joins the pilgrimage and is accepted as a chela of a Kalmyk priest, through whose influence she is initiated into "the secret tradition" in Lhasa. After this, she travels in Tibet, India, and Cambodia. Years later she is introduced to a fellow disciple, Dorzhiev, son of a Mongolian prince. He advises her, originates the doctrinal content of the Mahatma letters, and is the real person on whom the Master KH is based. Dorzhiev was a key figure in Russian intelligence during the Great Game, and became the tutor and advisor of the Thirteenth Dalai Lama. After 1915, he went to St. Petersburg, where he established a Buddhist temple. He died in 1938 in a Stalinist prison. The "Mongolian philosopher," apparently his student, escaped to Cambodia, where he instructed Paul Brunton and inaugurated a new phase of esoteric history.[26]

In *The Harmonious Circle,* James Webb identifies George Ivanovitch Gurdjieff as Dorzhiev's traveling companion Ovshe Norzunov, speculating thus that Dorzhiev provides the missing link between HPB and Gurdjieff. This identification, which has been disproven by other evidence, is not, however, a necessary part of the chain connecting Dorzhiev and HPB. The tale of the "Mongolian philosopher" is highly unlikely; HPB was in other places when this story would have her in Tibet. But while Gurdjieff was not Norzunov, and Dorzhiev was certainly not KH, there is sufficient evidence to suspect some connection among Dorzhiev, Blavatsky, and Gurdjieff.

Dorzhiev was a Buryat Mongol from the region north of Ulan Ude. The Buryats inhabit an area south and east of Lake Baikal, as well as adjacent regions in Mongolia, China, and Russia. In the early nineteenth century, they were converted from their traditional shamanism to Tibetan Buddhism. From a series of "loosely-connected nomadic pastoralist tribes" in the seventeenth century, they evolved into a distinct ethnic entity by the time Russian sovereignty was extended to their territory.[27] When the border between Russia and Mongolia was firmly established, most Buryats were on the Russian side. Yet their religious, racial, and linguistic ties were with the Mongolians. The Buryats were evolving from nomadic livestock herding to settled agriculture, with those in western Buryatia leading the assimilation into Russian culture. Many converted to Orthodoxy.

Dorzhiev spent his life in Mongolia, Tibet, and Russia, while HPB never returned to any of those lands during the time in which he could have influenced her. It would seem, then, that the Brunton story about Kalmyk pilgrims, Lhasa initiations, and an introduction to Dorzhiev via Tibetan sources, provides no reliable explanation. What, then, are the possible connections between the Buryats and Theosophical history? Esper Ukhtomskii is a promising source of clues.

Prince Esper Esperovitch Ukhtomskii was born to a wealthy family with extensive interests in Central Asia. He claimed to have been a practicing Buddhist from the age of fifteen, and acquired a large collection of manuscripts and art objects from Mongolia and

Tibet, which he housed in a museum in Irkutsk. His interest in Buddhism led to his appointment as Chief of the Department of Foreign Creeds, which controlled non-Christian faiths in the Russian empire. He later edited newspapers in Riga and St. Petersburg, and was a director of the Russo-Chinese bank.[28]

In 1890 and 1891 he accompanied the Czarevitch on a round-the-world trip which included stops at Adyar and Ceylon. His account of the journey includes frequent expansionist comments, such as, "We are, and must be supported by the idea of an ever-possible advance of the irresistable North over the Hindu Kush."[29] Ukhtomskii's *Travels in the East of Nicholas II, Emperor of Russia, when Czarevitch 1890–91* was translated into English and published in 1896. It provides a fascinating record of an elaborate journey, and yields considerable insight into the author. In two large quarto volumes, the book contains over five hundred illustrations, with almost every page enlivened by a vivid depiction of places and people encountered by the travelers. Joining Nicholas were five Russian princes, of whom the senior officer was Major-General Prince V. A. Bariatinskii, A. D. C. to his majesty. Only days before the outset, Ukhtomskii was given leave from his post in the Department of Foreign Creeds in the Department of the Interior and assigned to Bariatinskii as chronicler of the journey.[30] One can readily imagine that Ukhtomskii was the most able man for the job; his understanding of the religious and cultural background in the many countries visited is astounding. Although he writes sympathetically of each country visited, it is clearly among Buddhists that he feels most at home: "in Buddhism, with its simple, clear, and sober ideas, we find another East, the East of a reconciled past, of a more rational present, and a brighter and more active future."[31]

The education of the young Czarevitch demanded familiarity with the Eastern lands which Russian imperialism increasingly coveted. Passing through Vienna, the travellers embarked from Trieste, sailing through Greek waters to Cairo, where they spent several weeks exploring Egypt. Proceeding through the Suez Canal to Aden, the Russians next sailed for Bombay. It is in his description of the approach to that city that Ukhtomskii first expresses his religious emotions overtly:

> To-morrow, India! Sleep deserts mine eyes. I vainly sought it in the balmy night;—in the gold and crimson of the rising sun, the dawn greets the promised land, where the heavens are pervaded with the charms of love, but passion is con-

quered by an unspeakable sadness,—where life glows bright, yet all is as a dream, and breathes with beauty irresistible as death. O land of daring dreams and soaring thought! thou risest out of the azure deep, whose mournful moaning echoes sadly back the discord reigning in the weary heart. India lies before us! here holiness and peace appeared in visions unto men contemptuous of pleasure; since their age the people live the self-same life, yearning for the Divinity, for freedom and atonement. Here where the earthly realm of sorrow borders on the heavens, and when the soul is crushed by unceasing torments, this magic land calls us into a world of wonders, into the realm of the eternal mysteries and of boundless wisdom.[32]

After traveling in India, Ukhtomskii concluded that there was a deep affinity between the Russian and Indian peoples:

> Without doubt the deeper one's study of Indian history and of the individual qualities of the races inhabiting the peninsula, the more definite become certain theses concerning this land, which excites in us an ever-growing and almost instinctive interest. Once 'Russia' and 'the East' (taking the latter to include the combined peculiarities of the culture of Islam, Brahminism, Buddhism, Confucianism, etc.) are placed in a completed group of organically associated nations with a strong vitality, their marked difference from the nations of the West, in their past and their present, will become patent to every unprejudiced observer . . . [33]

During their long passage through India, the Russians were welcomed by virtually every major maharaja in the country, including all those with known Theosophical links. The British extended every hospitality and helped arrange all details of travel, so they must have been annoyed later to read Ukhtomskii's remarks:

> Clearly history is preparing new and complex problems in the East for the colonizing states of Western Europe, which are not really at home in Asia (as we Russians always have been, and still are, without being aware of it), but appear, in some measure, as fortuitous and abnormal excrescences on her gigantic body. . . . The journey of the Czarewitch through the civilized countries of the East is full of deep significance for Russia. The bonds that unite our part of Europe with Iran

> and Turan, and through them with India and the Celestial Empire, are so ancient and lasting that, as yet, we ourselves, as a nation and a state, do not fully comprehend their full meaning and the duties they entail on us, both in our home and foreign policy.[34]

During the journey through Bihar, the Russians visited Bodh Gaya just after the formation of the Maha-Bodhi Society:

> Buddha Gaya is now becoming a religious centre in the eyes of the local Theosophical Society and of Buddhists of different nationalities, who dream of building a monastery near the old temple, of opening colleges with theological and philosophical faculties, with an enlightened circle of cosmopolite zealots, the Maha-Bodhi Society, with its own periodical, libraries, and so forth; in fact, to found a whole city, a nursery of faith and knowledge in the spirit of the 'master,' aimed at influencing the Brahminized world of India, at taking advantage of the schisms arising in it, and again leading countless thousands into the path of the hermit prince.[35]

In Adyar on 7 February 1891, the imperial party visited the TS headquarters. Ukhtomskii's comments on this visit are informative:

> We must not forget, however, that we are in a land where it is difficult, and as yet perhaps wellnigh impossible, to define the connection and the boundary between phenomena of a perfectly natural character, and such as to European eyes partake of the miraculous. For this reason, perhaps, it was in India that, at the instance of H. P. Blavatsky, a Russian lady who knew and had seen much, the idea sprang up of the possibility, and even the necessity, of founding a society of theosophists, of searchers for the Truth in the broadest sense of the word, for the purpose of enlisting adepts of all creeds and races, of penetrating deep into the most secret doctrines of Oriental religion, of drawing Asiatics intro true spiritual communion with educated foreigners from the West, of keeping up secret relations with different high priests, ascetics, magicians, and so on.
>
> Here in Madras, in the suburbs of Adyar, the new and original brotherhood first saw the world *[sic].* Colonel Olcott, an American, was a most active assistant and friend to our

talented countrywoman, who is known to Russian literature as Radda-Bai.

A great number of branches of the Madras Theosophic lodge have sprung up in Asia, America and Europe. Several periodicals are specially devoted to the observation, and partly to the study, of the inexplicable psychic phenomena of yogism. H. P. Blavatsky called forth a whole storm of accusations of imposture, and on account of the suspiciousness of the English, was obliged to bid farewell for good and all to the wondrous peninsula which had become so dear to her; but her power of calling forth the sincere sympathy and devotion of the natives, their vague longing to group themselves together under the banner of this strange *northern* woman, belonging to a people radically strange to Albion, her constant journeyings through the land to come into closer relations with the wise men, and to penetrate into the sacred mysteries of the Brahmins and the Jains,—all these things have created an exceptional position for her, and one which has not been occupied by any one for ages. For the India of the present and the future, H. P. Blavatsky is not dead, and never will be.[36]

A chapter is devoted to describing the journey through Ceylon, which included two days of Buddhist ceremonies in Kandy. Ukhtomskii does not describe his meeting with Olcott in Colombo, but does mention him as "having been much occupied latterly with the idea of discovering the spiritual links between the lands in which Sakya Muni is revered as a divinity."[37]

Ukhtomskii's meeting with Olcott is described in detail in the fourth volume of *Old Diary Leaves:*

There was lying in Colombo harbor at that time a Russian frigate on which the Czarewitch, the present Czar, was making the tour of the world, accompanied by a staff of eminent men. One of these gentlemen, during the Prince's Indian tour, had called at Adyar during my absence in Burma, expressed much interest in Theosophy, and bought some of our books. I was sorry to have missed him, as also the ball at Government House, to which the new Governor, Lord Wenlock, had invited me "to have the honor of meeting His Imperial Highness the Czarewitch." Learning from the Russian Consul at Colombo that some of the Crown Prince's staff would be pleased to make my acquaintance, I went aboard the frigate and spent an hour in delightful conversation with Prince Hespere

> Ouktomsky, Chief of the Departement des Cultes, in the Ministere de l'Interieur, who was acting as the Prince's Private Secretary on this tour, and Lieutenant N. Crown, of the Navy Department at St. Petersburg, both charming men. I found myself particularly drawn to Prince Oukhtomsky because of his intense interest in Buddhism, which for many years he has made a special study among the Mongolian lamaseries. He has also given much time to the study of other religions. He was good enough to invite me to make a tour of the Buddhist monasteries of Siberia. He asked me for a copy of my Fourteen Propositions, so that he might translate them and circulate them among the Chief Priests of Buddhism throughout the empire. This he has since done.[38]

In discussing the potential success of Olcott's effort, Ukhtomskii implies that he will use his own influence on Olcott's behalf:

> In Japan, Burma, Chittagong, and Ceylon Colonel Olcott's programme and his fourteen fundamental propositions have been approved. It remains to be seen how Siam and Cambodia, China, Corea, and Thibet will regard his attempts at strengthening the ties between the Buddhist communions of the world. As far as concerns Thibet, and within Mongolia, the Buriats and the Kalmucks, the ideas of Madame Blavatsky's coadjutor will undoubtedly meet with attention and sympathy.[39]

Despite Ukhtomskii's extensive connections with the Buddhists of those countries, they receive surprisingly little coverage in his book. There are abundant illustrations of the inhabitants and art of Mongolia, Buryatia, Tibet, etc., but one seeks in vain for passages that reveal the author's associations and sympathies. Perhaps this is for reasons of state security; Ukhtomskii's links with the Buryats and Tibetans in any event were surrounded with secrecy.

Ukhtomskii's interest in "secret relations" is apparent in his 1896 comment that "The Tibetans, who keep up very near relations with our Buryats, are gradually but deeply imbibing identical ideas."[40]

Olcott met Ukhtomskii for the last time in Colombo on 23 April 1897. His account of this meeting provides an indication of the prince's continuing contacts with high-ranking Buddhists in several countries:

He was almost as deeply interested in the study of Buddhism as I, myself, and our meeting at Colombo on this occasion was the result of a request of his to that effect in a letter received by me from him some weeks before . . . His greeting to me was most cordial and at once prepossessed me in his favor. He had all that high-bred courtesy, ease of manner, and social polish which is so marked among the Russian nobility. He told me that he was on his way to China as a special ambassador to the Emperor . . . [after a ride in a dugout canoe together] I spent the whole day with the Prince, taking him to Kotahena Temple, to see Prince Jinawarawansa, to Mrs. Higgins' *Musaeus,* and the *Sanghamitta* Girls' schools, and to call on the High Priest, Sumangala, with whom the Prince had a most interesting conference, through a Sinhalese interpreter . . . At parting, Prince Oukhtomsky expressed to me his great delight with all that he had heard and seen during the day, and carried away with him several unique images and other Buddhistic curios, given him by Sumangala and by the Prince-priest, Jinawarawansa . . . it was his intention to revisit the Buddhist Lamaseries of Mongolia before returning home from his Chinese mission; at any rate, he gave me a cordial invitation to make the grand tour with him and personally discuss with the chief priests, the resemblances and differences between Northern and Southern Buddhism. He has translated into the Russian language my Fourteen Fundamental Propositions, and assures me that they have all been approved by the Mongolian and Tibetan Buddhist scholars . . .[41]

Zhamtsaran Badmayev (1851–1919) was from the Lake Baikal region, a Buryat Mongol like Dorzhiev, but he converted to Orthodox Christianity and became a major influence on the royal family. A scholar in Chinese and Mongolian languages, he was honored with the presence of Tsar Alexander III acting as godfather in his conversion ceremony. From 1875 to 1893 Badmayev held civil service posts, but his practice of Tibetan medicine is what endeared him to the Romanovs. He treated the hemophiliac Czarevitch and was on good terms with Rasputin. Webb concludes of him that he "stood head and shoulders above the crowd of magi and holy fools who clamored around the steps to the throne," and that even in jail after the Bolshevik Revolution, his charisma impressed his captors.[42]

In 1887, HPB wrote a letter to Sinnett which seems to refer to Badmayev:

> A Tibetan who came back with the Prjivolsky expedition (or after it) a "plant doctor" they call him as he produces mysterious cures with simples, told Soloview and others it appears, that they were all fools and the SPR asses and imbeciles, since all educated Tibet and China know of the "Brotherhood of the Snowy Range," I am accused of having invented; and that he, himself, knows several Masters personally. And when asked by General Lvov what he knew about the London Psychic R. Society since he had never been in Europe before, he laughed and told the General "looking him straight between the eyebrows" that there was not a book pro or contra Tibet and its wise men that remained unknown in Tchigadze. When the General, "much struck," asked him if the Brotherhood would not help Russia against England—the "doctor" laughed again. He said England or Russia were all one for the "Wise Men"; they left both to their respective Karma.[43]

The claim of indifference to the struggle between Russia and England hardly coincides with what is known of Badmayev's later activities. Given Sinnett's political attitudes, however, this may well have been edited by HPB for his consumption.

Another Mongol associate of Ukhtomskii was Ovshe Norzunov, who is mistakenly identified by James Webb with Gurdjieff. Norzunov appears in the records of British India as a Mongol travelling through India to Tibet with a shipment of golden bowls supplied by Joseph Deniker (1852–1918). Deniker is another link to the Kalmyks, as he was born in Astrakhan and was knowledgeable about the races and cultures of the region. He was also a specialist in Buddhism and Oriental languages, but had trained in chemistry and anthropology before becoming the librarian of the Museum of Natural History. He became "the chief means of communication between the Russian experts on Central Asia and the Western world," due to his translations.[44] He knew Ukhtomskii, and was introduced to Dorzhiev by the Orientalist Sylvain Levi. He remained a friend of Dorzhiev, for whom he "did many favors."[45]

Norzunov returned to Paris in 1901 and 1902, and provided Deniker with photographs which became the basis for Webb's effort to identify Norzunov and Gurdjieff. Norzunov's account of his travels to Tibet are closely analyzed by Webb, but he fails to convince on the subject of the Norzunov/Gurdjieff identity. This does not render any less likely Webb's conclusion that Gurdjieff had some communication with Dorzhiev, Badmayev, and Ukhtomskii. The same group is mentioned in Webb's appendix on "The Sources of the System" where, after discussing Notovitch's *The Unknown Life of Jesus,* the author speculates that:

> The idea that the real, the "esoteric," Christianity had derived from Buddhism would explain precisely what Gurdjieff was doing in Tibet as the pupil of Agwan Dordjieff. It may also explain quite a lot about the relationship between Dordjieff, the convert to Orthodoxy Shamzaran Badmaieff, and Prince Ukhtomsky, the Theosophist—who, although he announced himself as a practicing Buddhist, was once described by Badmaieff in a letter to Nicholas II as a good Christian.[46]

Additional information on the career of Dorzhiev was presented in *Theosophical History,* by Jeffrey Somers. The name Agwan Dorzhiev is a Russification of Ngawang Lobsang Dorje. He was born in the Trans-Baikal region as a Mongol subject of the Russian empire. At the age of fourteen, he began his studies at the San Ganden monastery in Urga (now Ulan Bator). At nineteen, he went to the Drepung Monastery in Lhasa, where he received a special assignment to the young Thirteenth Dalai Lama. Among his titles was Abbot of the Innermost Essence. He received inner teachings with the Dalai Lama, and gradually acquired influence over him. Dorzhiev became the most knowledgeable student of foreign affairs in Tibet, and acted as Foreign Minister. Seeing Russia and England as both intent on acquiring Tibet, he preferred Russian hegemony. He identified Russia with Shambhala and the Czar with the promised protector-king. In 1898, he toured the Kalmyk regions and then Paris as the guest of Deniker.[47]

At this point, Ukhtomskii emerges as the key figure who bridges Russian, Mongolian and Tibetan affairs. He was responsible for arranging an audience with the Czar for Dorzhiev, with the aim of improving relations between Tibet and Russia. Throughout the last decades of the nineteenth century, tension between Russia and England had been building over the question of Tibet. After British letters to the Dalai Lama in 1902 were not acknowledged, troops were sent to the border region. In 1903, three thousand British troops marched into Tibet, reaching Lhasa in 1904. There they found that the Dalai Lama had fled with Dorzhiev to Mongolia. After the Dalai Lama returned to Tibet in 1916, Dorzhiev went to St. Petersburg, where he was given permission to build a Tibetan Buddhist temple. The temple, which still stands, will be made a museum. Stalin had made it a vivisection research center after exiling Dorzhiev to Ulan Ude in 1937, where he died the following year. Somers concludes that Dorzhiev's linguistic breadth and wide travels made him unique among the lamas of his time.[48]

Four additional secondary sources provide further information on Ukhtomskii. The *Modern Encyclopedia of Russian and Soviet History* defines him as a "government official, diplomat, publicist and specialist on Oriental affairs" who was born into "an old family of the upper nobility" whereby he "inherited the title of prince and what was reputed to be immense wealth."[49] In 1896, he became editor and publisher of the St. Petersburg *News,* which he used to promote the cause of expansionism in Asia. Thereafter, his closest ally in the Russian government was Sergei de Witte, Minister of Finance and first cousin of HPB. Through Witte's influence, he became chairman of the Russo-Chinese Bank in 1896, which marked the beginning of Ukhtomskii's role in international finance:

> In the spring of that year, in order to expedite the proposed Chinese Eastern Railway across Manchuria, Witte dispatched him to the Suez Canal to escort Li Hung Chang, the Chinese envoy, to St. Petersburg before representatives of other powers could intercede. In 1897 he was sent to China for negotiations on the railway project, and it was he who conveyed a large sum, reputed to be one million rubles, to Li for past favors. Although his mission failed to gain the concessions that Witte desired, the line was built, and he became chairman of the Chinese Eastern Railway Company. He renewed his unofficial mission in 1900 at the time of the Boxer troubles, but again his efforts proved abortive.[50]

After Witte lost his position in 1903, Ukhtomskii's career as a diplomat came to an end. His literary career would soon end equally abruptly. His chauvinistic confidence during the Russo-Japanese war led to a "devastating blow" to his reputation when Russia was defeated.[51] This marks the end of his public life. Ukhtomskii survived until 1921, but the *Encyclopedia* provides no details of his whereabouts or activities in his last sixteen years.[52] Other sources provide further understanding of the nature of the disillusionment which led to Ukhtomskii's retirement to private life. In *Russian Affairs* (1904), British author Geoffrey Drage gives colorful details of the extent of Ukhtomskii's Russian chauvinism. He is quoted as threatening to "crush, if necessary with a giant's foot, the proud young state of Japan."[53] Drage describes Ukhtomskii as one who "wields immense influence in many quarters, can promote Russian interests in the East, and secure a hearing for his views at home."[54] Britons must have been disquieted to read of his belief that "In our organic connection with all these lands lies the pledge of our future, in which Asiatic Russia will mean simply all Asia."[55] Ukhtomskii believed that this would come about via "painless identification," yet he implicitly proposed a war of extermination against Great Britain.[56] In *Russian Far Eastern Policy, 1881–1904,* Andrew Malozemoff reveals the extreme extent of Ukhtomskii's folly in 1904, and the reaction that ensued. He is quoted as claiming that "We have nothing to conquer. All these peoples of various races feel themselves drawn to us, and are ours, by blood, by tradition, and by ideas. We simply approach them more closely. This great and mysterious Orient is ready to become ours."[57] Even the initial defeats suffered at the hands of Japan failed to quench the Prince's enthusiasm:

> . . . Ukhtomskii broke out in expressions of blatant and unabashed chauvinism. He forecast that Russia would defeat Japan and compensate herself for the expenses of the war by taking a large section of China. This would lead to a Russo-Chinese war in which the Chinese would be conquered. The English would then intervene, and Russia would have to drive the English out of India.
>
> Ukhtomskii had many critics who lampooned him with derisive remarks. He was labeled a "superpatriot" and a "faddist," and contemporary critics sarcastically attacked his "yellow Russia" *(zheltorossiia)*. . . .[58]

Buddhism in Russia, John Snelling's 1993 biography of Dorzhiev, answers many questions that have been raised about the elusive Buryat by other recent studies, and provides a detailed portrait of Ukhtomskii. The Thirteenth Dalai Lama, Tubten Gyatso, was about twelve years old when Dorzhiev entered his life. From 1888 through 1913, Dorzhiev was the strongest influence over the Dalai Lama, who viewed him as his "true guardian and protector."[59] Some Tibetans pressured the Regent to exile Dorzhiev, but the Dalai Lama himself prevented this. The previous four incarnations had been murdered by their regents before attaining maturity; Snelling attributes to Dorzhiev some of the responsibility for Tubten Gyatso's escape from this fate. In his discussion of the minority of the Thirteenth Dalai Lama, the author mentions that one crucial event was Sarat Chandra Das's penetration of Tibet. He gives the personal name of Das's sponsor as Losang Palden; other sources identify him only by his title, Sengchen Tulku. Losang Palden was arrested and drowned as punishment for aiding Das, which confirms the evidence presented in *The Masters Revealed* concerning these tragic events.[60]

Most relevant to the present investigation are Snelling's discoveries concerning Ukhtomskii's role in Dorzhiev's life. His characterization of the prince is based on the most extensive research to date. Ukhtomskii's childhood background may explain his later preoccupations to some extent; his father "founded a steamship company to link the Baltic with India and China via the Black Sea."[61] Ukhtomskii's interest in Buddhism had developed during his university studies in philosophy, and soon after graduation in 1884 he entered government service in the Department of Foreign Creeds. Contact with Russian Buddhists led to the beginning of his art collection, called by Snelling the "first of its kind in the world."[62] Ukhtomskii's love for Buddhism was based on his appreciation of its humanitarianism and moral idealism. But, adds Snelling, "above all he believed that a revitalized Buddhism, perhaps based at a restored Bodh-Gaya and under the spiritual leadership of the Dalai Lama of Tibet, could reawaken and unify the disparate Buddhist groups of Asia and initiate a regeneration . . . "[63] In the four years preceding his journey with Nicholas II, Ukhtomskii had made repeated trips to Buryatia, Mongolia, China, and Sri Lanka. The latter is the most likely site of his first encounter with Theosophists, sometime in the late 1880s.[64]

Through his scholarly affiliations, Ukhtomskii was acquainted with all the other leading Orientalists of Russia. Although his original interest in Buddhism was scholarly, he became personally involved with the Buryats and acted as their advocate in St. Petersburg. Snelling notes that he "called for better health care . . . and defended them against both forcible conversion to Christianity and the arbitrary excesses of local officials."[65] Despite his fanatical expansionism, Ukhtomskii was a liberal reformer, incurring the wrath of government censors who eventually forbade him to sign his editorials. After 1900, he increasingly lost favor with the court, and by the time Rasputin appeared on the scene, Ukhtomskii had "completely lost the Emperor's ear."[66]

In 1898, Dorzhiev left Lhasa to begin the journey which would eventually lead to St. Petersburg. Ukhtomskii received reports of the lama during his travels in Buryatia, and was so intrigued that he invited Dorzhiev to the capital. Snelling surmises that Ukhtomskii's appeal to Dorzhiev was attributable to his search for channels to the Dalai Lama that might promote Russian interests.

Within the next two years, Dorzhiev would have two interviews with the Emperor.

Snelling's research unearths several facts relevant to Theosophical history. In 1900, Dorzhiev's Kalmyk disciple Ovshe Norzunov, with whom he had traveled in Mongolia, was sent on a commercial mission to Tibet. He carried part of a large shipment of steel begging bowls with him, and sent the remainder on another ship. The bowls, made in Paris, were shipped via Marseilles, Calcutta, and Darjeeling. While in Darjeeling awaiting the second shipment, Norzunov stayed at the Ghum monastery outside the city. This is the same monastery where HPB found refuge on her mysterious 1882 pilgrimage. Norzunov's host at Ghum was Sherab Gyatso, a Buryat lama who had been an attendant of Sengchen Tulku. Yet another connection to the Theosophical Masters is that Sarat Chandra Das, who lived in Darjeeling, was familiar with Norzunov and Dorzhiev, and advised the British on their possible political affiliations. (He mistakenly thought the mission to Russia to have been instigated in Mongolia rather than Tibet.)[67] While at Ghum, Norzunov was ordered by the government to remain in the vicinity, and required to report regularly to the District Commissioner in Darjeeling. Although Dorzhiev also passed through the area and visited Norzunov at Ghum, this was not discovered by the British until well after the fact. After being escorted to Calcutta and held in detention there, Norzunov was deported to Russia. Although his shipment of bowls eventually reached its destination, Norzunov returned with his other objectives unsatisfied. But he did not have to wait long to return to Lhasa. Norzunov, Dorzhiev, and six companions arrived there in early 1901, to a heroes' welcome.

Snelling provides further information on Ukhtomskii's later years than has heretofore been available in English. He reports that after the revolution, Ukhtomskii was Assistant Curator of the Far Eastern Department of the Russian Museum. Since he had given both of his collections of oriental art to the state before the revolution, he was perhaps regarded with greater approval by the Soviet authorities than he otherwise might have been.[68] Ukhtomskii died peacefully in 1921, after a period of illness. Some links between Ukhtomskii's Buryat associates and HPB are suggested by the evidence presented by Godwin and Webb. But evidence suggests that Ukhtomskii's most interesting role in Theosophical history was as a mentor to George Ivanovitch Gurdjieff.

George Ivanovitch Gurdjieff

George Ivanovitch Gurdjieff had a career which parallels that of HPB in a striking number of details: birth and early childhood in the southern reaches of the Russian Empire, with exposure to the varied races and religions of the Caucasus; youthful rebellion, followed by years of wandering in search of ancient wisdom; claims to have visited Egypt, Persia, India, Tibet, and the Far East, but vagueness as to details of time and place; reported injury in battle; sudden emergence as a public teacher after age forty; attraction of a circle of European and American intellectuals; scandals including accusations of fraud and espionage; seemingly endless capacity to offend Western sensibilities; troubled relations with disciples; final years of calm spent teaching a circle of private students; fragmentation of the movement he founded in the years immediately following his death.

These parallels are indeed striking, but may give a false picture unless considered in light of equally striking contrasts. Blavatsky was a Russian aristocrat; Gurdjieff was a Greek/Armenian whose father was a cattleman, then a lumberyard owner, and finally a woodworker. HPB was fluent in French, English, Italian, and later Arabic and Sanskrit, but limited in her mastery of Asian vernacular languages; the reverse appears true of Gurdjieff. Gurdjieff indulged freely and openly in alcohol and sexual pleasure; HPB denounced both in no uncertain terms. Theosophy, despite its occult atmosphere, was a universalistic movement open to all; Gurdjieff's disciples believed that only a few could profit from his teachings, which should be kept hidden from the outside world. The movements they founded have shown scant mutual respect; Gurdjieff was condescending at best in his comments on Theosophy, while Theosophists have been highly suspicious of his claims. Due to his extreme care to conceal his sources, any solid identification of Gurdjieff's Masters would be much more difficult than in the case of HPB. Yet despite the "automythological" character of his writings, they provide the only possible starting point for an investigation.

The passages in Gurdjieff's writings that most specifically cite a source for his teachings are in *Meetings with Remarkable Men.* This book describes the young Gurdjieff's discovery, in the ruins of an ancient Armenian town, of a collection of letters from one monk to another. A society called the Sarmoung brotherhood is mentioned in the letters as a "famous esoteric school, which, according to tradition was founded in Babylon as far back as 2500 B.C."[69]

Gurdjieff and his associates in a group called the "Seekers of Truth" proceed to travel throughout Central Asia in search of the Sarmoung brotherhood. At the conclusion of *Meetings with Remarkable Men,* the pilgrims arrive at the Sarmoung monastery located near Chitral, in the mountainous region north of the Khyber pass, along the present border of Pakistan and Afghanistan. Gurdjieff declares, "As we later ascertained, among the adepts of this monastery were former Christians, Jews, Mohammedans, Buddhists, Lamaists, and even one Shamanist. All were united by God the Truth."[70] He quotes Father Giovanni, a former missionary, about the brotherhood to which he belongs: "Our brotherhood has four monasteries, one of them ours, the second in the valley of the Pamir, the third in Tibet and the fourth in India."[71] *The Teachers of Gurdjieff,* by the pseudonymous Rafael Lefort, describes the author's efforts to contact the sources of Gurdjieff's teachings within the decade following his death. In the course of exploring various leads in Gurdjieff's writings, the author finds himself travelling among Sufi teachers of the Middle East. His search culminates in Northern Afghanistan, near the site of the Sarmoung monastery as described in Gurdjieff's account. There he is told that this is indeed the center where Gurdjieff had studied under Sufi masters more than fifty years earlier.[72] It appears likely that Idries Shah is the author of this book, which seems to have been written to attract Gurdjieff's followers to Shah's version of contemporary Sufism. John G. Bennett's autobiography, *Witness,* describes Mr. Shah's successful effort to claim the allegiance of a Gurdjieffian group under Bennett's direction in the 1950s.[73]

In *The People of the Secret,* author Ernest Scott relates varied references to trans-Himalayan masters of the Khwajagan order, affiliated since the 14th century with the Naqshbandi Sufis. In an inaccessible spot there is said to be a center of Khwajagan activity known as the Markaz or powerhouse of the "People of the Tradition."[74] Scott cites a traveller's encounter with a center which he equates with the Sarmoung monastery. This article, "Solo to Mecca," by Omar Burke, describes a month spent at a Sufi monastery located three days' travel north of Karachi.[75] Scott suggests that the Sarmoung brotherhood is a specialized subdivision of the Naqshbandi Sufis. The author is affiliated with the "Shah school" of neo-Sufism, and follows its insistence on Gurdjieff's Sufi sources. In *Gurdjieff: Seeker of the Truth,* by Kathleen Speeth and Ira Friedlander, it is suggested that the Sarmoung brotherhood is distinct from the Naqshbandis but closely related.[76] Both books assert that the Sarmoung ("the bees") are preservers of pre-Christian

Middle Eastern occultism, working within the context of Naqshbandi Sufism.

The first comprehensive book on Gurdjieff and the movement he established is *The Harmonious Circle* by James Webb, published in 1980. James Moore's *Gurdjieff: the Anatomy of a Myth* (1991) provides a more sympathetic and reliable account, but does not address Gurdjieff's links to Theosophy in any detail. While Webb identifies some of the forms adopted by Gurdjieff as Sufic (e.g., the Stop exercise, the sacred movements), he stresses a distinction between form and content, and tries to derive the content of Gurdjieffian teaching from Western occult traditions. Although Webb establishes that Gurdjieff's writings show ample evidence of familiarity with the languages and cultures of Central Asia, including Tibet, he regards Gurdjieff more as a self-taught innovator than as an emissary of any esoteric fraternity.[77]

Gurdjieff and Blavatsky present similar problems to biographers. There appears to be a deliberate effort in both cases to appear untrustworthy and suspicious and to render the biographer's task impossible. Gurdjieff and HPB seem to be incarnations of the same archetype, successive acts in the same play. Each exemplifies the same model of the spiritual teacher, which has been called that of the magus. It is characterized by a heroic quest, usually involving years of travels, culminating in self-transformation, followed by a return to "the world." After this return, the magus cannot or will not directly describe what he has experienced. His personal history is presented in such a mysterious and confusing manner that posterity is left with scant clues regarding mundane details like spouses and children. He also seems somehow compelled to provoke censure from society, and to stimulate turmoil among his followers. The Sufi doctrine of instrumental teaching demonstrates a possible explanation of the apparently "outrageous" and "fraudulent" aspects of HPB and Gurdjieff. Instrumental teaching stresses the effect on consciousness, rather than the information conveyed, as the essence of a spiritual teacher's role. This has led to Malamata, the "path of blame," in which, at appropriate times, the teacher acts out negative roles in order to test and awaken the student more effectively than can be done through verbal instruction. Sufi teaching-stories abound in examples of this theme.[78] It can be argued that Blavatsky and Gurdjieff both demonstrated mastery of this technique, with comparable results. The Mahatma letters include the following passage explaining why the writers present themselves in ways likely to arouse suspicion:

> . . . I wish I could impress upon your minds the deep conviction that we do not wish Mr. Hume or you [Sinnett] to prove conclusively to the public that we really exist. Please realize the fact that so long as men doubt there will be curiosity and enquiry, and that enquiry stimulates reflection which begets effort; but let our secret be once thoroughly vulgarized and not only will sceptical society derive no great good but our privacy would be constantly endangered and have to be continually guarded at an unreasonable cost of power.[79]

In another letter, Koot Hoomi remarks:

> The chela is at perfect liberty, and often quite justified from the standpoint of appearances—to suspect his Guru of being a "fraud" as the elegant word stands. More than that: the greater, the sincerer his indignation—whether expressed in words or boiling in his heart—the more fit he is, the better qualified to become an adept.[80]

Among contemporary students of Gurdjieff, Sufism is generally regarded as the dominant influence on his teachings although esoteric Christianity, as practiced in the Orthodox tradition, is also recognized in his works. His extensive travels also provided ample opportunity to learn about Buddhism, and its influence can also be discerned in his teachings. Like Blavatsky, Gurdjieff synthesized a wide variety of traditions encountered in his travels. In his analysis of Gurdjieff's sources, James Webb draws attention to the Occult Revival of the late nineteenth century as an influence. The American P. B. Randolph's theories in particular are suggested as sources of the Gurdjieff system. But it is the Theosophical tradition which Webb believes was the single most important source for Gurdjieff. In *The Secret Doctrine,* he points out, are "references to the four bodies of man, to the 'ray' of creation, to number symbolism . . . applications of the octave to the chemical elements and the musical scale . . . and the renaming of the four elements 'hydrogen,' 'nitrogen,' 'oxygen,' and 'carbon.' "[81] A comparison of the teachings of Blavatsky and Gurdjieff leads to the conclusion that both are equally indebted to another source, Isma^cili Shi^cism, but how either contacted it remains mysterious. Isma^cili elements in Shaykhism may link the Baha^ɔi tradition to the same source.

There can be little doubt that Gurdjieff was well acquainted with HPB's teachings. The mystically inclined European intelligentsia of the early twentieth century was fairly well saturated with Theosophy, both in Russia and in Western Europe. In *Beelzebub's Tales to His Grandson,* Gurdjieff refers to Theosophy, Spiritualism, occultism, and psychoanalysis as "pseudo-teachings" which "are means only for the obscuring of their already, without this, obscured psyche."[82] His comments on the definition of "initiate" clarify the object of his ire. One sense of the term, which he approves, is for those who "thanks to their personal conscious labors and intentional sufferings" are able to "acquire in themselves objective merits which can be sensed by other beings irrespective of brain-system, and which also evoke in others trust and respect."[83] But increasingly common were self-proclaimed initiates who were in reality members of "criminal gangs," whose aim was theft of the "essence-values" of their followers.[84]

Theosophy was familiar to the most prominent of Gurdjieff's disciples. The first exposure of Gurdjieff's ideas in England came through P. D. Ouspensky's lectures to the Quest Society in London in 1919. This group was founded by G. R. S. Mead, Blavatsky's former secretary, after his alienation from the TS following Annie Besant's election as president in 1907.

Ouspensky had been a highly visible Theosophical writer and lecturer in Russia between 1907 and 1911, prior to his first encounter with Gurdjieff.[85] As the leading figure in promulgating Gurdjieff's thought, he inevitably made connections between the two systems. In *No Religion Higher Than Truth,* Maria Carlson explains Ouspensky's transition from Theosophist to Gurdjieff disciple. She defines him as "the most important and visible Theosophical thinker in Russia" despite the fact that he was only active in the TS for seven years. In Ouspensky's own words, Theosophy produced a "strong reaction" in him although he immediately recognized its "weak side":

> The weak side was that, such as it was, it had no continuation. But it opened doors for me into a new and bigger world. I discovered the idea of esotericism, found a possible approach for the study of religion and mysticism, and received a new impulse for the study of "higher dimensions."[86]

During his years of Theosophical apprenticeship, Ouspensky synthesized a wide range of ideas with those he encountered in Theosophy; Nietzche, Darwin, and Vladimir Solovyov were stronger and more lasting influences on his thought than Blavatsky. Just before meeting Gurdjieff, Ouspensky had made a lengthy tour of the East, visiting Egypt and Ceylon *en route* to India, where he spent two months. While in India, he visited Adyar and met Annie Besant, but returned disillusioned with the TS. In a series of Theosophically-sponsored lectures on his travels, Ouspensky "talked only about disillusionment in seeking the miraculous," and accused the TS of "arrogance and sectarianism," according to a newspaper account.[87] Around this time, in early 1915, he told a friend of his intention to leave the TS because its members were "just sheep, showing no evidence of independent thought."[88]

A. R. Orage, the chief exponent of Gurdjieff's ideas in America, had been an active TS member and lecturer in England, joining the Society in 1896 and continuing as an active participant through 1907.[89] Thus, it might be suggested that their influence on Gurdjieff provides the key to correspondences between his thought and the doctrines of Theosophy. However, it is unlikely that two Theosophical scholars of the magnitude of Orage and Ouspensky (both of whom were renowned as writers prior to meeting Gurdjieff) would have been initially attracted to his ideas unless they found compelling evidence of the intrinsic relevance of his teachings to those of HPB. *In Search of the Miraculous,* Ouspensky's record of his years of study with Gurdjieff, is widely regarded as the authoritative introduction to Gurdjieff's thought. At no point does Ouspensky suggest that Gurdjieff's ideas were not fully developed by the time of their first encounter in 1914. Ouspensky and Orage were both fully convinced of the reality of Gurdjieff's contact with a secret brotherhood in Central Asia. What might have compelled them to this conclusion after years of Theosophical study?

The starting point in understanding the Fourth Way teachings is Gurdjieff's proposition that man is asleep, and that in his state of sleep, he is a machine. Implicit in these statements is the possibility of awakening and thereby being liberated from this mechanical state. The flashes of heightened awareness which lead to awakening are referred to by Gurdjieff as "self-remembering," and, combined with the effort to understand the mechanical reactions of the "False Personality," form the basis of "the Work." The first and most insidious obstacle to awakening is the illusion of "Imaginary I," defined in J. H. Reyner's *The Gurdjieff Inheritance* as the belief that "our affairs are managed by a single intelligence which one calls oneself."[90] In fact, according to Fourth Way teachings, we are fragmented into multiple and mutually unconscious selves, each of which calls itself "I." Blavatsky teaches that contemporary humanity's existence is driven by *kama-manas,* the lower mind conditioned by desire for sensation. The ever-shifting desires and sensations distract the personality from its immortal essence, the Higher Triad of Atma-Buddhi-Manas. Thus the concepts of "imaginary I" and "False Personality" correspond with Blavatsky's teaching that humanity is deluded by kama-manas, which is the governing principle in this phase of human evolution. Both teachings postulate higher levels of consciousness which characterize more permanent aspects of human identity. The main contrast between Gurdjieff and Blavatsky on this point is the angle of approach; the former proceeds inductively, the latter deductively. With Gurdjieff, the starting point (and constant point of reference for all subsequent doctrines) is the immediate experience of the human individual. Blavatsky, on the other hand, generally discusses the human individual in light of cosmic correspondences and principles, which provide the foundation of her Theosophical psychology. The focus of Theosophy has been on transformation of culture and society, while the Fourth Way movement has explicitly dismissed such objectives. Gurdjieff's aim was solely to aid the individual to awaken from illusions of "imaginary I," "internal considering," "identification," and "false personality."

Both Gurdjieff and HPB were attracted from an early age to magic and occultism, and each embarked in youth on a series of journeys lasting around twenty years. Egypt, Turkey, and Central Asia figure prominently in both itineraries. Most important, each claimed to have encountered "Masters of Wisdom." In Gurdjieff's teaching, our planet is part of a cosmic system of "reciprocal maintenance," and human affairs are controlled by a hierarchy called the "Conscious Circle of Humanity." This is completely congruent with the Theosophical doctrine of hierarchies. According to Gurdjieff, the Conscious Circle of Humanity continually seeks to influence humanity to awaken from its state of sleep. Those who respond to these influences are drawn to esoteric schools where secret knowledge is preserved.

An obvious divergence between the Theosophical and Fourth Way teachings is the approach to reincarnation. Ouspensky grafted the Nietzchean idea of "recurrence" onto Gurdjieff's system of ideas, providing a very bleak view of the process of death and rebirth; he taught that we relive exactly the same lifetime repeatedly, until an awakening to higher influences liberates us from this mechanical repetition. However, Gurdjieff is silent on the subject of reincarnation, which for HPB is the cornerstone of all understanding of human existence. This may reveal Gurdjieff's conclusion that an emphasis on reincarnation is psychologically counterproductive. In his system, the all-important goal is immediate awareness of our own inner processes and resources.

The strongest evidence of a basic link between the doctrines of Gurdjieff and Blavatsky is their use of septenary divisions to describe the human constitution, the stages of human evolution, and the structure of the cosmos. In both systems of thought, each of these models corresponds harmonically to the other two. The individual human constitution is described by Blavatsky as composed of seven principles which correspond to cosmic principles. Gurdjieff describes seven human "centers." Below is a tentative list of correspondences between these:

Gurdjieff "Centers"	**Theosophical "Principles"**
Higher Intellectual	Atma (Divine)
Higher Emotional	Buddhi (Spiritual)
Intellectual	Manas (Mental)
Emotional	Kama (Desire)
Moving	Prana (Energy)
Instinctive	Linga Sarira (Astral)
Sexual	Sthula Sarira (Physical)

The identifications of Manas with Intellectual Center or Kama with Emotional Center are transparent. The two higher centers clearly correspond to the two higher principles of Atma and Buddhi, but the one-to-one correspondences here are less obvious. The three lower centers of Gurdjieff's system and the three lower principles in Blavatsky's both serve as vehicles through which the higher energies operate. The distinction between the moving and instinctive centers seems parallel to that between the peripheral and autonomic nervous systems. Blavatsky's principles of prana and linga sarira play comparable roles in her system; prana is the flow of psychophysiological energy which maintains all life, while the linga sarira is the etheric model upon which the physical body is modelled. In either case, the model postulates an active/passive pair mediating between the conscious energies "above" and the physical body "below." Identifying the sex center in Gurdjieff's system with the sthula sarira or dense body of the theosophical tradition is plausible since the physical body is reproduced sexually. Reyner describes the main function of the sex center as "coordination of all the individual energies in the fulfillment of the overall design."[91]

Gurdjieff emphasized that the centers are generally unbalanced and improperly functioning, and that only by recognizing this through self-observation can one advance on the path to harmonious development. "The Work" stresses that the primary goal is the gradual purification of negative emotions through self-observation. Theosophists tend to object to this emphasis as being overly self-oriented and lacking in altruism, but Gurdjieff's followers would respond to this charge by arguing that the main aim of this process it to replace "internal considering" with "external considering," learning to think of others before oneself. Until one becomes moderately self-aware, efforts at altruism may do more harm than good.

Peter Washington, in *Madame Blavatsky's Baboon,* presents Gurdjieff as HPB's most important successor in a process he calls the "emergence of the Western Guru." He sees the primary distinction between them as the transition from optimism to pessimism: "If Theosophy represents the idealistic tendencies in early-twentieth-century Europe—the currents of feeling which gave birth to the League of Nations, social democracy and youth movements—Gurdjieff is part of the complementary fascination with barbarism and primitivism which colours the politics of fascism and works of art from Lawrence's novels to Stravinsky's early ballets."[92] Examining each movement as an expression of the historical circumstances of its birth suggests some reasons for the difference in emphasis. Theosophy, a product of the late Victorian era, reflects a belief in progress that was a keynote of the period. Although HPB's definition of progress was hardly mainstream, she nonetheless shared certain basic assumptions. Gurdjieff, beginning his teaching in a collapsing Russian Empire and fleeing to an uneasy inter-war Europe, cannot have retained much faith in human progress through the horrors he witnessed.

Contradictions are as apparent as correspondences between Gurdjieff and HPB on the subject of the "bodies" of man. Gurdjieff insists that one has no permanent "I" or a "causal body" until it is earned. This is corroborated by Blavatsky's teaching that the lower manas is entirely mortal and that only higher thought nourishes the immortal essence. Blavatsky emphasizes that only in an adept are the higher principles expressed fully or harmoniously. Gurdjieff likens the human condition to a carriage being pulled by runaway horses, which are out of control because the coachman is drunk and the Master is asleep inside. He stresses self-observation because without thereby developing a nucleus of Permanent I and Real Conscience, we can never develop harmoniously all our potential capacities.

Gurdjieff's doctrine that there are seven evolutionary stages for the individual corresponds to Blavatsky's derivation of seven evolutionary stages of humanity, the earth, the solar system, and the cosmos. For Gurdjieff, men nos. 1, 2, and 3 are dominated by the moving, emotional and intellectual centers respectively, while man number 4 is beginning to harmoniously develop all three. Man 5 is possessed of True Conscience, and numbers 6 and 7 are beyond the range of our understanding. HPB's typology is that of "fourth-rounder," "fifth-rounder," etc. This refers to the doctrine that the present cycle of earthly evolution represents the fourth round (four passages of life through the solar system), and that those who have outstripped the pace of the rest of humanity have by so doing become more typical of the humanity of the future. Many creative geniuses are defined as fifth rounders, while Gautama Buddha is the only sixth rounder named in the *Mahatma Letters*. HPB states that humans are dominated by the fourth principle, kama, because the earth is in its fourth round. (The Hopi cosmology also focuses on the idea that the present world and humanity are the fourth in cyclical progression.) Both models postulate the joint action of a sevenfold process of energy transformation, a sevenfold human constitution through which the process takes place, and a seven-stage pilgrimage for individual and racial evolution.

To describe the workings of cosmic intelligences, Gurdjieff proposes a second sentenary model, called the "Ray of Creation." This hierarchy is a series of increasingly dense stages of matter, through which energy is constantly transformed in a bidirectional flow. The seven stages of the Ray of Creation are: the Absolute, which is governed by one law; All Possible Worlds, governed by three; the Galaxy, governed by six; the Sun, governed by twelve; The Planetary System, governed by twenty-four; the Earth, governed by forty-eight, and the Moon, governed by ninety-six. Thus, in this system, the issue of freedom vs. determinism is seen as implicit in the structure of the cosmos, in which increasingly dense materiality is equated with loss of freedom for the beings moving down the Ray. The involutionary process is thus a "fall" into material enslavement, a gnostic idea which is also echoed by HPB. The return flow in the Ray of Creation implies that conscious evolution leads to gradual liberation from this enslavement.

The writings of HPB contain repeated assertions of a balance of involutionary and evolutionary processes, and the concept most often used to illustrate this is the "planetary chain," which is held to correspond to similar processes at all levels of evolution. The "shadowy arc" is the downward semicircle of spirit involving into matter, while the "luminous arc" is the upward semicircle of matter evolving back to spirit. Although Gurdjieff uses "energy" rather than "spirit" to refer to that which descends the Ray of Creation, the basic principles of involution and evolution are the same as those described in the Mahatma letters and the Blavatsky writings. Both are related to the scheme depicted in the Kabbalistic Tree of Life.

The repeated stress on the numbers three and seven is a factor connecting both Gurdjieff and HPB to the Kabbalistic tradition. For Gurdjieff, the two fundamental laws of the universe are the Law of Three and the Law of Seven. The Law of Three postulates that all manifestation results from three forces he called affirming, denying, and reconciling. Reyner relates this Law of Three to the Christian trinity and the Hindu trimurti; however, the three gunas of rajas, tamas, and sattva are closer correspondences. Hegel's dialectic of thesis, antithesis, and synthesis approximates this Law of Three, as does the triad of proton, neutron, and electron. Blavatsky teaches of the three successive logoi in *The Secret Doctrine.* One could proliferate instances of the widespread fascination with tripartite divisions of reality, but these are less structurally important to Theosophy and the Fourth Way movement than sevenfold models.

The Law of Seven, according to Reyner, is illustrated by a musical octave, supposedly "devised by an ancient esoteric school for the purpose."[93] The Ray of Creation said to "conform to this but in a descending order so that the will of the Absolute constitutes the upper DO and the successive stages then progress towards the lower DO, representing increasingly coarse manifestation."[94] The creative or descending octave governs the realization of intention in practical form while the ascending octave is concerned with "progress from the lower to a higher level."[95]

The major significance of the Law of Seven lies in the fact that at two points in the major scale, between MI and FA and between TI and DO, there are half-tone rather than full-tone intervals. These are said to represent stages at which "progress is impeded and has to be reinforced by some additional means."[96] All organic life is said to express a cosmic effort to transcend such an interval (between the all-planetary and earthly levels) in the Ray of Creation.

Searching for Theosophical analogies to the Ray of Creation leads to abundant possibilities. Using Blavatsky's septenary model, the breakpoints in the scale are between the linga and sthula sariras

(TI/DO) and between manas and kama (MI/FA). These do indeed seem to represent points at which there is special stress—the points at which the "first and second death" divide the human constituents. Physical death occurs with the separation of the other six principles from the physical body; a "second death" takes place when the higher triad of Atma-Buddhi-Manas is freed from its temporary vestures.

Gurdjieff's ideal of the Fourth Way provides another numerical point of comparison to Theosophy. Gurdjieff designated three traditional methods of spiritual discipline. The Way of the Fakir focuses on asceticism, mastery of the physical body. The Way of the Monk focuses on worship, an exercise of the emotional center. The Way of the Yogi is said to focus on pursuit of knowledge and exercise of the intellectual center. All involve a certain withdrawal from life, but the Fourth Way as taught by Gurdjieff is lived in the midst of life and exercises all the centers harmoniously. (The four ways can thus be seen as parallel to hatha, bhakti, jnana, and karma yoga respectively). A search for Theosophical correlates to Gurdjieff's prescription of a Fourth Way yields little which applies to the level of the individual aspirant. Blavatsky portrays these various approaches as being appropriate at varied times and places according to the needs of individuals, and does not make the radical critique of their imbalance implied in Gurdjieff's teaching. However, there is an obvious Theosophical correspondence to the ideal of a "Fourth Way." This is revealed in *The Secret Doctrine*'s subtitle: "the Synthesis of Science, Religion and Philosophy." HPB makes much the same point about the collective aspect of human spiritual evolution that Gurdjieff makes about individual spiritual development. She regards science, religion, and philosophy as three inherently limited, fragmentary approaches to truth and reality, which can best be approached through a fourth way, Theosophy, that incorporates, harmonizes, and balances them all.

The structural similarities in the teachings of Blavatsky and Gurdjieff point inevitably to Isma^cili influences in their systems of cosmology and psychology. The centrality of the number seven is a major clue which points toward Isma^cili doctrines as an important source for both Blavatsky and Gurdjieff. Henri Corbin's *Cyclical Time and Isma^cili Gnosis* describes the doctrine of a septenary historical scheme, paralleled by a septenary initiatory path for the individual adept:

> From the summit to the base of the mystical hierarchy, the movement of perpetual elevation propagates itself. Finally, in

> the same way that the Seven periods of a cycle are closed by the Great Resurrection . . . at the end of the Cycle of his individual life, at the Seventh grade of his ascension, the adept finds himself at the threshold of perfect angelhood of the Tenth Intelligence. This is the dawn of the Great Resurrection . . . The vision finishes by embracing all the universes . . . [97]

These passages from the Mahatma letters are strikingly similar: "as man is a seven-fold being so is the universe," and, "The degrees of an Adept's initiation mark the seven stages at which he discovers the sevenfold principles in nature and man and awakens his dormant powers."[98] The doctrine of the Resurrection acquires a specific meaning in Isma῾ili gnosis, which relates it to Blavatsky's teachings. Each of the seven principles of the individual is "resurrected" by the influence of the next higher principle. HPB's sevenfold breakdown of human principles was presented variously as Chaldean, Tibetan, and Chaldeo-Tibetan. But in fact its closest historical analogue is Isma῾ili.

The Isma῾ili are the second major branch of Shi῾a Islam. The Shi῾a differ from the mainstream Sunni in their belief that spiritual authority after Muhammad rests with a series of Imams rather than with the Caliphate. The two main branches of the Shi῾a are called the Twelvers and the Seveners, based on the number of Imams they recognize. The Seveners are called Isma῾ilis due to their recognition of Isma῾il as the last Imam before the seventh, who went into occultation. Their sect arose in Arabia, attained political power in Egypt under the Fatimid dynasty (eleventh century) and later in Persia before the Mongol invasion. Since then, they have been a persecuted minority, often preserving their teachings in the guise of Sufism. The Druze of Lebanon are an offshoot of the Syrian Isma῾ilis. Present Isma῾ili leadership is by the Aga Khan, who lives in India, where the majority of his followers are located. Dan Merkur's *Gnosis* summarizes the role of seven in Isma῾ili thought:

> Pre-Fatimid Isma῾ilism extended theosophical analyses to the Arabic alphabet, the Quran, and universal history, as well as cosmology. The theosophy relied primarily on groups of two, seven, and twelve. Seven letters composed the name of God (Bism᾿ullah), corresponding to the seven verses of the first sura, and the seven natiqs, or "prophets," whose activities each commenced an epoch in world history. The seven letters also generated the seven heavens, seven earths, seven seas,

> seven days of the week, and so forth. By different manipulations, the systems of seven letters and their consequences were made to generate systems of twelve in the alphabet, Quran and cosmos . . . Muhammad was counted as the sixth *natiq,* and Ismaᶜilism anticipated the arrival of a seventh, a messianic Qaᶜim or Mahdi, who would inagurate the seventh and final epoch of world history.[99]

In 1878, HPB wrote in a letter to Professor Hiram Corson of Cornell University, "I belong to the secret sect of the Druzes of the Mount Lebanon and passed a long life among dervishes, Persian mullahs, and mystics of all sort."[100] Her friend and travel companion Albert Rawson supported this claim, writing that HPB had been "made acquainted with many, if not quite all, of the rites, ceremonies and instructions practiced among the Druzes of Mount Lebanon in Syria; for she speaks to me of things that are only known by the favored few who have been initiated."[101] In the *Theosophical Glossary,* HPB called the Druze the "Sufis of Syria."[102] In *Isis Unveiled,* she cites the Druze among those who have inherited Sufi occult lore. One of HPB's most explicit references to Sufi sources of her own doctrines appears in the posthumously published article "The Eastern Gupta Vidya and the Kabalah": "[T]he Kabalah of the Jews is but the distorted echo of the Secret Doctrine of the Chaldaeans, and that the real Kabalah is found only in the Chaldaean Book of Numbers now in the possession of some Persian Sufis."[103] As this Chaldean Book of Numbers is frequently cited in *The Secret Doctrine,* and is unknown to scholars in the West, HPB's knowledge of it might have been acquired in study with the Sufis to whom she attributes its possession. The above passage illuminates two less specific references in *The Secret Doctrine.* In Volume I she writes: "the public knows nothing of the Chaldaean works which are translated into Arabic and preserved by some Sufi initiates."[104] In Volume II, she adds that "except in an Arabic work, the property of a Sufi, the writer has never met with a correct copy of these marvellous records of the past, as also of the future, history of our globe."[105] To summarize HPB's claims about the *Chaldean Book of Numbers,* it is the original source of the Kabbalah, and contains passages in Hebrew and Greek, although she has only seen it in Arabic translation. She claims to have heard of other versions preserved by Polish and Palestinian rabbis. Its wisdom is of "Chaldean" origin, yet the meaning of this term is never satisfactorily explained. It solves many scientific and religious mysteries through numerological theories emphasizing threes and sevens.

Several texts known to scholars correspond to part of this description; the *Chaldean Oracles* was a Hellenistic work teaching a cosmology based on threes and sevens. Various Kabbalistic works bear some resemblance to HPB's claims about her unknown source. But it is in Isma^cili literature that is found the peculiar overlay of Hellenistic, Sufi, and more ancient doctrines in a single work.

Some of the most ancient texts are preserved by the Isma^cilis of the Pamir region on the borders of India, China, Pakistan, and Afghanistan. An important example is the *Umm al-Kitab,* which is a product of the early phase of Central Asian Isma^cilism. According to Pio Filippani-Ronconi, this text may have begun as "a sort of catechism of an aberrant kind of Manichaean sect, strongly affected by Yoga practices and theoretically influenced by Vajrayana theology."[106] It is still regarded as a most holy scripture by the Isma^cilis of the Upper Oxus and the Pamir range. In spite of its mixed origins, the author notes:

> it is worth observing, however, that the syncretic content of this Book, with all its irregularity, bears notwithstanding such an Isma^cili orientation as to transform it into an authentic document of the school . . . (whose members) not only did not refuse previous revelations, but were able to make them fit into the picture of their own religious ideology, in the same way that they had already absorbed into their doctrines the Pythagorean, Neo-Platonic, Sabean and Hermetic beliefs and tenets. With this work, the Isma^cili da^ɔw produces a conscious effort to present itself as the summary and coronation of all preceding creeds."[107]

In the *Umm al-Kitab,* the seven intelligences are portrayed as " 'the limbs, or members, of God' . . . or the seven forms . . . symbolizing the seven divine periods . . . of ontological meta-history, reflected beneath in the seven cycles of prophecy in human history."[108] These intelligences of the Pleroma are described as "corresponding, as reflections, to the luminous entities imprisoned within the planetary bodies . . . "[109] The *Umm al-Kitab* also "explicitly maintains the theory of the repeated lives of man on earth, not only in the future but also during cycles of past time."[110]

Scholarship on the sources of Blavatsky and Gurdjieff is in its infancy, and can be expected to advance with increasing knowledge of such texts as the *Umm al-Kitab.* While it remains at present impossible to specify all the historical connections between Theosophical and Fourth Way doctrines, the evidence is sufficient to imply strongly that they draw on common sources.

The Lubovedsky Mystery

In *The Harmonious Circle,* James Webb speculates on the possibility of Gurdjieff's acquaintance with Dorzhiev and Ukhtomskii:

> If Gurdjieff had wanted to study Tibetan Buddhism at the source, he could have had no better tutor than Dordjieff, a Tasnit Khanpo at the right hand of the Dalai Lama. Prince Esper Ukhtomsky, with a personal and long-standing commitment to Buddhist practice, and his belief in the "necessity" of the brotherhood of seekers for the truth, would also have been able to further the young man's quest. Ukhtomsky is the most likely original of the character "Prince Lubovedksy" in *Meetings with Remarkable Men.*[111]

The identification of Prince Lubovedsky with Prince Ukhtomskii is not explained by Webb; it may have been part of the oral tradition uncovered in his researches for *The Harmonious Circle.* Although this may have emanated from Gurdjieff himself, it is unverified. A chapter of *Meetings with Remarkable Men* is devoted to Lubovedsky, however, and it suffices to demonstrate the plausibility of Webb's hypothesis.

It should be recognized at the outset that Gurdjieff took great pains to confuse the reader as to which of his characters were historical, and which were fictional. Perhaps all were a combination of the two, rendering any solid identification impossible; this was his apparent intent.

Gurdjieff introduces Prince Yuri Lubovedsky as "remarkable and out of the usual run of men . . . much older than I and for almost forty years . . . my elder comrade and closest friend."[112] He recounts the tale of the prince's interest in Spiritualism following the death of his young wife in childbirth. This led to a complete withdrawal from the usual social life of his class, and a total preoccupation with occultism. The extremely wealthy prince was soon visited by a mysterious elderly man, with whom he held a lengthy private conversation. Shortly thereafter, Prince Lubovedsky left Moscow to spend "almost all the rest of his life in Africa, India, Afghanistan and Persia."[113] Gurdjieff declares:

> The prince was a very rich man, but he spent all his wealth on 'searches' and on organizing special expeditions to the places where he thought he might find an answer to his questions. He lived for a long time in certain monasteries and met many persons with interests similar to his own.
>
> When I first met him, he was already middle-aged, while I was still a young man. From then on until his death we always kept in touch with each other. Our first meeting took place in Egypt, at the pyramids . . .[114]

While serving as tour guide to a Russian archaeologist, Gurdjieff encountered the prince, who became very agitated upon seeing an ancient map which Gurdjieff had brought from Armenia. When the prince revealed that he had vainly attempted to buy this map, a conversation unfolded which led to a correspondence which lasted "almost thirty-five years."[115] Gurdjieff describes their "last meeting but one" in Istanbul.[116] Although Lubovedsky had a home in that city, Gurdjieff had expected him to be in Ceylon at the time of his visit. Lubovedsky explains the reason for his delay; Vivitskaia, a young Polish woman whom he had met on the ship, was being taken into white slavery in Egypt. He rescued her, and she becomes a key member of the "Seekers of Truth," which includes Gurdjieff and Lubovedsky. This group pursues a series of explorations in Central Asia, visiting monasteries, obscure tribes, and masters of various occult traditions.

After recounting Vivitskaia's life story, Gurdjieff resumes with the information that after this Turkish encounter, his only contacts with Lubovedsky for several years were through letters. The prince wrote from Ceylon, Afghanistan, and Baluchistan, but then his letters ceased. It was only after several years that the two were reunited in Central Asia.[117]

The account of this final meeting follows a long digression into Gurdjieff's recollections of his friend Soloviev, "later an authority on what is called Eastern medicine in general, and on Tibetan medicine in particular, and . . . also the world's greatest specialist in the knowledge of the action of opium and hashish on the psyche and organism of man."[118] This characterization recalls Badmayev's status as an expert on Tibetan medicine, and provides another reason to suspect that the group of Ukhtomskii's associates is connected to Gurdjieff's Seekers of Truth. Webb stresses Ukhtomskii's use of the phrase "seekers of truth" in his description of the TS.

A dervish named Bogga-Eddin becomes the channel whereby Gurdjieff and Soloviev are reunited with Lubovedsky. In Bokhara,

Gurdjieff meets Bogga-Eddin after not seeing him for several months, and inquires as to his whereabouts during that time. Bogga-Eddin tells of his encounter with an old man who belongs to the Sarmoung Brotherhood. The old dervish reveals to Bogga-Eddin that he is fully aware of Gurdjieff and his explorations, and is interested in meeting him. Their meeting is the first of several, involving very long conversations, which ultimately lead to an invitation for Gurdjieff to visit the main Sarmoung monastery. After a lengthy journey in which Gurdjieff and Soloviev are blindfolded with hoods, on the eighth day, the hoods are removed. The terrain appears to be that of one of the river valleys east of Bokhara. After several more days' ride, the travellers arrive at the monastery, on a slope facing snow-capped mountains. They are left in a guest house for several days, provided with food and left to their own devices. After they have rested and started to explore the monastic complex of buildings, a young boy comes running to Gurdjieff with a note written in Russian:

> My dear child: I thought that I would have a stroke when I learned that you were here! I am distressed that I cannot rush at once to embrace you, and that I must wait till you yourself come to me. . . . Come to me soon, and we will talk about everything! . . .[119]

Following the young boy to the cell where the prince is waiting, Gurdjieff is delighted to be reunited with the old mentor whom he had thought dead. Lubovedsky reports that he is mending well after a bout with blood poisoning. He asks how Gurdjieff came to be there, and upon hearing of his travels, launches into his own story.

Lubovedsky describes himself as a victim of inner apathy and disillusionment at the time of his last meeting with Gurdjieff. During his subsequent trip to Ceylon, he met a famous Buddhist monk, with whom he traveled up the Ganges. This expedition turning out to be "just another chase after a mirage," the prince lost faith in his quest. After proceeding to Kabul for an extended visit, the prince devoted himself "entirely to oriental idleness," spending much time at the home of his "old friend," the Aga Khan.[120] Gurdjieff's Prince Lubovedsky claiming the Aga Khan as an old friend suggests Ukhtomskii as a possible channel for Isma^cili influences in the Fourth Way teachings. In Kabul, Lubovedsky met a venerable but poorly dressed Tamil, who surprised him by speaking Russian very correctly. The old Tamil declared that he had spent much time in

Russia, and invited the prince to go with him to a *chaikhana* (teahouse). There the Russian conversation proceeded, but after some minutes of small talk, the old man abruptly changed his tone, astounding the prince with his uncanny knowledge of his past:

> Eh, Gogo, Gogo! Forty-five years you have worked, suffered and laboured incessantly, and not once did you decide for yourself or know how to work so that, if only for a few months, the desire of your mind should become the desire of your heart. If you had been able to attain this, you would not now in your old age be in such solitude as you are![121]

"Gogo" was the prince's childhood nickname, and he was amazed at the old man's knowledge of this. He asked "But who are you, who know me so well?" to which the Tamil responded:

> Is it not all the same to you, just now, who I am and what I am? . . . Is there really still alive in you that curiosity which is one of the chief reasons why the labours of your whole life have been without result?[122]

After an initial feeling of despair, saying "it is already too late," the prince is encouraged by the old Tamil to try once more, promising his assistance on condition that he "consciously die to the life you have lived until now, that is to say, break away at once from all the automatically established practices of your external life and go where I shall indicate."[123]

Lubovedsky's acceptance of this condition was followed three days later by the appearance of a Tadzhik guide, who informed him that he had been hired to accompany the prince on a journey lasting one month. After two weeks of travel, they arrived at the Sarmoung monastery.

At this point, Gurdjieff's account resumes, and he describes his stay at the monastery in the company of the prince. The sacred dances which are the basis for the "movements" taught by Gurdjieff are witnessed by the pilgrims, as is a mysterious seven-branched mechanism used for learning the dances. The last encounter with Lubovedsky comes at the end of Gurdjieff's three-month stay. Having been told by the shaykh that he has only three years to live, the Prince agrees to spend those years at the Olman monastery, on the northern slopes of the Himalayas, as the shaykh advises. After spending three days in intense conversation, Gurdjieff and the prince part for the last time:

> The caravan began to move, and as it passed behind the mountain, the prince turned, looked at me, and three times blessed me. Peace be to thy soul, saintly man, Prince Yuri Lubovedsky![124]

It may be impossible to determine which elements of this story are fictional, but internal contradictions provide some helpful clues. The most obvious false note is the length of the acquaintance between Gurdjieff and the prince. At the end of this chapter the reader is informed that Soloviev, Gurdjieff's travelling companion, died in 1898. This dates the Sarmoung visit to within a year or so before that date. The prince's death would then have taken place around 1900. But how can Gurdjieff have had a friendship of 35 to 40 years with a man who died in 1900? This would place their meeting in Egypt in the early 1860s, well before Gurdjieff's birth. Either the length of the acquaintance or the date of the Sarmoung meeting is false, and perhaps both are. *Gurdjieff: Seeker of the Truth,* by Kathleen Speeth and Ira Friedlander, contains an appendix giving an approximate chronology of his early life. According to this, the Sarmoung visit occurred before 1900, the year of the dissolution of the Seekers of Truth and of Gurdjieff's solo travels in Tibet, which lasted until 1902. In 1905, however, he "spent two years in a Sufi monastery in Central Asia, studying the laws of human suggestion."[125] This latter date is likely to be that of the Lubovedsky/Ukhtomskii encounter, if indeed they are the same man. But there are so many false elements in the story that the truth will probably remain forever elusive. Nonetheless, the parallels to Lubovedsky are formidable. Both are extremely wealthy princes, both completely retire from public life in Moscow, both are explorers of Central Asian monasteries, and both are older than Gurdjieff. Although not much can be proven on the basis of a semi-fictional account, these parallels strongly indicate that Ukhtomskii is the original of Prince Lubovedsky. The interest in Ceylon demonstrated by both, and their intimacy with Sinhalese Buddhists, strengthens the case for their identity. Nonetheless, the hypothesis brings some formidable problems. Ukhtomskii and Gurdjieff could have been acquainted for thirty-five years only if they met in 1886, when Gurdjieff was 20. The date of the Sarmoung visit also remains a problem.

The only full-scale biography of Gurdjieff to date is James Moore's *Gurdjieff: Anatomy of a Myth.* Far more sympathetic than Webb, Moore is no less scholarly, although he devotes considerably less attention to the sources of Gurdjieff's ideas. Moore provides a chronology which is the most reliable yet produced, although many dates are approximate. He gives 1887 as the date of Gurdjieff's first meeting with Lubovedsky in Cairo, and 1888 as the year of their journey to Thebes together. The acquaintance between Gurdjieff and Dorzhiev is given as occurring in 1897, and the following year is hypothesized as the date of Gurdjieff's arrival at the Sarmoung monastery where he finds Lubovedsky. This, of course, is incompatible with the Ukhtomskii hypothesis, but rests on such fragmentary evidence as to leave plenty of uncertainty.[126]

In light of facts found in other sources cited above, before 1905 Ukhtomskii could not have become Gurdjieff's world-weary but newly-inspired Seeker of Truth. Therefore, it is possible that the 1905 date given as a second trip to a "Central Asian Sufi monastery" by Speeth is actually that of the Sarmoung encounter with Lubovedsky/Uktomskii. The probable beginning of the acquaintance is around 1896, as suggested by the same source. This was the year in which Ukhtomskii was sent to Egypt on official state business. If indeed Gurdjieff remained in contact with Ukhtomskii until his death in 1921, the latter could have played the role of "Hidden Master" for the first nine years of his friend's public work.

The nature of the evidence makes it impossible to determine the truth about Gurdjieff's sources. He, like HPB and the Bahaʾi leaders, exemplifies a pattern of genealogical dissociation. This term, coined by David C. Lane, is illustrated in his study of the roots of the Eckankar movement. It describes the practice of concealing the real origins of an emergent spiritual tradition and supplanting the truth with more appealing mythical genealogies. HPB did so by exalting her human sponsors into quasi-divine supermen, but was paradoxically generous with accurate information about them that undermines Theosophical mythology. The Bab, Bahaʾuʾllah, ʿAbduʾl Baha, and their disciples insisted that their teachings were direct messages from God, and that any apparent indebtedness to Shaykhism, Naqshbandi Sufism, or Theosophy was coincidental. Bahaʾuʾllah and ʿAbduʾl Baha progressively distanced themselves from the militancy and fanaticism of the Bab; contemporary Bahaʾis have no access to his *Bayan,* with its prescriptions for widespread book burning and confiscation of infidels' property. Gurdjieff's Seekers of Truth and Conscious Circle of Humanity were carefully fictionalized to prevent historical scrutiny of his sources. In each case, the scholar's effort to unravel the truth is frustrated by deliberate occultation of history. What is unique about Gurdjieff is his honesty about the process; he makes it clear that he is concealing history and promoting mythology. Therefore, it is not surprising that the historical connections between Gurdjieff and the Theosophical Masters are elusive, while the strongest evidence of a relationship is found in the congruence of doctrines.

Mrs. Annie Besant

PART FOUR.

The Great White Sisterhood

An unmistakable theme that emerges in the study of HPB's Masters is the parallel pilgrimages made by a series of European women throughout the nineteenth century. HPB, Lydia Pashkov, and Lady Jane Digby all traveled in Lebanon and Syria in search of magic and antiquities. Their exploits were equalled in audacity and drama in the twentieth century by Isabelle Eberhardt, Mirra Alfassa, Alexandra David-Neel, Annie Besant, and Alice Cleather. The most successful of the female occult explorers carried out their exotic journeys in remarkably similar ways, implying a cultural common denominator linking their distinct pursuits in some wider evolutionary purpose. A striking forerunner of all these pilgrims died when HPB was still a child, yet her spiritual pilgrimage may well have involved contacts with adepts who were later contacted by Blavatsky.

Lady Hester Stanhope

Lady Hester Stanhope was the eldest daughter of Charles, third Earl of Stanhope, and his wife Lady Hester Pitt, sister of Sir William Pitt. Her father was a maverick in the political climate of late eighteenth-century England, opposing the war against the American colonies and later favoring the French republicans. Such positions caused his ostracism in Parliament, where he was known as a "minority of one."[1] He has even been called the "first socialist or labor peer," and his enthusiasm for the French revolution was such that for a time he discarded his title and insisted on being called "Citizen Stanhope."[2] Sir Charles was also a noted inventor, his accomplishments including a calculating machine, a process of stereotyping, a monochord for tuning musical instruments, a hand-operated iron printing press, a microscopic lens, and a way to fireproof buildings.[3] His first wife, Lady Hester's mother, died when Hester was four years old, leaving three young daughters. Lord Stanhope remarried, and three sons resulted from his second marriage. Lady Hester was unhappy under the domestic tyranny of her eccentric father, and at the age of twenty-four left her home to live with her grandfather. Three years later, she went to live with her uncle the Prime Minister, where she served as hostess until his death in 1806. During the years following her uncle's death, she was reputed to have had a series of unhappy love affairs. In 1809, she bore the double blow of the death of her intended husband Sir John Moore, who died with her name on his lips, and that of her favorite brother Charles, in the battle of Corunna.[4] At this point, having quarreled with most of her relatives, she decided to leave England for a time. She first settled in Wales, where she met the man who was to be her lifelong private physician, Dr. Meryon. During the following year, she left England forever, proceeding with Dr. Meryon and a large retinue of servants to Istanbul via Gibraltar, Malta, and Athens. In Malta, she joined forces with Michael Bruce, a younger man of equally aristocratic English origin. They became lovers, and their relationship continued for several years. After spending many months in Malta, they sailed for Alexandria, but were shipwrecked *en route* near the island of Rhodes. Rescued after being stranded without food or shelter on a large rock for thirty hours, she "was forced to change her torn and dripping raiment for the attire of a Turkish gentleman—a dress which she never afterwards abandoned" according to Lytton Strachey.[5]

For the rest of her life, Lady Hester remained in the Middle East, increasingly rejecting European culture. From 1811 to 1813 she was engaged in what Strachey calls a "triumphal progress" that included Cairo, Jaffa, Jerusalem, Acre, and Damascus.[6] In Cairo, she was received in state by Muhammad Ali, the Pasha, who conversed with her for an hour. She always dressed in scarlet clothes with gold trimming, covered by a burnous when on horseback. Her arrival in each new village or city was astounding to the population, which hailed her as a queen. During this period of travel, she was most often accompanied by Michael Bruce, but this relationship remained unknown to historians until a collection of their letters was published in 1951 under the title *The Nun of Lebanon.* He shared the great adventure of her career, a journey to Palmyra, which she was the first European woman to visit. Only a few intrepid travelers had made the week-long journey in the desert. Strachey reports:

> The Pasha of Damascus offered her a military escort, but she preferred to throw herself upon the hospitality of the Bedouin Arabs, who, overcome by her horsemanship, her powers of sight, and her courage, enrolled her as a member of their tribe. After a week's journey in their company, she reached Palmyra, where the inhabitants met her with wild enthusiasm, and under the Corinthian columns of Zenobia's temple crowned her head with flowers. This happened in March, 1813; it was the apogee of Lady Hester's life. Henceforward her fortunes gradually but steadily declined. The rumour of her exploits had spread through Syria, and from the year 1813 onwards, her reputation was enormous. She was received everywhere as a royal, almost as a supernatural, personage: she progressed from town to town amid official prostrations and popular rejoicings.[7]

At the end of 1813, Lady Hester rented an empty monastery on the slopes of Mount Lebanon, where she fell ill with the plague on the very day she moved in. Michael Bruce was at this time *en route* to Europe. After her recovery she became increasingly involved with the Druze, whom she later protected from Ibrahim Pasha when he invaded Lebanon.[8] She wrote to Michael that she had acquired "the bible or koran of the Akel Druses," which "might go to my life, should it be known that I possessed it," adding that she had obtained "many other curious manuscripts, which I am almost certain no one ever got hold of before."[9] According to Strachey, from the Druze she acquired belief in transmigration. *Travels of Lady Hester Stanhope,* written after her death by her physician, Dr. Meryon, contains considerable information on the teachings and activities of the Druze, but contradicts Strachey on the subject of their teaching of transmigration, "for they say the soul is of too divine nature to take up its habitation in the body of a beast."[10] Perhaps this is merely a semantic argument, as Lady Hester apparently believed in human reincarnation, but not rebirth in animal forms.

In 1816, she moved to the home where she was to remain for the rest of her life, near the village of Djoun. Her final home was beautifully situated with a view of the mountains and the Mediterranean. She maintained a large garden and entertained guests regularly. Here the religious aspect of her pilgrimage to the East increasingly came to the fore. Perhaps her imagination had been permanently inflamed by the prophecy made in her youth by Samuel

Brothers, that she was "to visit Jerusalem, to pass seven years in the desert, and to become the Queen of the Jews, and to lead forth a chosen people."[11] In her Djoun establishment she made a special study of astrology, as well as demonology. Her astrological system emphasized "what she called people's nijems or stars" which were associated with corresponding beings at many levels of existence:

> A man's destiny may be considered as a graduated scale, of which the summit is the star that presided over his birth. In the next degree comes the good angel attached to that star; then the herb and the flower beneficial to his health and agreeable to his smell; then the tree, and such other things as contribute to his good; then the man himself: below him comes the evil spirit, then the venomous reptile or animal, the plant, and so on; things inimical to him.[12]

To the sympathy of the stars of two persons, or the lack thereof, she attributed all the variations of human relationships. She claimed to be able to read a person's face and determine his ruling star, and demonstrated to the satisfaction of observers her ability to read character by this method. Her interest in occultism extended to the field of prophecy, and the results of this obsession led to the eccentricities for which she is best remembered:

> But more remarkable was her faith in the early coming of a Messiah, or Mahedi, on which occasion she expected to play a glorious part . . . a native soothsayer, Metta by name, . . . brought her an Arabic book which, he said, contained allusions to herself. Finding a credulous listener, he read and expounded a passage relating to a European woman who was to come and live on Mount Lebanon at a certain epoch, and obtain power and influence greater than a sultan's. A boy without a father was to join her there, whose destiny it was to be fulfilled under her wing; while the coming of the Mahedi, who was to ride into Jerusalem on a horse born saddled, would be preceded by famine, pestilence and other calamities.[13]

In her Djoun monastery, Lady Hester kept a stable of Arab horses, one of which gave birth to a foal with a spinal deformation that had the appearance of a saddle.[14] This foal, Laila, was believed to be the horse on which the Mahdi would ride into Jerusalem. Lady Hester kept Laila and her own mount Lulu ready for the Great Day. When the young boy she had believed to be her prophesied companion for the coming of the Mahdi died, she settled upon another candidate. Among the many visitors to her establishment was Harriet Livermore, who as an Adventist shared Lady Hester's belief in the coming of the Lord. She lived for some time with Lady Hester, until they quarreled, at which point she proceeded to spend several years among Syrian tribes. Throughout Syria, both Lady Hester and Harriet Livermore were known as prophetesses. Although she constantly alluded to the coming Messiah, she adhered to neither Christianity, Judaism, Islam, nor the Druze religion, saying, "What my religion is nobody knows."[15] She emphasized the wisdom of the ancients, and taught a complex angelology to those willing to listen to her theories. Frequently visited by learned shaykhs, she absorbed bits and pieces of many esoteric systems. Interpreting all reports of wars and political struggles as signs of the coming advent, she believed that the Freemasons of the world spied on her and wanted her to become part of their conspiracy. Elaborate in her enthusiasm for magic and charms, she was regarded as a madwoman by many of her acquaintances. A colorful account of a visit to her Djoun establishment was given by Alexander Kinglake in *Eothen* (1844). He recalls:

> Lady Hester talked to me long and earnestly on the subject of Religion, announcing that the Messiah was yet to come; she strived to impress me with the vanity and falseness of all European creeds, as well as with a sense of her own spiritual greatness; throughout her conversation upon these high topics, she skillfully insinuated, without actually asserting, her heavenly rank.[16]

Kinglake differs from those who called her mad, noting that she was not "an unhesitating follower of her own system," and that one could "distinguish the brief moments during which she contrived to believe in Herself, from those long and less happy intervals in which her own reason was too strong for her."[17] After many years of gradually deepening debt, poverty and loneliness, Lady Hester died on 23 June 1839. The greatest moment of her declining years was her taking in and feeding hundreds of refugees following the battle of Navarino in 1827. But she has been remembered more for her eccentricity than for her philanthropy, at least in Europe.

One perplexing reference to Lady Hester is found in Volume I of the Blavatsky *Collected Writings* series, where she is allegedly quoted. The compiler writes "Lady Hester Lucy Stanhope (1776–1839), the famous English traveller who had circled the entire world dressed as a man, says in her book on Russia: 'In that barbarian land I met an outstanding woman-scientist, who would have been famous in Europe, but who is completely underestimated due to her misfortune of being born on the shores of the Volga river, where there was none to recognize her scientific value.' "[18]

This refers, according to de Zirkoff, to HPB's maternal grandmother, Helena Pavlovna de Fadeev. However, there is no bibliographic citation provided, and examination of accounts of Lady Hester's life reveals no evidence of her ever visiting Russia, much less writing a book about it. Certainly this visit, if it did take place, preceded HPB's birth, as by 1831 Lady Hester was poverty-stricken and unable to leave Djoun. In alleging that Lady Hester circled the entire world and wrote a book on Russia, the compiler may have confused her with someone else. Or perhaps it was Helena Pavlovna who was the traveller, meeting Lady Hester in the Middle East. If this meeting took place, regardless of the time and setting, it would have introduced into HPB's family the awareness of Lady Hester as a role model. If stories of Lady Hester formed part of HPB's upbringing, this might account in part for her youthful eagerness to explore the Middle East and to delve into the secrets of Druze and Sufis. Even if de Zirkoff's account is entirely mistaken, Lady Hester did pave the way for HPB in another sense. She made a tremendous public impact on the people of the region, generally being favorably regarded. The previous passage of an eccentric European aristocratic woman through the same regions that HPB was to visit shows that she was not the first to break this ground. In *Isis Unveiled,* HPB admitted that she had failed to equal one of Lady Hester's exploits:

> Lady Hester Stanhope, whose name was for many years a power among the masonic fraternities of the East, is said to have witnessed, personally, several of these Yezidean ceremonies. We were told by an Ockhal, of the sect of the Druses, that after having been present at one of the Yezidis' "Devil's masses," as they are called, this extraordinary lady, so noted for personal courage and daring bravery, fainted, and notwithstanding her usual Emir's male attire, was recalled to life and health with the greatest difficulty. Personally, we regret to say, all our efforts to witness one of these performances failed.[19]

Thus, HPB contacted a Druze leader who, years earlier, may have been involved in Lady Hester's Oriental education. In any case, Blavatsky was initiated by the Druze of the same region, an honor which may have been partly due to her illustrious English predecessor.

The significance of Lady Hester Stanhope to Theosophical history is substantial for another reason, however. Lady Hester's conviction that the "day of the Lord" was at hand is part of a very widespread phenomenon. In America, the Millerites selected 1843 and then 1844 as the year of the return of Christ. In the Middle East, a variety of movements emerged during the nineteenth century which included the Ahmadis, followers of Mirza Ghulam Ahmad of Qadian, India, who claimed a revelation direct from God. In 1881, Muhammad Ahmad of the Sudan claimed the title of Mahdi and the leadership of an independent state which survived his 1885 death by thirteen years. The greatest expression of the Messianic anticipation of the nineteenth century, however, took place in Iran during the emergence of the Babi and Baha'i faiths, and the Baha'i book *Thief in the Night* presents Lady Hester as a forerunner of the Bab and Baha'u'llah.

Isabelle Eberhardt

Isabelle Eberhardt's short life is a case study in the transcendence of gender as a barrier to a life of adventure. There are intriguing correspondences between the early environments of Isabelle and HPB. Isabelle's mother, Natalia Nicolaevna Eberhardt, was a product of the same German/Russian nobility as were the Hahns, HPB's father's family. General Pavel Karlovitch de Moerder, husband of Natalia Nicolaevna, was old enough to be her grandfather. When they married in 1858, she had just turned twenty, while he was in his mid-sixties. Another parallel to HPB's marriage to Blavatsky is that Moerder's career, which began in the Napoleonic wars and included heroic action in the Crimea, included a long period in the Causasus, where he was based in Yerevan. This is the same city to which HPB was taken as a bride. Nikifor Blavatsky and Pavel Karlovitch de Moerder were both assigned to the Caucasus in the same year, 1829, but Blavatsky remained there in civil posts for the rest of his career, while Moerder continued his military exploits throughout the empire. The ostracism that Natalya Nicolaevna suffered for her adulterous relationship with Aleksandr Trofimovskii was similar to that suffered by Lydia Pashkov for her divorce, or by HPB for her many sins against public opinion.

Trofimovskii was born a serf in the province of Kherson in 1826. He was educated in a theological seminary, but never became a priest or even a believer in any traditional sense. If he ever met HPB it was probably during the 1860s, when she lived in the same region. At this time, he was a free-thinking intellectual quite frustrated with his life in the backwaters of the Ukraine. Since, during this period, HPB was crisscrossing the Ukraine in the company of Agardi Metrovitch, an opera singer and revolutionary, her social status would not have placed her outside the range of Trofimovskii's acquaintance. Nevertheless, their acquaintance remains a matter of speculation. However, Trofimovskii's long-term acquaintance with Lydia Pashkov lends some weight to the supposition that he had met HPB. The educational techniques he applied to the rearing of his daughter insured that she would be comparably independent and contemptuous of convention. HPB's friend Lydia Pashkov and Afghani's disciple James Sanua remained in close contact throughout their lives. Both, in their later years, played quasi-godparent roles for Isabelle. After the suicide of her half-brother Vladimir, Abou Naddara wrote:

> There remain to you two brothers of whom my son Ali is the elder. And I? Incapable, alas, despite the treasure of paternal love which I consecrate to you, I can render you no service. What can I say? The humble abode of the proscribed Egyptian is open to you, you will be treated there as the elder sister of our children . . . Write to me, dear daughter, for your letters pour a salutary balm on my heart which is mourning for the sorrows of my city . . . [20]

Indeed, when Isabelle agreed to marry Rechid Bey, a Turkish diplomat who had changed his name from Archavir Gaspariantz to disguise his Armenian origins, her father wrote to Abou Naddara requesting a background check of the mysterious young man. Upon receipt of his favorable response, the marriage was approved, but subsequent events rendered it impossible. Lydia, too, expressed maternal sentiments in her letters: "Believe that I think of you as an adoptive daughter" and "Believe that I feel the heart of a mother for you."[21]

Lesley Blanch's *The Wilder Shores of Love* (1954) includes an account of Isabelle's life which provides another view of her relationship with Lydia, as well as her connection with Si Mahmoud and the Qadrya. Isabelle visited Lydia in 1900 in Paris, and received useful advice for the aspiring travel writer. Lydia, characterized by Blanch as "exotic and worldly, an ardent feminist and warm-hearted," warned Isabelle that "To live the life you and I prefer one needs fifty thousand francs' income."[22] Her salon provided many new acquaintances for Isabelle, whom she advised to always dress as an Arab male in order to promote her image as an eccentric genius.

"Si Mahmoud," Isabelle's Arab male persona, was not her first pseudonym. In her Swiss years, she wrote letters and articles under the name "Nicolas Podilinsky." But it was as Si Mahmoud that she lived the most enthralling moments. Her collection of journals, *The Passionate Nomad,* translated into English in 1988, includes passages which powerfully evoke the spirit of the Great White Sisterhood:

> [T]he farther behind I leave the past, the closer I am to forging my own character. I am developing the most unflinching and invincible will, to say nothing of integrity, two traits I value more than any others, and, alas, ones that are so hard to find in women . . . I have given up the hope of ever having a corner on earth to call my own, a home, a family, peace or prosperity.[23]

This passage was written in Cagliari, Sardinia, in January 1900, as Isabelle awaited her next voyage to Algeria, which took place in July. She spent a few months in Geneva en route, where she reflected on the qualities that attracted and repelled her in others:

> People who interest me are those who are subject to that lofty, fertile form of suffering known as dissatisfaction with oneself; the thirst for an 'Ideal,' something mystical and eminently desirable that fires their souls . . . Self-satisfaction because of some accomplishment will never be for me, and as I see it, truly superior people are those preoccupied with the quest for better selves.[24]

So intensely committed to spiritual aspiration was Isabelle that within a month of her arrival in Algeria she began to frequent the Qadrya Sufi order in the company of her intended husband, Slimene Ehnni. After a few happy months together, Slimene was transferred to Batna, leaving Isabelle in El Oued. There she was the victim of a murderous attack that left her hospitalized for many weeks with injuries to her head and arm. Isabelle attributed this to a rival Sufi order to which the attacker belonged, but it may have been inspired from within the Qadrya ranks. In either case,

Isabelle's penetration of the order in male disguise (albeit recognized as such) may well have aroused outrage in that or other orders. Although her attacker was tried and convicted, Isabelle was expelled from North Africa and separated from her beloved Slimene in May 1901. While staying with her brother Augustin in Marseille, her commitment to Islam grew stronger and she was seized with the vision of becoming a *maraboute,* or holy woman. This was probably an impossible goal for an impoverished, cross-dressing foreigner, but in any case Isabelle's death at twenty-seven prevented her attainment of her spiritual goal. In light of HPB's attainments in this direction after a comparably tempestuous youth, it is conceivable that Isabelle might have evolved into someone quite different from the promiscuous drug and alcohol abuser she was in her twenties. The sincerity of her faith in Islam and her own mission is unquestioned. The flash flood which took her life might also have aborted a literary career and a spiritual pilgrimage which would have been an extension of HPB's work. The fact that Isabelle was advised by two mentors who had also been involved in HPB's preparation for her public mission is a striking coincidence.

Blanch presents Slimene and Si Lachmi in considerably greater detail than does Isabelle in her diaries. The husband-to-be is, in her account, an unworthy object of Isabelle's interest, lacking any claim to significance except for his apparent amatory skills. The Qadrya chief, on the other hand, was quite a distinctive character who had wrested leadership of the order from his father and brothers. Si Lachmi combined his religious role with frequent military exploits. He had opponents within his own order as well as among other Sufi groups. Thus, the attack on Isabelle's life can be explained as an indirect attack on Si Lachmi from within his own sect.

Annette Kobak's biography, *Isabelle,* provides additional background on Isabelle's father that relates him to Theosophical concerns. He was appointed tutor to the de Moerder children around 1870, sixteen years after his marriage in Akilin Polgorow in Kherson. He was "an erudite man, well versed in the classics, and fluent in French, German, Italian, Arabic and Hebrew as well as Russian."[25] He had been an Orthodox priest but rejected this role and became devoted to the anarchist movement. After his removal to Switzerland, he was associated with Bakuninists, whose publications he helped to finance. During Isabelle's childhood at the Villa Neuve, the family was regularly visited by political exiles from Russia and Turkey.[26]

Isabelle's half-siblings uneasily suspected the nature of their mother's involvement with the tutor, and fiercely resented his power over their lives. Nicolas and Natalie, the older de Moerder children, became involved with Alexandre Perez-Moreyra in a series of threats against Trofimovskii which involved the police. Augustin, the youngest of the de Moerders, began to run away from home at fifteen and continued to do so regularly until his final departure years later. Isabelle and her sickly half-brother Vladimir were the only children in the household who maintained a good relationship with Trofimovskii, whom the others regarded as a criminal usurper. Closeness to her father may explain in part Isabelle's attraction to Islam, for according to Kobak "Culturally the 'oriental' world and its history were closer to Trophimowsky's background than the European."[27] He taught Isabelle about the Caucasus and the Kalmyk Steppes, implanting in her a nostalgic bond with places she had never seen, which later emerged in her writings. It was not apparently until his old age that Trofimovskii formally embraced Islam, and even then his anti-religious attitudes remained:

> Trophimowsky's interest in Islam seems to have revived in the early 1890's, during Isabelle's adolescence, partly no doubt through re-reading the Koran with her, and partly because by the 1880s Islam, under its charismatic leader Jamal al-Din al-Afghani, was beginning to present itself as a radical force for the Arab peoples' liberation from the expansionism of the European colonial powers. The methods of Al-Afghani . . . must have recalled those of Trophimowsky's revolutionary days: secret societies, people's solidarity, assassinations; and his agnostic's view of Islam as a civilization rather than a religion coincided with Trophimowsky's own.[28]

Isabelle later claimed her father to be a "Muslim Russian" who died shortly after her birth, a story which Kobak believes was told her by her parents. Indeed, her father was a Russian Muslim, but very much alive. Although she flirted with underground politics during her late teens, she soon lost patience with this environment and concentrated on the Muslim world to which she had always been attracted. Then, at nineteen she initiated correspondence with Abou Naddara, who introduced her to another correspondent who was to teach her Islamic theology. Ali Abdul-Wahab was a wealthy Tunisian whose epistolary friendship with Isabelle was followed by personal acquaintance after her arrival in Africa. Her alter ego, Si

Mahmoud, was a Tunisian student travelling in Algeria. Apparently, her studies with Ali Abdul-Wahab prepared her to play this role well.

While Isabelle went to Africa a Muslim, she did not become a Sufi until after arriving in El Oued in August 1900. Her husband, Slimene Ehnni, was an officer there in the native cavalry regiment called the *spahis*. Spahis were part of the French military, and Slimene was a fully gallicized Muslim who was entitled to French nationality by virtue of his father's naturalization. Not long after meeting Slimene, Isabelle found another reason to value life in El Oued, her acquaintance with the Qadrya sheikhs.

Isabelle had met Abdul-Aziz Osman the previous winter in Marseilles, where he was exiled from his native Tunisia for his political views. He fell in love with her and helped her entrance into Algerian life, referring her to the Qadrya Sufi fraternity. Four sons of the late Sidi Brahim had established, according to his wishes, *zawiyas* ("monastery-cum-lodges") in the surrounding area. Isabelle was welcomed by all, and in November 1900, became a *khouan* or initiate of the lodge:

> They gave her the black rosary or chaplet of the order, and this, together with the particular dhikr or ritual prayer of the order, would identify her to fellow Qadryas wherever she went in Algeria, enabling her to count on their practical and spiritual help.[29]

By the middle of 1901, Isabelle was feeling called to martyrdom for Islam or a mystical mission of unknown dimensions, and Slimene was encouraging her in this feeling. After Slimene's release from the army in February 1902, the couple settled in Tenes, where Isabelle developed several literary friendships which were to lead to her posthumous fame. In Robert Randau (an anagram of his original name Arnaud) and Victor Barrucand, Isabelle found her first real friends among the French Algerians. Among the happy moments in Tenes was a beach party at which Isabelle fed couscous to Randau, his wife and two friends. She danced on the sand, sighed, "Yes, I am happy, because you're all happy and because the wine is good! Damn it, if I were always happy I would never write a line, you know, because I would be completely satisfied!"[30]

But on the way home, Isabelle lamented to Randau that she felt irresistably drawn back to the desert:

> Oh, my dear Arnaud, I loathe this countryside, how it stinks; I hate cultivated fields, and countryside full of greenery and corn. Why have I got this unhealthy taste for dead landscapes and salty sand? Why do I prefer the nomad to the Harratin, the beggar to the rich man? Aye aye aye! Suffering is a spice for me, enriching the flavor of existence. Ah! I'm very Russian, underneath! I love the knout! . . . [31]

By 1903, the love between Isabelle and Slimene had begun to unravel, and political events attracted her into new adventures which separated her from her husband. Brigadier-General Hubert Lyautey was pursuing policies oriented toward the eventual French acquisition of Morocco. A "hearts and minds" approach was designed to win over all the irresolute tribes and to deny access to oasis markets to those who did not submit to French friendship. On assignment for *l'Akhbar,* edited by Victor Barrucand, Isabelle went to Ain Sefra which she used as a base for exploring the southwestern desert. She rode among the oases with French soldiers and local tribesmen. Lyautey arranged for her to visit, in November 1903, a Sufi monastery of the Ziania order in the town of Kenadsa. This was within Moroccan territory, and Lyautey hoped for useful information about the inclinations of the local peoples toward French occupation. Kobak concludes that Isabelle was being used not only for intelligence gathering but also to promote collaboration with the French.[32]

As Si Mahmoud, the Tunisian scholar, Isabelle was installed in the zawiya, where, after acquiring Moroccan clothes, she was free to wander. Some may have suspected her gender, but she claimed, "If anyone has suspicions, they would be very careful not to let me sense them, because it would represent a grave dereliction of Muslim etiquette."[33] Increasingly ill, Isabelle left Kenadsa to recover in a hospital at Ain Sefra. After leaving the hospital, she was reunited with Slimene, with whom she was living when a flash flood took her life on October, 1904. In an undated note, perhaps written in her final hospital stay, Isabelle reflected on her life:

> . . . I've tasted ecstasy in all its forms, the most refined as well as the most primitive . . . None of these forms has fooled me, and I've rejected them all . . . I have never believed in the possibility of absolute happiness, and I have never bent my head, free of shackles, to any kind of idol. My life passes by like this, and this is the way it will end . . . And so, without

> illusions and without hope, I shall carry on until the day I disappear into the shadows I came out of one day, an ephemeral and vain creature.[34]

In these words to posterity, Isabelle reveals herself as if conscious of her impending doom. Having rebelled against all social conformity, experienced all the delights of the senses, and written enough to insure her posthumous reputation, she was ready at twenty-seven to "slip into the abyss."[35] Ever since her death, French readers have had access to her pioneering writings which have remained available throughout the twentieth century. Only recently has the English-speaking world had the opportunity to learn much of Isabelle's quest. Kobak summarizes her life as a journey "from the new world to the old, from clutter, mental and material, to space, from inherited guilt to redemption, from seething complications to some measure of peace, and from mystery back to mystery."[36] This description characterizes all the members of the Great White Sisterhood. But Isabelle, and Lady Hester before her, were so eccentric that they could make only minor contribution as cultural seed-bearers. They have been remembered for their daring, audacity, and vision, rather than for any lasting accomplishment. Although their quests for initiatory wisdom were as sincere as HPB's, they were no match for her intellectual power or ability to convey her values to the masses. Another member of this sorority of travelers did, however, equal Blavatsky's achievements in many ways, and exceed them in one important aspect. Alexandra David-Neel may well be HPB's greatest occult successor.

Alexandra David-Neel

Born in 1868 in Paris, Alexandra David moved to Brussels with her parents in 1873, when her father's leftist political involvements made it impossible for him to remain in France. At the age of nineteen, she went to London where she was involved with an occult group called The Supreme Gnosis. There she became familiar with Theosophy, and may have encountered the London TS during the lifetime of HPB. Whether or not she ever met Blavatsky, her biographers acknowledge her debt to Theosophical ideas:

> the influence of theosophical thought on David-Neel was greater than she cared to admit. In her time, Blavatsky the person and her concepts were not to be evaded . . . She created

> the image of Tibet as Shangri-La, the mother lode of ancient lore.[37]

After returning to Paris in 1889, Alexandra attended the salon of Lady Caithness regularly.[38] In 1891, she made her first trip to Asia, a brief visit to India during which she studied yoga with a Brahmin named Bashkarananda. In the winter of 1892–93, Alexandra returned to Europe, where for the next several years she pursued a career as an opera singer. Her leftist associations during this period caused the police of Paris and Brussels to open dossiers on her. In 1900, at age thirty-two, she met a French engineer in Tunis, Philip Neel, who she married after a four-year courtship. The marriage would be marked by long separations. In London in 1906 to work on a book about Chinese philosophy, she became affiliated with Anagarika Dharmapala's Buddhist entourage. It was not until 1911, however, that Alexandra returned to Asia. Her first stop was in Ceylon, where she lectured to the TS before proceeding to India. This may have been inspired in part by her involvement with Dharmapala, her first teacher of Buddhism. In Pondicherry, she met Aurobindo Ghosh, whom she called "an interlocutor of rare intelligence belonging to that uncommon breed of rational mystics with which I am in sympathy."[39] This acquaintance was probably due to Alexandra's close friendship with Mirra Alfassa, who was later to become Aurobindo's partner in the Pondicherry ashram he established.

Mirra Alfassa, who grew up in Paris in the late nineteenth century, discovered the occult as a disciple of the Master "Max Theon" between 1905 and 1908. Mirra, now known to her disciples as The Mother, spent the last fifty-three years of her long life at the Aurobindo Ashram in Pondicherry, India. But preceding that were forty-two eventful years of preparation. She first encountered Max Theon, teacher of the Cosmic Philosophy, through a college friend of her first husband. Theon and his wife lived in Algeria, where they welcomed seekers attracted by their periodical, *The Cosmic Review*. Although Theon was the teacher of the Cosmic Philosophy, his English wife's trance readings provided the bulk of the magazine's contents. When the couple visited France in 1905, they met Mirra, who was immediately drawn into their orbit. She later remembered of him, "He had two assumed names. He had adopted an Arab name when he took refuge in Algeria—I don't know for what reason—after having worked with Blavatsky and founded an occult society in Egypt."[40] The first name he adopted, Aia Aziz, was supplanted by Max Theon after his arrival in Algeria. The Cosmic

Philosophy was based on the Kabbalah, according to Mirra's recollections. Theon, who was born Louis Maximilien Bimstein, son of a rabbi in Warsaw, may have been the source of some of HPB's Kabbalistic doctrines. He died in Algeria in 1927, long after Mirra had become Aurobindo's partner. Although in a sense she was his disciple, Aurobindo exalted Mirra to semi-divine status. After his death, she tried to exemplify his teachings in Auroville, city of the future, located near Pondicherry.

In 1912, Alexandra met Sidkeong Tulku, Maharaja of Sikkim, who was to be her sponsor for the next several years. In the same year she also met the Dalai Lama. From late 1914 through August 1916, she studied Tibetan while living as a hermit in Sikkim. After touring Japan and Korea in 1917, Alexandra returned to the Himalayas, where she lived for two years at the Kum Bum monastery in Tibet. During this period, with her Tibetan perfected, she determined upon the goal of being the first European woman to penetrate Lhasa. This she accomplished, after a four-month journey with her Tibetan companion Yongden, in February 1924. The following year, she returned to France, where she remained for most of the rest of her long life. Except for an interval from 1937 to 1945 when she lived in China, Alexandra remained in her native country until her death on 8 September 1969, at the age of one hundred.[41] She was honored as the preeminent scholar/explorer of Tibetan religion and culture in France. Her biographers Barbara and Michael Foster define her "ultimate contribution to world knowledge":

> In the tradition of the scholar adventurer, she went, she saw, she recorded. For many centuries the Tibetans amassed much of the knowledge of the ancient world, carrying it on their beasts of burden over the deserts from China, or on their backs over the Himalayas from India. Alexandra began the reversal of that process, a transfer of the *dharma,* which today has been accelerated by the outflow of refugees from Tibet . . . Are we presently again on the threshold of a fusion of Eastern and Western thought and art? If so, Alexandra's place is in the center of humanity's historical progress.[42]

Alexandra's travels were devoted to her search for secret teachings of Hindu and Buddhist Tantra. Two of her best-known books, which remain in print in English, are *My Journey to Lhasa* and *Magic and Mystery in Tibet.* Alexandra's first teacher of Buddhism was Anagarika Dharmapala, who was set on the path of working for Buddhist revival by his encounter with Madame Blavatsky twenty-five years earlier. The two maintained regular communication until the end of Dharmapala's life. Throughout Alexandra's early years of search she was a Theosophist, and she stayed for long periods at Adyar in 1892 and 1911. Although she later downplayed her indebtedness to Theosophy, Alexandra David-Neel's role in history was clearly parallel to that of HPB. Each focused Western interest in the initiatory traditions of Asia through eyewitness testimony in compelling accounts, without identifying fully with any specific lineage. Alexandra began her Buddhist studies with the Sinhalese Theravada, but became known for her work with the Tibetan Mahayana. Helena moved from Masonic Masters to Sufi teachers, from Rosicrucian adepts to Sikh and Hindu Mahatmas, all the while proclaiming herself a Buddhist. The dubious claims made by HPB regarding her travels and studies in Tibet provided a stimulus for Alexandra, who exceeded in reality all the feats that HPB had attained only in imagination. Measured in terms of audacity, endurance, and intellect, Alexandra may well be HPB's greatest and truest successor.

Daniel Caracostea, Archivist of the French Section of the TS, unearthed documents clarifying David-Neel's early contacts with Theosophy. Although in her later writings she was sarcastic and dismissive in her attitude to the TS, at the time she was a devoted member. Her TS diploma, dated 7 June 1892, was received in London. In March 1893, Annie Besant wrote Alexandra a letter which reveals that she had requested admission to the Esoteric Section. Caracostea's researches in Adyar, however, indicate that David-Neel (Mlle. David at the time) never became an ES member.[43]

In *Magic and Mystery in Tibet,* Alexandra confirms HPB's general view of the powers of Tibetan occultists, but rejects their alleged Theosophical manifestations. On the basis of her extensive contacts with Tibetans, she concludes that "Telepathy is a branch of the Tibetan secret lore . . . the subtler ways of sending messages 'on the wind' remain the privilege of a small minority of adepts in that art . . . [who] are unanimous in ascribing the cause of the phenomena to an intense concentration of thought . . . "[44] But after describing Tibetan theories and practices, she continues:

> One thing I must say, however, is that communications from mystic masters to their disciples through gross material means, such as letters falling from the ceiling or epistles one finds under one's pillow, are unknown in lamaist mystic circles. When questions regarding such facts are put to contemplative

> hermits, erudite lamas or high lamaist dignitaries, they can hardly believe that the inquirer is in earnest and not an irreverent joker.[45]

Alice Leighton Cleather

One of the most arduous initiatory journeys undertaken by a Theosophist was made by Alice Leighton Cleather. Although Cleather had been a personal pupil of HPB in London in the 1880s, her search for the Masters reached its climax in the 1920s. Perhaps the most incredible feature of Cleather's quest is that it began in earnest when she was seventy-two years old and was followed by continued travels until her death at ninety-two.

In 1885, when she joined the TS, Cleather was thirty-nine years old and living in Eastbourne with her husband and two sons. She met Bertram Keightley soon after becoming a Theosophist, and through him she first encountered HPB in 1887.[46] In Alice's own words, "From that moment I became her devoted disciple."[47] By late 1888, she had joined the Esoteric Section, and on 17 September 1888 was admitted to HPB's Inner Group. This remarkable but short-lived occult order consisted of six men and six women disciples. Cleather took notes of the meetings and subsequently provided the fullest available record of its teachings.[48]

When the TS was divided by the Judge/Besant conflict, Cleather sided with Judge and later accompanied his successor Katherine Tingley on her worldwide Theosophical Crusade in 1896–97. By 1899, she had lost faith in the Point Loma experiment, and rejected organized Theosophy completely. For the next two decades, her time was occupied largely by her partnership with Basil Crump, twenty-one years her junior. Crump, a barrister who retired after a nervous breakdown, had previously published studies of Wagnerian opera from a Theosophical perspective, and the two created a slide lecture program with musical accompaniment which they repeated for more than twenty years in locations around the world.[49]

Cleather's books, and the biographical sketch of her in the Blavatsky *Collected Writings,* shed no light on the whereabouts of her husband, Col. Gordon Cleather, during these wanderings. This period of her life remains elusive, but de Zirkoff discovered evidence of her presence in Egypt in 1911, and residence in Italy from that year through early 1918. At age seventy-two, Cleather began a life of adventure that lasted for the next twenty years. Accompanied by Crump and her son Graham, she set sail for India in a ship that was sunk *en route* by German torpedoes. The three survived in a life raft and were rescued, arriving in India in late 1918. An additional blow fell in 1919 when Cleather was widowed. In January 1920, Cleather followed the example of HPB by taking pansil, the five vows of Buddhism. This fulfilled her premonition, during the 1896 Theosophical Crusade's passage through the subcontinent, "that India alone was the true field for lasting and effective work in the cause of 'Theosophy'—which is that of the Wisdom Religion."[50] She describes the circumstances of her formal conversion to Buddhism:

> We were so fortunate as to obtain the great privilege of making our public profession of the Precepts binding on the Buddhist laity, at Buddha Gaya, under the sacred Bodhi Tree, in the presence of "Yellow-cap" (Gelugpa) Tibetan Lamas, their Chief—Geshe Rimpoche, the Head Lama of the Dongkar Monastery, in the Chumbi Valley, performing the Ritual. Later, we learnt that we were the first and only Europeans who had ever taken the Five Precepts at this sacred spot.[51]

Alice Cleather is best known for the three books she published in 1922 and 1923: *H. P. Blavatsky, a Great Betrayal, H. P. Blavatsky, Her Life and Work for Humanity,* and *H. P. Blavatsky as I Knew Her.* All were published in Calcutta, which became the headquarters of the Maha Bodhi Society in 1912. While living there, she was associated with Anagarika Dharmapala, who was responsible for inducing her to write her second and longest book. She writes in its preface that it "is an expansion of a series of articles written for the Journal of the Maha Bodhi Society (Calcutta), a Buddhist monthly, at the request of the Editor, the Venerable the Anagarika Dharmapala, who also asked me to preface them with a short account of myself and the nature of my connection with the wonderful woman who forms the subject of this book."[52]

The first of the three booklets, *H. P. Blavatsky, a Great Betrayal,* is an extended protest against the policies and activities of the TS under Annie Besant. Leadbeater is particularly singled out for opprobrium. The second, and longest, *H. P. Blavatsky, Her Life and Work for Humanity,* provides a more complete view of Cleather's unique interpretation of Theosophy. She was a fanatical partisan of HPB, to the extent of being disdainful of virtually everyone else in Theosophical history. The death of her "spiritual mother" is interpreted in a variety of ways, none of them reassuring. At one point HPB's demise (from influenza) is attributed to her enemies:

> Like a light brought into a dark place full of the creatures which "love darkness rather than light," so was the real H. P. B. . . . Instantly, like moths attracted to a lamp, all the denizens of this dark place which is our earth . . . were irresistably attracted round her. Not only did they obscure the Light—this they did abundantly—but finally in 1891 they put it out; i.e., it was withdrawn from our midst, returning to the realm from whence it came.[53]

Cleather's solution to the succession controversy is to conclude that HPB had no successors, since Besant, Judge, Olcott, and Sinnett were all unfit to carry on the TS. Moreover, HPB's death is taken as proof of this:

> H. P. B. had been withdrawn; and, as I have shown, without their chosen Agent the Masters could no longer give their direct aid and guidance. Nay more, the Agent's recall was the sign of the final failure of the T. S. as a body.[54]

Thus the Masters "recalled," or in other words killed, HPB as punishment for the sins of her fellow-Theosophists. Olcott is especially severely condemned, despite the conclusion that "there can be little doubt that the work which Colonel Olcott was destined to accomplish for Southern Buddhism in the East, was foreseen by the Masters, and that his selection at this time and the special privileges he enjoyed were very largely due to this fact."[55] Because Olcott failed, in Cleather's view, to support HPB properly in the face of the Hodgson investigation, he was cut off thereafter from the Masters. Although there is some justification for Cleather's sense that the death of HPB marked the closing of a door to the Masters, her writings convey an impression that bitter resentment of the subsequent history of the TS caused her to become unbalanced. While the record of later claimants to communication with the Masters tends to support Cleather's view, her judgment of Olcott is ill-informed and one-sided. His extensive direct dealings with the Masters are barely acknowledged in her diatribes. To some extent her attitude may have been derived from HPB herself; Dharmapala, however, was probably a contributing factor, in light of his conflicts with the Colonel.

The last of Cleather's studies of HPB is the most valuable by far, giving an intimate portrait of Blavatsky in the role of occult teacher in London. *H. P. Blavatsky as I Knew Her,* written in the first person, constitutes primary source material of unique value. Only here is found a thorough account of the Inner Group to which Cleather belonged. In the year of its publication, Cleather and Crump established the Blavatsky Association, devoted to defending the memory of HPB and promoting study of her works. In later years, Cleather collaborated with Crump on *The Pseudo-Occultism of Mrs. Alice A. Bailey* and *Buddhism the Science of Life.* But the triumph and climax of her career was the role she played in producing a 1927 reprint of HPB's *The Voice of the Silence,* endorsed by the Panchen Lama. *The Voice* is comprised of three fragments that HPB claimed to have learned by heart during her years as a chela. All three are clearly genuine Asian religious texts, not inventions by HPB. Cleather explains the circumstances of the 1927 edition in an editorial foreword:

> Reaching Peking in December, 1925, after studying for seven years in India, we were privileged to come into close touch with H. H. the Tashi [Panchen] Lama, who had left Tibet in 1924 on a special mission to China and Mongolia. As members of his Order, part of the work we undertook at his request for Buddhism was the present reprint, as the only true exposition in English of the Heart Doctrine of the Mahayana and its noble ideal of self-sacrifice for humanity.[56]

This refers to the Tibetan Gelugpa sect, as Cleather's 1920 initiation was through its auspices. No more is said about the circumstances of the Panchen's request for the reprint, which seems likely to have been inspired by Cleather and Crump's description of the book. Whatever the reasons for his interest, he lent support to the project:

> . . . All the Tibetan terms and references have been checked with the assistance of members of the Tashi Lama's suite . . . we publish this edition under the auspices of the Peking Buddhist Research Society, who recognize in it the highest and most sacred teachings of their own "contemplative" schools. It was not until we came in contact with Chinese and Tibetan Buddhists that we obtained this striking confirmation of the truth and value of H. P. Blavatsky's work.[57]

Therefore, according to Cleather and Crump, their reprint is issued "with the strongest and most authoritative Tibetan and Chinese endorsement."[58]

The preface is dated May 1927, when Cleather had just passed her eighty-first birthday. Incredibly, it marks only the beginning of the most dramatic adventures of her life. The Panchen Lama's endorsement reads, "All beings desire liberation from misery. Seek, therefore, for the causes of misery and expunge them. By entering on the Path liberation from misery is attained. Exhort, then, all beings to enter the Path."[59] When the Tibetan recognized the genuineness of *The Voice of the Silence,* Cleather and Crump seem to have overinterpreted this as a full endorsement of all HPB's claims, writing that "During many years of study and initiation in Tibet, H. P. B. spent a considerable time at Tashi-llum-po, and knew the predecessor of the present Tashi Lama very well."[60] Although Blavatsky may well have visited regions where Tibetan Buddhism was practiced, for example Ladakh and Mongolia, there is no evidence supporting her claim to years of study and initiation in Tibet, especially residence at Tashilhunpo. In *The Masters Revealed,* evidence is presented suggesting that her greatest access to Tibetan scriptures came through the Bengali explorer Sarat Chandra Das, who, after his extensive travels in Tibet, was befriended by Olcott. Since the more reliable references to Tibetan matters appear in HPB's writings rather late in her career, her connections to that country were apparently later and less direct than Cleather and other Theosophists were led to believe. Indeed, Cleather unwittingly provides a bit of evidence for the Das hypothesis in her endnotes:

> We are particularly indebted to the encyclopaedic dictionary of Rai Bahadur Sarat Chandra Das for confirmations of H. P. B., especially regarding Esoteric *Mahayana* and the living Initiates, generally disputed or ignored by Western Orientalists. As he obtained all his material personally from the best authorities at Tashi-llum-po and other important centres . . . where H.P.B. also claimed to have studied, his confirmation is the more valuable.[61]

During her stay in Beijing, Cleather, her son, and Crump received passports for Tibet from the Panchen Lama, whom they planned to meet later at Lake Kokonor in Western China. He gave Cleather a document which read "Special Gelukpa Buddhist of the English race, Faithful and devoted, to be treated as a Buddhist, to be afforded every assistance and help, and not to be injured or wrongfully opposed."[62] The three English travelers were also provided with letters of introduction from two generals to the military governors of the provinces through which they passed. But their journey, while perhaps successful as an initiatory trial, ended in disaster:

> After an extremely arduous journey of many months on camel and by foot, traversing the barren Mongolian desert, they discovered the Buddhist leader had been detained, and would not arrived as expected. Thus they were required to embark upon the Yellow River at flood stage in a small junk, were stripped of valuables by marauding bandits, and arrived at Sining in North West China 6 months later.[63]

The exhausted band of Theosophists returned to Beijing after Cleather had sufficiently recuperated, and remained there until 1937. Coincidentally, Alexandra arrived in the same city, accompanied by Yongden, at the beginning of 1937. In light of their common acquaintance with Dharmapala, it seems possible that the two women were acquainted. But their attitudes toward HPB were so diametrically opposed that it is hard to imagine them as particularly cordial. In March of 1937 Cleather, almost ninety-one years old, attended a Parliament of Religions in Calcutta, making side trips to Ceylon and Darjeeling. The Panchen Lama died in November 1937, followed six months later by Alice Cleather, who had returned to Darjeeling after spending several months in Calcutta.[64]

The Blavatsky Association went out of existence in 1947, the year that Crump died. Since then, Cleather has been little known within Theosophical circles and virtually unknown elsewhere. Her dismissal of Olcott, Judge and Besant put her at odds with the entire Theosophical movement, while her hagiographic attitude toward HPB makes her books unconvincing to outsiders. But despite her flaws, it is regrettable that Alice Cleather has been almost forgotten. Her lonely crusade against the self-appointed Theosophical successors became an initiatory journey of astounding scope and vigor.

Annie Besant

The death of HPB marked the beginning of a tension-filled period of five years during which the TS was rent asunder by a power struggle between its president and vice-president. William Q. Judge had been a very successful exponent of Theosophy, simultaneously editing the *Path* magazine and heading the American Section. He wrote concise, accessible explanations of Theosophical teachings, and gradually attracted several thousand new members in the period after his return from India. After HPB left Adyar, her relationship with Olcott was competitive and tense, while she grew fonder of Judge. It was at the latter's instigation that she formed the Esoteric Section in 1888, over Olcott's strenuous objections. When Annie Besant became a Theosophist in 1889, she also emerged as HPB's most trusted disciple and the most visible member of the society. She was already one of the best-known women in England, having been in the headlines for much of her adult life. As a young wife and mother, she scandalized the nation by rejecting the Church of England and leaving her clergyman husband. This resulted in a notorious legal case in which custody of her two children was taken from her. After several years as a leader in the Secularist movement, closely linked to Charles Bradlaugh, Besant began to change her outlook. Passing through Fabian Socialism, she arrived at Theosophy when she read *The Secret Doctrine* in 1889. After HPB's death, Judge and Besant became co-heads of the ES, and were closer to each other than either was to Olcott. For American and European Theosophists, Judge and Besant were seen as HPB's spiritual successors while Olcott's influence waned. In the months after HPB's death, Judge and Besant combined forces against Olcott and induced his resignation on the basis of charges of sexual immorality which were never made public. The accuser was Henrietta Muller, according to the anonymous history *The Theosophical Movement 1875–1925.*[65] The circumstances of the resignation remain unclear to this day, but the crucial fact is that Judge was the heir apparent, and Besant was in full sympathy with his effort to supplant Olcott. The Colonel surprised them both by withdrawing his resignation, however, after allegedly receiving a clairaudient message from his guru on 10 February 1892, described in *Old Diary Leaves:*

> Its impressiveness was enhanced by the fact that he told me things which were quite contrary to my own belief, and hence it could not be explained away as a case of auto-suggestion. He told me (a) That a messenger from him would be coming, and I must hold myself ready to go and meet him; (b) That the relationship between himself, H.P.B., and myself was unbreakable; (c) That I must be ready for a change of body, as my present one had nearly served its purpose; (d) That I had not done well in trying to resign prematurely: I was still wanted at my post, and must be contented to remain indefinitely until he gave me permission to abandon it; (e) That the time was not ripe for carrying out the scheme of a great International

> Buddhist League, and that the Maha-Bodhi Society, which I had intended to use as the nucleus of the scheme, would be a failure; (f) That all stories about his having cast me off and withdrawn his protection were false, for he kept constant watch over me, and would never desert me.
>
> As regards the first point, I shall show, at the proper time, how exactly the predicted messenger came; as regards the second, this was a great surprise, for H.P.B. had been behaving in such a way about me, and had made such reckless assertions about the influence of the Masters having been withdrawn from Adyar, that I really supposed that all was at an end between us; and as I had not heard directly from my Guru for some time, I did not know but that he was so displeased with me that he had withdrawn his protection.[66]

The hypothesis that Ranbir Singh was Olcott's Master Morya may shed light on the psychological mystery of this message. If Morya had been alive in 1892, Olcott would presumably still have been able to contact him by ordinary means. Whatever the truth behind Olcott's experience, there does seem to be a discrepancy in a later passage in *Old Diary Leaves* in which he describes Norendro Nath Sen introducing the Colonel to a huge meeting 24 October 1892:

> Alluding to my offer to retire from office and give way to a younger man, and to my having withdrawn my resignation at the entreaty of friends, the chairman said: "His retirement would not only have been a heavy blow to the Society, but also a serious loss to all India, for whatever of religious or spiritual progress . . . this country had made in recent years was mainly, if not solely, due to Colonel Olcott's untiring efforts. He had been for the last twelve years the standard-bearer of light and life for the Hindus."[67]

This makes the entreaty of Indian friends rather than the interference of the Master responsible for Olcott's change of heart. Although his clairaudient experience may have been genuine, there seems to have been another factor in the withdrawal of the resignation. Olcott retained the faith and support of a very large and influential contingent of Indian leaders, whose sentiments were expressed by Sen. Soon he was to use such evidence of support to win over Annie Besant. In 1891, Besant had begun to receive Mahatma letters through Judge which she at first accepted as genuine. After the debacle of the Olcott resignation, she began to have doubts about Judge's relations with the Masters, and when in late 1893 she finally made her first journey to India, it resulted in a complete change of allegiance.

The circumstances of Judge's effort to keep Besant and Olcott apart remain somewhat unclear. In *Old Diary Leaves* the Colonel remarks that his esteem for Judge suffered a sharp decline when, during an 1891 visit to New York, he found a Mahatma letter on the table of his room, which he concluded was "a palpable fraud" performed by Judge.[68] But it was only when he concluded that Judge was deceiving Annie Besant that the rupture became complete. After having agreed to attend the 1892 convention of the TS in Adyar, Besant changed her plans, which Olcott later attributed to "Judge's schemes to prevent my meeting with her, and by comparing notes, jointly discover the heartless trickery he was playing upon her, and the treachery to me he was then plotting."[69]

The basis for these charges becomes somewhat clearer when Olcott explains the role of Walter Old in the affair:

> Nothing of a sensational kind occurred until the 22nd [December 1892], when Walter R. Old, of the London working staff, arrived and joined our Headquarters organization. Almost immediately there was an interchange of confidences between us, which for the first time opened my eyes to the treacherous policy that Mr. Judge had been following up with regard to the Society and myself in the matter of his relations with the Masters. I cannot tell how shocked I was to discover his lack of principle, and to find that my previously more or less vague suspicions fell far short of the reality. Without making any pretensions to exceptional goodness, I certainly never did anything to warrant him in making, in a forged letter, my own Teacher and adored Guru seem to say that, if Mrs. Besant should carry out her intention of visiting India, she might run the risk of my poisoning her! Let any of my honorable colleagues picture to themselves how they would feel if such cruel and baseless imputations were made against their character.[70]

In his exposé of the Judge case, *Isis Very Much Unveiled,* which ran as a serial in the *Westminster Gazette,* Edmund Garrett explained the circumstances leading up to this climax. As Besant was preparing to go to India, she received from Judge a cablegram warning "You are desired not to go to India remain where you are grave danger Olcott await further particulars by an early mail."[71]

Initially, Besant and others in London thought this referred to a danger *to* Olcott, but the "further particulars" made the message quite the reverse. Judge wrote a letter in which a Mahatma message was enclosed, which warned that the danger was *from* Olcott and *to* Besant. Garrett comments:

> But what could this danger from Colonel Olcott be? Mr. Judge and his Mahatma left that darkly vague. Some of their friends in England dotted the i's and crossed the t's for them. It is hardly credible, but the suggestion was nothing less preposterous than that Colonel Olcott intended to poison Mrs. Besant![72]

For a time this was believed by the London Theosophists around Besant, as well as by Annie herself, who wrote to Indian members that "Master had forbidden her to come."[73]

Without the text of the original letter, it is impossible to evaluate the issue of the poison threat. Garrett and Olcott make it quite clear, however, that Besant was given a vague threat that a trip to India would place her in danger, and that this effectively controlled her behavior. But eventually, Besant decided to disregard the alleged warning, and fulfil her promise to visit India.

Annie Besant and Constance Wachtmeister arrived in Colombo, Ceylon, on 9 November 1893, late at night. The next day they proceeded with Olcott by train to Kandy, where Besant gave a lecture to a large audience that evening on "The World's Great Needs."[74] After several ceremonial visits and sightseeing, the Theosophists returned to Colombo the next morning, where Mrs. Besant again spoke to a packed hall, including the leading British government officials. On 12 November they proceeded by train to Galle where they were received with enthusiasm by a large crowd to whom Besant lectured. The next day, after another lecture by Besant, Olcott spoke on the Maha Bodhi Society. On the 14th, the Theosophists returned to Colombo via Panadura, where Mrs. Besant lectured yet again. The last full day in Ceylon, 15 November, was marked by a visit to the Buddhist High Priest Sumangala. Of all the Mahatma figures identified in *The Masters Revealed,* Sumangala appears to have been the most accessible. Visits to him were a regular feature of Theosophical pilgrimages to Ceylon until his death in 1911.

For more than a month, the party toured South India, visiting Tuticorin, Tirunelveli, Palayankottai, Madurai, Tiruchchirappalli, Thanjavur, Kumbakonam, Erode, Bangalore, Gooty, Hyderabad, and points in between. Besant's lectures were received with acclaim at every stop. Some representative titles of her speeches are "Karma," "The Dangers of Materialism," "Theosophy and Science," "Pilgrimages of the Soul," "Adepts as Facts and Ideals," and "Hinduism and Theosophy." On 20 December, the Theosophists returned to Adyar where the annual convention was about to begin. During her first month in India, Besant had seen evidence of Olcott's intimate connections with native princes and spiritual leaders. In Madurai, the Raja of Ramnad provided a mansion for the travellers. In Tiruchchirappalli, the Prince of Pudukkotai, a Theosophist, hired a house for their accommodation. In Bangalore, the group visited the Maharaja's palace. On the last day in Bangalore, the Theosophists were visited by K. Sheshadri Iyer, Dewan (Prime Minister) of the state, who was accompanied by other high officials "who vied with each other in assurances or personal regard and affection for one who had shown as great a love as any Hindu for their native country."[75] In Hyderabad the travelers were "housed at Bashir Bagh, a splendid palace of the late Sir Asman Jah, ex-Prime Minister of the Nizam."[76] Yet all this was no more than a foretaste of what lay in store for Annie after her arrival in Adyar.

Perhaps the most crucial events of the entire journey occurred during the convention, where Olcott, Wachtmeister, Bertram Keightley, E. T. Sturdy, William Edge, and Walter Old met privately to consider documents emanating from Judge. Their unanimous conclusion was that he was producing fraudulent Mahatma letters, and should be deposed from both the vice-presidency and the position of General Secretary of the American Section. This marked the beginning of one of the most tumultuous years in Theosophical history. In the spring of 1894, Judge was summoned to London to a meeting of a Judiciary Committee to be held that June. This was a fiasco for the anti-Judge forces, who were unable to answer Judge's objection that the charges against him violated the TS's constitutional ban on making belief in Mahatmas obligatory. To try Judge for fraudulently forging their letters would assume the Masters' existence, as Olcott was forced to admit. The committee therefore disbanded without taking any action. A series of satirical articles on the case appearing in the *Westminster Gazette* kept the issue in the public eye, and produced further polarization for and against Judge. In November, Judge issued a circular headed "By Master's Direction" in which he deposed Besant as co-head of the ES. The American Section declared autonomy in March 1895, and Olcott responded by canceling the charters of the pro-Judge branches and reconstituting the Adyar loyalists into a new, much smaller American section.

The relevance of the Judge case to the present investigation is its role in bringing together Olcott and Besant. Because his own position was insecure, the Colonel apparently felt an urgent necessity to convince Besant of his intimacy with Asian adepts. During the remaining months of her first Indian tour, Annie was treated to an almost royal welcome, orchestrated by Olcott and his Indian allies. The cast of characters involved in the northern half of this tour included several with close links to the secret world of the Theosophical Mahatmas.

Annie Besant began 1894 in Madras with an open air lecture on "India" to an audience of 6000. Around this time, Olcott, in Tiruchchirappalli, received another message from his Master which explained the previous one of February 1892. Early one morning, he heard the voice of Morya tell him "This is the messenger whom I told you to be ready and go meet: now do your duty."[77] Olcott again was delighted to know that he was still under the watchful guidance of the Mahatma. Ever since February 1892, he had expected the reappearance of Damodar, who had written to a few Theosophists since he vanished seven years before. Olcott was therefore quite surprised to learn that Annie was the promised messenger.

The group next sailed from Madras to Calcutta, where they arrived 10 January to a magnificent welcome. Among the local dignitaries waiting on the jetty was Norendo Nath Sen, longtime President of the Calcutta Branch TS. The welcoming party of several hundred was awaiting them amid greenery arches, flowers, and flags. On the next evening, Mrs. Besant lectured on "India's Place Among the Nations" to an audience of 5000. After a whirlwind of receptions and lectures, Besant ended her Calcutta schedule with a final lecture at Town Hall.

The next stop on the Bengal itinerary was Berhampur, where another royal welcome awaited them:

> Mrs. Besant was carried in a tomjon, an uncovered arm-chair attached to poles which rest upon the bearers' shoulders, with an accompaniment of fluttering flags and gaudily dressed mace-bearers, supplied by the local Jain branch of the T.S. We crossed the river in a houseboat and found an elegant carriage . . . supplied by H. H. the Maharanee Surnomoyee.[78]

Annie's first lecture was on "India, Past, Present and Future" which was attended by the usual throngs and scheduled amid the obligatory visits to local dignitaries and schools. On the Theosophists' final evening in Berhampur, Annie was honored with chants of welcome and farewell which Olcott reproduces in *Old Diary Leaves:*

The Song of Welcome

Welcome sister, the ever unfortunate mother India takes you to her bosom. Now she has nothing precious of which she can make a present to you; but she is ready to receive you with Shamit (sacrificial fuel), Kushahan (a seat made of sacrificial grass), Padya (water for washing the feet with), Arghya (respectful oblation) and sweet words.

What has brought you sister, here? India is now lifeless. Here is now no chanting of the Vedas, no Tapobana (garden for practicing religious austerities), no twice-born, no uttering of Mantras (mystical incantations). Now the cry of famine-stricken people rends the sky.

We, the inhabitants of Berhampore, give a garland of flowers round your neck; please take it, simple sister, with your characteristic affability.

You are now a learned daughter of mother India, you are honored throughout the world and your reputation is worldwide. We are glad to see you.

The Farewell Song

You have sacrificed, sister, all you had for the sake of your mother with the simple hope of infusing life into fallen India.

You have seen the condition of India with your own eyes; the sons of India look sullen and gloomy. None has an iota of happiness here; the heart of every one is heavy with feelings of miseries.

Sing, sister, the song of India's miseries in your own country. The minds of famishing people can have no inclination to God.

Sing the song of India's glories with fresh energies; we would console our heavy hearts hearing that song from far beyond the ocean.

Farewell sister, go to your own country with the blessings of 200 millions of people and distribute there with sound health the treasures of Aryan religion.

The parting is embittering; do not fail, sister, to come here again with the remembrance of your fallen brothers.[79]

On 19 January, the group's last day in Berhampur, Annie lectured on "Theosophy and Hinduism" in the morning, after which the Theosophists visited the aged Maharanee. Following an address from students at the college, the group departed for Bankipur, Bihar.

The Maharaja of Darbangha provided the travelers the use of his palace in Bankipur, where they remained for two days before proceeding to Varanasi. Here the group was joined by Professor G. K. Chakravarti, who had acquired considerable influence over Besant at the Parliament of Religions, and whom Judge would soon accuse of leading her astray. There the crowds attending Besant's lecture were so overwhelming that the second such event was limited to ticket holders. After an excursion to Sarnath and a third lecture, the Theosophists proceeded to Allahabad, and thence to Agra. In each of these cities they remained for two or three days. Next they headed south to Muttra, where on February 10 they were lodged in a house belonging to the Maharaja of Bhurtpur. This was one of the earliest royal sponsors of the TS, mentioned in correspondence by HPB prior to her departure from New York in 1878. From Agra the travelers headed to Delhi and Meerut. On the 17th, they left for Ambala, entering the Punjabi heartland. Due to their rushed schedule the Theosophists had regretfully turned down invitations to visit the Sikh-ruled states of Patiala and Jind. The rulers of both states had been involved in the conspiracy led by Thakar Singh Sandhanwalia to restore his cousin Dalip Singh to the throne as ruler of an independent India. Jind in particular was identified as a financial supporter of the plot. Heading northwest through Ludhiana and Jalandhar, in each of which the group held its usual salon and lecture, the Theosophists reached Kapurthala around the 21st. Here the hospitality of the maharaja was particularly noteworthy:

> H. H. the Maharajah sent his carriages to meet us at the railway . . . on arrival, [we] were put up in the richly decorated guest-house . . . The present and former Dewans of Kapurthala, Messrs. Mathura Das and Ramjus, son and father, and Sirdar Bhaktar Singh, C. I. E., the most active of the State officers, came and talked Hinduism with us. [At this time many Sikhs still regarded Sikhism as a Hindu sect] . . . Our party had an audience with the Maharajah, who speaks English and French, a rare accomplishment in India, and is almost equally well-known in London and Paris. He took us for a drive through the town and in the evening

> presided at Mrs. Besant's lecture on "Ancient Aryan and Modern Civilization," in a splendid Durbar Hall, profusely decorated and a fine place for public functions. I was much struck with the appearance of the officers of State, who sat before us in rich and picturesque dresses and followed the speaker's eloquent discourse with close attention. We took leave of our audience on the next day and Mrs. Besant was invited into the interior of the Palace to meet the Maharani. Just before our getting into the carriages to depart, an officer of the State presented to each of us, with the compliments of his master, a handsome Kashmir shawl. The Countess left us at Kartarpur, where we took train to the famed city of Amritsar, the chief town of the Sikhs. On our arrival we were driven to the Golden Temple, that lovely architectural creation, which, with its gold-plated domes that sparkle in sunlight and moonlight, stands at the centre of a great tank, and is reached and surrounded by a pure white marble causeway with handsome forged iron railings . . . [80]

After a lecture that evening, the group proceeded the next morning to Lahore. Here they were welcomed by a large party at the station, and then headed for the bungalow provided by the Maharaja of Kapurthala. On the evening of the 24th, Besant gave an address on "Theosophy and Modern Progress" which was heard by 5000. This was followed by what Olcott calls a conversation-meeting at the Town Hall.

The centrality of the Maharaja of Kapurthala in the Punjabi phase of the tour is relevant to the initiatory status of the trip for Mrs. Besant. Kapurthala was the home town of Bhai Gurmukh Singh, who had been educated at the maharaja's expense. Gurmukh Singh was a leader of the Singh Sabha who remained on close terms with Olcott until his death in 1898. When, on her first Indian tour after becoming President of the TS in 1907, Besant sought donors for her Central Hindu College project, the most generous donors were the maharajas of Kapurthala, Varanasi, and Kashmir.[81]

On her second day in Lahore, Besant lectured twice, gave a durbar between the two lectures, and finally visited the headquarters of the orthodox Hindu group the Sanatana Dharma Sabha. There her address was translated by Pandit Gopi Nath, who had earlier sided with the Singh Sabha against the Arya Samaj when the latter group began to oppose the TS. By 1894, this disagreement was resolved, as on the Theosophists' last day in Lahore the president of the local Arya Samaj was taken into TS membership.

On the 28th February the group arrived in Bareilly, where they were rejoined by Chakravarti. After the usual round of lectures, ceremonial visits, and conversaziones, the Theosophists proceeded to Lucknow, where Olcott departed for Adyar 3 March and Besant headed toward Bombay. On the 12th, Olcott was reunited with Besant outside Poona, after having collected materials on the Judge case for her to take back to London. In Bombay, just before her departure, Besant was introduced to Shyamaji Krishnavarma, who had been on intimate terms with the founders during the period of their allegiance to Swami Dayananda. Krishnavarma remained friendly to the TS for many years, but ultimately became a political enemy of Mrs. Besant. During the same period she met Prince Harisinghji Rupsinghji, described in Part One. On a surprising note, Olcott and Besant encountered A. O. Hume and his daughter, both still Theosophists, on shipboard in Bombay just prior to Besant's departure for Europe.

As in the cases of Blavatsky and Olcott, opinion on Besant has been polarized around extremes based on the perceived reality of her contacts with the Masters. Those who believe that she and Olcott rather than Judge were the true initiates of the Mahatmas tend to accept a set of corollaries which are highly debatable: that her later reliance on Leadbeater's clairvoyance was justified, that his portrayal of the Theosophical Masters (despite its extensive conflicts with that given by HPB and Olcott) was reliable, and that therefore the Krishnamurti Messiah craze was inspired by the same Masters as those of the early TS.

Particularly implausible in the beliefs of Besant's most fervent admirers is her alleged progression, along with Leadbeater and other leading Adyar figures, in a series of nocturnal initiations leading through the "Arhat" stage and beyond, conducted in Shambhala and conferring bizarre honors such as the Mahachohanship of Mercury. It is beyond the scope of the present inquiry to analyze Leadbeater's neo-Theosophy; the reader is referred to Gregory Tillett and Arthur Nethercot for colorful portrayals of its excesses.

At the opposite extreme is the view that Besant's rejection of Judge was tantamount to a rejection of the real Mahatmas, and that henceforth the only genuine initiates of Theosophical Masters are found in Judge lineages. This viewpoint fails to take into account Olcott's extensive and continuing contacts with adepts who had taught HPB and served as secret sponsors of the TS. These two positions have dominated Theosophical history, although they by no means exhaust the possibilities. Other alternatives include: 1) the skeptical consensus that the Theosophical Masters were nonexistent and thus all their alleged initiates either deluded or fraudulent; 2) Alice Cleather's position that HPB was the Masters' only true instrument and her death evidence of their rejection of the entire Theosophical movement; 3) the position implied by the evidence examined in this book and its predecessor. This is that after HPB's death, Olcott retained the confidence of many surviving adept sponsors of the TS, as well as an unparalleled knowledge of the secrets of Theosophical history. When Judge began using his influence over Besant to undermine Olcott's position, the power struggle set into motion a chain of events which led to her transformation. Olcott's effort to persuade her that he rather than Judge deserved her support was elaborate, extensive, and supported by a huge cast of characters throughout India and Ceylon. Through the attention showered upon her during this journey, Besant was awakened to her destiny as a leader of the Indian nation.

Among the many eminent Indians Besant encountered on her journey, a few stand out as particularly relevant to her initiation into the world of the Mahatmas. Sumangala and Krishnavarma are among those nominated as Theosophical Mahatmas in *The Masters Revealed.* Through her encounter with Sumangala, Besant would have been impressed with the strength of Olcott's ties to Sinhalese Buddhism. As High Priest, Sumangala was arguably the most influential Theravadin of his time, and was a Theosophist until the end of his life. But Besant's religious allegiance was to Hinduism, and her loyalty to India was the keynote of her later career. In meeting Krishnavarma, Besant encountered a witness to the transfer of TS headquarters to India in response to the Masters' invitation. As in the case of Sumangala, Krishnavarma's continuing links to Olcott demonstrated the extent to which the Masters retained confidence in his leadership.

But perhaps more important symbols of the continuity of Mahatmic sponsorship of the TS were Norendro Nath Sen, Pandit Gopi Nath, and the Maharaja of Kapurthala. Sen had been involved with Theosophy since its early days in India, and in 1882 had advised Koot Hoomi about the *Phoenix* venture to establish a newspaper with native capital. As a journalist himself, Sen presumably was considered a qualified advisor to KH, who quoted him in a letter to Sinnett about the venture. Sen was twenty years old when he first became editor of *The Indian Mirror* in 1863, although this was a temporary assignment. He continued to write for the paper and again became editor after it became a daily. In 1883 Sen became proprietor as well as editor, and continued in this capacity until his death in 1911. His TS membership continued throughout his life. According to Surendranath Banerjea he was the "most moderate among the political leaders of Bengal."[82] Both Banerjea and Besant were allied to the moderate wing of the Freedom Movement and disavowed extremism and violence. When several Singh Sabha leaders and maharajas had conspired in the mid-1880s to restore Dalip Singh to his throne with French and Russian support, Sen explicitly rejected their overtures. In the late 90s he served in the Bengal Legislative Assembly, and was later active in the anti-partition movement of 1905–06. But his firm rejection of terrorism brought him into such conflict with his fellow Bengalis that he abandoned the political scene in his final years.

Pandit Gopi Nath was an orthodox Brahmin from Lahore who had been deeply involved in Olcott's 1883 tour through northern India to meet the Mahatmas. Nath wrote the *Theosophist* description of the group's stay in Lahore, where he was editor of the *Mitra Vilasa*. He proceeded with Olcott, Damodar and Brown to Jammu, and served as translator at various points of the tour.[83] Thus he was one of the best qualified witnesses to the events of that remarkable journey; presumably Besant's contact with him deepened her appreciation for the continuity of Olcott's relationship with Indian adepts.

Kapurthala also figured significantly in the same crucial 1883 trip. On their last day in Lahore, Olcott and company spent hours in discussion with the representatives of the Maharaja of Kapurthala, and a week later they visited his kingdom after leaving Jammu. The fact that ten years later Olcott recapitulated so much of this journey in the company of Besant and Wachtmeister suggests an initiatory intent; it seems that he wanted to reveal to them as fully as possible the world of the real Mahatmas who had sponsored the society.

But despite the genuineness of her initiatory journey, under Besant's leadership the TS promoted the occultation of the Masters in a way that would have horrified Olcott and Blavatsky. The reality of Olcott's and Besant's visions of the Masters is beyond confirmation or disproof. Their knowledge that the real Morya and Koot Hoomi were dead may have contributed to the quasi-Spiritualistic devolution of the TS in the twentieth century. Both Olcott and Besant were made susceptible to exploitation by clairvoyants and alleged initiates, due to their yearning for renewed contact with the defunct Mahatmas.

Regardless of her later mistakes, Annie was to some extent a genuine initiate of the Theosophical Masters. Her initiatory travels and role as a Western exponent of Eastern spirituality made her an exemplary member of the Great White Sisterhood. Moreover, her work for India fulfilled the major objectives of the Mahatmas Morya and Koot Hoomi, defined by HPB as "the real, practical good the Society is doing . . . for the natives."[84]

In 1906 another scandal disrupted the TS, casting a dark shadow on Olcott's last year in office. Helen Dennis, a leading Chicago Theosophist and official of the American branch of the ES, accused Leadbeater of sexual abuse of two adolescent boys, her son Robin and Douglas Pettit. Such accusations were to recur in India in 1917 and in Australia in 1925. Both boys claimed that Leadbeater, in the guise of a benevolent spiritual advisor, had taken advantage of them sexually. In an Executive Committee hearing, Leadbeater admitted not only that he had taught masturbation as a means of sexual release but had given indicative action. Olcott and the committee, horrified, demanded Leadbeater's resignation, which was immediately given. At the time, Besant sided with Olcott against her colleague and denounced his behavior toward the boys. But Leadbeater had a strong hold on Besant, having led her in clairvoyant investigations of such matters as occult chemistry and past lives. Almost immediately after his resignation, CWL began a campaign to restore his intimacy with Besant, bombarding her with friendly letters. Less than a year after her election to the TS Presidency, Besant welcomed him back into the society. For the next twenty-five years, Leadbeater was the strongest influence on Besant's Theosophy, and his clairvoyance dominated her conception of the Masters and their qualities.

Biographers have unfailingly noted Besant's recurring tendency to hero-worship of male figures in her life. In *The Fabians,* Norman and Jeanne Mackenzie summarize her pattern of conversions:

> In each of the spiritual crises which punctuated her anguished pilgrimage through life . . . a change of mind was associated with a change of heart. Conversion was personified in an attachment to a new male idol, preferably a man who seemed a victim of hostile circumstances and was forced to vindicate himself against great odds. Though she was herself a magnetic personality, a powerful orator, and able journalist and author, and an effective organizer, her temperament seemed

> to demand a masculine partner whom she could both admire and patronize, a focus for powerful emotions which required all the elements of a marriage except sexual intimacy.[85]

From her husband Frank, through Charles Bradlaugh, Edward Aveling, George Bernard Shaw, Judge, Olcott, Chakravarti, and Leadbeater, to Krishnamurti, Annie remained focused on male external authority. Certainly in the cases of her Theosophical male partners, there was a consistent theme of support for someone she saw as a victim of hostile circumstances. But ironically, she herself contributed to these circumstances in most cases. When she was reconciled with Olcott, her feelings may well have been influenced by a sense that she had wronged him in siding with Judge. After Olcott's death, Besant welcomed Leadbeater back into the TS despite having been actively involved in getting him out. She remained loyal to Krishnamurti long after he rejected the phantasmagoria with which she had surrounded him.

The strain of this situation contributed to her gradual entry into a twilight period of senility which lasted until her death in 1933. Although her Theosophical teachings were dominated by Leadbeater, her political mission was her own, an area in which he rarely became involved. As founder of the Central Hindu College, which became a university in 1916, she was the foremost leader of her time in Indian higher education. In the same year, she founded the Home Rule League, devoted to gradual attainment of Indian autonomy within the British Empire. After being interned by the government in 1917, she was elected president of the Indian National Congress the following year. But soon thereafter, she lost her prestige among young Indians due to her moderate views at a time when political extremism was becoming widespread.

Henry Steel Olcott has never been listed among the influential mentors of Annie Besant, yet he may have been the most crucial figure in her life. Until she toured India with him, she had only a vague sense of her destiny as a political and religious leader. After 1894, her commitment to India was absolute, her role as future president of the TS fairly well assured, and her loyalty to Olcott firmly established. Their extended tour accomplished a radical modification of her religious and social status; this is the keynote of initiatory experience. The rites performed in town after town in her honor contributed to her transformed identity. But another element of initiation, oral teachings, may have played a more important role in making this journey the turning point of Besant's life. The secrets confided to her by Olcott and his many

Indian friends remain inaccessible to historical research. It is impossible to know how much she learned during this period about the real Mahatmas and the true history of the TS. But it is safe to conclude that during her three month journey of 1893–94 Annie Besant acquired the understanding of India that would carry her through forty years of struggle, triumph, and defeat.

Despite the harmonious relationship between Besant and Olcott, there was a basic disagreement between them concerning the nonsectarian status of the TS. After the Hodgson report, Olcott tried to end all sensationalism about the Masters. HPB felt abandoned and resentful, as shown in her letters at the time. In a letter from the 1880s, signed by KH but written in HPB's handwriting and apparently addressed to her, the Master complains that "the Society has liberated itself from our grasp and influence" due to Olcott's effort to save the TS through deemphasizing the Masters. This, according to KH, saved its body, but "he allowed through sheer fear, to *[sic]* its soul to escape, and it is now a soulless corpse, a machine run so far well enough, but which will fall to pieces when he is gone" since "it is no longer a brotherhood, nor a body over the face of which broods the Spirit from beyond the Great Range."[86]

This view of Olcott's relations with the Masters has long been accepted among those Theosophists following the Judge lineages. But even in the Adyar TS, a view that he had wronged HPB and misled the Society has been promoted by the leadership. This is due in part to a Mahatma letter mysteriously received by Olcott in August 1888, en route to London from Bombay aboard the *Shannon.* In this lengthy message, KH warned Olcott that his "revolt . . . against her infallibility—as you once thought it—has gone too far and you have been unjust to her . . . "[87] In regard to immediate problems in the administration of the TS, KH wrote that HPB had "next to no concern with administrative details, and should be kept clear of them, so far as her strong nature can be controlled. But this *you must tell to all: With occult matters she has everything to do.* We have *not* abandoned her; she is *our direct agent.* I warn you against permitting your suspicions and resentments against 'her many follies' to bias your intuitive loyalty to her."[88]

In Jinarajadasa's commentary on this letter, he defends the ES, which was the object of Olcott's concern at the time, and explains that the letter sufficed to modify the Colonel's opposition to it. He adds that "It was not, however, till 1908 that the T.S. fully regained its original position, with the Masters of the Wisdom as once more the "First Section" of the Society.[89] Jinarajadasa had been expelled from the TS for his support of Leadbeater and insubordination to Olcott, so one may suspect a certain bias in his attitude toward the Colonel.

Despite their mutual admiration, Olcott and Besant were fundamentally divergent in their attitudes toward religion, as indicated by the Colonel in *Old Diary Leaves:*

> Unlike as H.P.B. and I were in many respects, we were akin in more ways than Annabai and myself can ever be. My praise of her is not tinged with blind partiality. She is religious fervor and devotion personified, the ideal female devotee who in time evolves into the saint and martyr . . . H.P.B. and I had none of this love of worship in our constitutions . . . A more consistently religious woman I never met, nor one whose life is a more joyful self-sacrifice.[90]

Olcott expressed his own attitudes toward the religious neutrality of the TS in his annual address of 1892, reprinted in *Old Diary Leaves* in 1900 because he concluded that his "views as to the non-sectarian basis of our Society and the evil of intolerance" still needed to be defended. He cites 1900 in particular as a year in which he had been obliged to restate his views in opposition to "a prevalent misconception in several countries," adding:

> I do especially protest against and denounce a tendency which is growing among us to lay the foundations of a new idolatry. As the co-Founder of the Society, as one who has had constant opportunities for knowing the chosen policy and wishes of our Masters, as one who has, under them and with their assent, borne our flag through sixteen years of battle, I protest against the first giving way to the temptation to elevate either them, their agents, or any other living or dead personage to the divine status, of their teachings to that of infallible doctrine. Not one word was ever spoken, transmitted, or written to me by the Masters that warranted such a course, nay, that did not inculcate the very opposite. I have been taught to lean upon myself alone, to look to my Higher Self as my best teacher, best guide, best example, and only savior. I was taught that no one could or ever would attain to the perfect knowledge save upon those lines; and so long as you keep me in my office, I shall proclaim this as the basis, the only basis and the palladium of the Society. I am led to make the above remarks by what I have seen going on of late. . . .

> As her tried friend, then; as one would worked most intimately with her, and is most anxious that she may be taken by posterity at her true high value; as her co-worker; as one long ago an accepted, though humble, agent of the Masters; and finally, as the official head of the Society and guardian of the rights of its Fellows—I place on record my protest against all attempts to create an H.P.B. school, sect or cult, or to take her utterances as in the least degree above criticism . . . [91]

Later in the same volume, he comments that although the creation of a Blavatskyite sect had been averted, "let no one suppose that this vicious tendency towards hero-worship has been rooted out from our natures, for a new idol is being fashioned in the form of that dear, unselfish, modest woman, Annie Besant."[92]

Despite Olcott's apprehensions about the worship of Masters and their disciples, Annie Besant was soon to promote an atmosphere in which the TS would exemplify religious mania. Her propensities in this direction were discussed in a letter she received, allegedly from KH, in 1900:

> A psychic and pranayamist who has got confused by the vagaries of the members. The T.S. and its members are slowly manufacturing a creed. Says a Thibetan proverb "credulity breeds credulity and ends in hypocrisy." How few are they who can know anything about us. Are we to be propitiated and made idols of. Is the worship of a new Trinity made up of the Blessed M. Upasika [HPB] and yourself to take the place of exploded creeds. We ask not for worship of ourselves. The disciple should in no way be fettered. Beware of an Esoteric Popery. The intense desire to see Upasika reincarnate at once has raised a misleading Mayavic ideation. Upasika has useful work to do on higher planes and cannot come again so soon. The T.S. must safely be ushered into the new century. You have for some time been under deluding influences. Shun pride, vanity and love of power. Be not guided by emotion but learn to stand alone. Be accurate and critical rather than credulous. The mistakes of the past in the old religions must not be glossed over with imaginary explanations. The E.S.T. must be reformed so as to be as unsectarian and creedless as the T.S. The rules must be few and simple and acceptable to all. No one has a right to claim

authority over a pupil or his conscience. Ask him not what he believes. All who are sincere and pure minded must have admittance. The crest wave of intellectual advancement must be taken hold of and guided into spirituality. It cannot be forced into beliefs and emotional worship. The essence of the higher thoughts of the members in their collectivity must guide all action in the T.S. and E.S. We never try to subject to ourselves the will of another. At favourable times we let loose elevating influences which strike various persons in various ways. It is the collective aspect of many such thoughts that can give the correct note of action. We show no favours. The best corrective of error is an honest and open-minded examination of all facts subjective and objective. Misleading secrecy has given the death blow to numerous organizations. The cant about "Masters" must be silently but firmly put down. Let the devotion and service be to that Supreme Spirit alone of which one is a part. Namelessly and silently we work and the continual references to ourselves and the repetition of our names raises up a confused aura that hinders our work.

You will have to leave a good deal of your emotions and credulity before you become a safe guide among the influences that will commence to work in the new cycle. The T.S. was meant to be the cornerstone of the future religions of humanity. To accomplish this object those who lead must leave aside their weak predilections for the forms and ceremonies of any particular creed and show themselves to be true Theosophists both in inner thoughts and outward observance. The greatest of your trials is yet to come. We watch over you but you must put forth all your strength.

K. H.[93]

This letter was written in the familiar KH handwriting on the margins of a letter dated 22 August 1900, addressed to Annie Besant from B. W. Mantri, a Bombay resident who expressed confusion about the Society's tenets. Besant was in London at the time, and found KH's annotations upon opening the letter. Although it was later published by the Adyar TS as a presumably genuine Mahatma letter, there has been little discussion of its accuracy or implications. Whether or not the author was KH, he or she was definitely an ideological ally of Olcott in the doomed struggle against worship of the Masters.

Initiated Women

How do the relationships among these women justify the phrase "Great White Sisterhood?" All pursued their personal visions of the occult quest. In search of the Masters, they travelled vast deserts. In pursuit of ancient wisdom, they contacted many teachers who shared of varied traditions. In very different ways, they felt compelled to share their discoveries with others, usually through their writings. Lady Hester Stanhope was the first and most spectacular case of a nineteenth-century European female abandoning her homeland to plunge into the life of the Near East. Isabelle Eberhardt, with Lydia and Abou Naddara as mentors, pursued the same destiny at the close of the century. Excellent horsewomen, they rode where no European women had been before, opening to the West new insights into the Orient. Their partnerships with male brotherhoods show that some Oriental Masters were eager to share their wisdom with European female disciples. The expansion of the Bahaʾi Faith in the West was due in large part to the spirit of Western women who travelled to the Holy Land to meet ʿAbduʾl Baha and returned home as Bahaʾi missionaries. Annie Besant's passion for India and her adoration of Krishnamurti were both symptomatic of this same desire for the Orient, which also motivated Katherine Tingley to travel to Egypt and India in search of contacts with the Masters. Later in this century, Alexandra David-Neel became world famous for her unprecedented penetration of Tibetan Buddhism. Alice Cleather sought relentlessly for the truth behind HPB's mysterious life. Annie Besant led the TS into international prominence. What made this possible, in every case, was self-liberation from the constraints of the traditional female role. Leaving husbands behind in their pursuit of liberation and enlightenment, these remarkable women provided a distinctly new role model for their twentieth century sisters.

In *Masculine and Feminine: the Natural Flow of Opposites in the Psyche,* Gareth Hill provides a Jungian interpretation of initiation which may shed some light on the historical role of the Great White Sisterhood. Hill proposes a model with four poles of psychic opposites, in which the psychological principles of masculine and feminine are present in every woman and man. The four poles described by Hill provide a basis for his definition of initiation, which is helpful in understanding the special role of female initiates like Blavatsky, Eberhardt, and David-Neel.

The static feminine pole is the Great Mother, organic wholeness and oneness, Nature as the womb from which all life emerges.

Positively, it signifies self-acceptance in harmony with the natural order. Negatively manifested, the static feminine is inertia, resistance to all innovation and change.

The opposite of the static feminine is the dynamic masculine. It manifests as initiative, goal-directedness, linearity, and technology. Positively expressed, it is the dragon-slaying hero, but its negative side is willful destruction and disregard for ecological balance. When one consciously focuses energy through one pole of the psyche, there is an unconscious compensation with the opposite.[94]

Western imperial conquest of the "backward" nations of Asia and Africa can be seen as an expression of this polarity. Non-Western cultures had the static feminine qualities of resistance to change and reverence for natural cycles. They were powerless in the face of the dynamic masculine war technology of the European powers, whose initiative was directed to the goal of commercial exploitation. But the later phases of colonialism focused on consolidation and control over what had been seized, which brings into play the complementary polarity between static masculine and dynamic feminine.

The static masculine manifests as order, standards, regulations, value systems. Negatively, it expresses rigidity and self-righteousness. Its polar opposite is the dynamic feminine, which is creativity, imagination, and altered states of consciousness. Negatively, the dynamic feminine is hysteria, chaos, emptiness, despair, and identity confusion.[95] During the late nineteenth and early twentieth centuries, the Western attitude toward colonial subjects had evolved from a dynamic masculine exploitation to a more static masculine paternalism. Native peoples were seen as needing the Western imperialists to impose order on their chaos. This was especially manifest in the effort of European missionaries to Christianize the East and thereby bring the entire world under the domination of their religion.

In the context of prevailing masculine energy directed from Europe to Asia and Africa, the initiated women sketched in these pages were a counterbalance. A key concept of Jungian psychology is enantiodromia, the tendency of things to turn into their opposites. The authoritarian static masculine energy directed at the Orient was opposed by the dynamic feminine energy embodied by Lady Hester, HPB, Isabelle Eberhardt, Alice Cleather, and Annie Besant. They went to Asia and Africa not to impose Western values but to transform themselves by experiencing altered states and unfamiliar customs. Their imagination and creativity were unleashed by their travels, and the expression of their personal transformation in writing provided a catalyst for cultural transformation which continues to the present. Where their compatriots went to preach and convert, they went to discover and revere.

This is not to say that only women can express feminine energy or that only men express masculine. There were indeed men—Blunt, Browne, and Olcott to name three—who received inspiration from their contact with Asian and African cultures. And most Western women in Asia or Africa undoubtedly shared the static masculine paternalistic attitudes of their male compatriots. Nevertheless, the gender of HPB and her successors in the Great White Sisterhood appears more than coincidental. Women who had rejected male domination at home were unlikely to share prevailing cultural biases when they went abroad. Moreover, esoteric brotherhoods in Asia and Africa seem to have been surprisingly willing to initiate Western women in preference to their male compatriots. Such fraternities were generally closed to women of their own societies as well. Western females thus seem to have been perceived as less threatening than either native women or Western men.

Hill's theory of initiation builds on the two polarities of dynamic/static and masculine/feminine. The transition from dynamic to static masculine is called the fiery initiation, which features submission of individual will to the collective. One's personal drives are integrated into a life structure sanctioned by one's culture. The passage from the dynamic to static feminine is the watery initiation, in which the limited, separated self is reborn into an expanded selfhood identified with the cosmos.[96]

An outstanding trait of the women who became initiates of Theosophical Masters is their passage through trials of a sort rarely accomplished by anyone of either sex. Their travels involved feats of endurance and bravery that tested their limits physically, emotionally, and spiritually. The Druze leaders who taught Lady Hester, the Tibetan lamas who instructed Alexandra, the Sufi teachers who initiated Isabelle, all seem to have been impressed by the dynamic masculine qualities shown by these women. They proved themselves equals of men in such traits, but after their initiations their behavior was quite different from that of native male disciples. The pattern of static masculine authority structures, secret or open, is to demand total commitment and loyalty. But while idealizing the Masters, Western female initiates were generally free to innovate and adapt the teachings they received.

In contemplating their accomplishments, one must recognize how differently they perceived Eastern spirituality from most of their male compatriots. Their receptivity to discovery evoked creative imagination. By yielding to the apparent chaos of alien cultures and relinquishing their native cultural identities, they became wayshowers for spiritual seekers of the twentieth century. Passing through the watery initiation, they were reborn into a new identification with humanity, the earth and the cosmos.

Occult Succession

The connections among many of the initiates portrayed in these pages remain elusive. While it is can be established that they are in various ways heirs of HPB's adept sponsors, generalizations are difficult. The story of HPB and her Masters is one of convergence; her Theosophy synthesized a lifetime of initiatory encounters with a global cast of characters. Tracing those encounters in *The Masters Revealed* provided a relatively coherent and satisfying explanation of her sources. By contrast, the story of Theosophy's initiatory legacy is one of divergence. Following the pathways of the characters in the present investigation leads to all points of the compass, and at the end of the journey the reader may feel that it has been incoherent and fruitless. But in the course of the investigation, some themes emerge which may justify the inclusion of these diverse characters in the same book.

First is the theme of HPB's Theosophy as a point of convergence and subsequent divergence, and therefore as a turning point in religious history. The richness of Theosophy's legacy is largely a function of the scope of HPB's mind. None before or after her has made a more audacious attempt to reconcile science, religion, and philosophy while bridging East and West. In drawing on Hindu, Islamic, Buddhist, and Western occultism in her synthesis, she created a vehicle whereby each of those traditions could be in turn influenced. Indeed, it would be difficult to say in which of these domains Theosophy's impact was greater. In each case, HPB made traditional followers of varied spiritual paths aware of their connectedness to the entire human religious heritage. In a parallel manner, Jamal ad-Din was a point of convergence for Shiᶜite esotericism, Western political ideals, and Sunni pan-Arabism. Virtually every subsequent development in Islamic history can be seen to have felt his impact. But because so much of his influence was concealed, many aspects of his role in history remain mysterious. HPB's impact on the work of Anagarika Dharmapala for the revival of Buddhism has been one of her least-recognized contributions, perhaps because Dharmapala was unsympathetic to the later TS.

Until recent years, neither Theosophists nor Buddhists fully appreciated the importance of his relationship with HPB and Olcott. Theosophy's impact on the changing role of women has only now begun to receive the attention it deserves. Perhaps the most occult succession of all is that of the Great White Sisterhood. HPB was a forerunner of many Western female disciples who received initiatory secrets formerly withheld from both females and foreigners. In light of all these avenues for further exploration, it seems likely that HPB's place in history will be enhanced by the work of future scholars.

A corollary theme that emerges in this investigation is the ubiquity of "genealogical dissociation," to use the term coined by David Lane. Just as Theosophy itself rests on hidden sources, it became in turn a concealed foundation for many subsequent developments. Neither Baha'is, Fourth Way disciples, nor New Age believers acknowledge the debt they owe to Theosophy and its Masters. Because HPB concealed her own sources, and was then concealed as a source by others, her historical significance has been drastically underestimated. In most cases, the linkages documented in these pages have either been forgotten or deliberately suppressed.[97]

To most Theosophists, "occult succession" has meant a linear progression of spiritual teachers equivalent to Hinduism's "Guruparamapara" or chain of gurus. "Occult" in this usage may refer to the knowledge, doctrines or spiritual status of the teachers. But from a historical point of view, it is equally appropriate to see "occult" as describing the way in which succession occurs. In most cases, HPB's spiritual influence has been transmitted in an underground manner, with neither Theosophists nor others being aware of its scope and complexity.

In the closing pages of her last book, HPB predicts two possible evolutionary paths for the Theosophical movement through the twentieth century. The less desirable option is described first:

> Every such attempt as the Theosophical Society has hitherto ended in failure, because, sooner or later, it has degenerated into a sect, set up hard-and-fast dogmas of its own, and so lost by imperceptible degrees that vitality which living truth alone can impart. You must remember that all our members have been bred and born in some creed or religion, that all are more or less of their generation both physically and mentally, and consequently that their judgment is but too likely to be warped and unconsciously biassed *[sic]* by some or all of these

> influences. If, then, they cannot be freed from such inherent bias, or at least taught to recognize it instantly and so avoid being led away by it, the result can only be that the Society will drift off on to some sandbank of thought or another, and there remain a stranded carcass to moulder and die.[98]

The partial accuracy of this prediction is confirmed by the fragmentation of the Theosophical movement after HPB's death. No branch of the movement has escaped the spirit of dogmatism and authoritarianism in the twentieth century. Few observers would deny that there has been a drastic loss of vitality throughout the movement. But Theosophists may have been paradoxically blessed by Krishnamurti's defection. Leadbeater's neo-Theosophy had successfully displaced HPB's original teachings, and only the crisis caused by Krishnamurti reversed the inertia. Until 1929, the Adyar TS had indeed drifted onto the sandbank of Leadbeater's clairvoyance, but since that time it has gradually returned to serious study of the original source teachings and the traditions from which they are drawn. In recent years, the Pasadena TS and the ULT have similarly emphasized points common to all Theosophists, becoming less dogmatic and doctrinaire in attitude. All have cooperated in a series of ventures, including Sylvia Cranston's biography of HPB and the 1993 Parliament of Religions in Chicago. Therefore, when HPB predicts what will happen if the Theosophical movement survives as a vital force, some of her remarks ring just as true as in the previous passage:

> Then the Society will live on into and through the twentieth century. It will gradually leaven and permeate the great mass of thinking and intelligent people with its large-minded and noble ideas of Religion, Duty, and Philanthropy. Slowly but surely it will burst asunder the iron fetters of creeds and dogmas, of social and caste prejudices; it will break down racial and national antipathies and barriers, and will open the way to the practical realisation of the Brotherhood of all men. Through its teaching, through the philosophy which it has rendered accessible and intelligible to the modern mind, the West will learn to understand and appreciate the East at its true value.[99]

In these passages, HPB's hopes and fears for the results of her lifework are clearly stated. Although her fears were grounded in awareness of past failures, her hopes were inspired by the monumental changes she witnessed. In the century since her death, HPB's initiatory successors have labored to make her vision a reality. Although the extent of their achievements falls short of her hopes, the general direction of their efforts has been true to her inspiration. In reference to an earlier theosophist, Jakob Boehme, his biographer Andrew Weeks defines a pivotal figure as "one into whom all the earlier currents flowed and out of whom these currents spread after being transformed by the force of his inspiration."[100] The spiritual journeys of HPB's occult successors reveal abundant evidence of the pivotal character of her remarkable life.

NOTES

Introduction: Initiation in Theosophical History

1. H. P. Blavatsky, *Theosophical Glossary,* p. 156.

2. C. J. Jinarajadasa, *Letters from the Masters of the Wisdom,* Second Series, p. 11.

3. *Encyclopedia of Religion,* vol. 6, p. 137.

4. Ibid., vol. 7, p. 225.

5. Ibid.

6. Bruce Campbell, *Ancient Wisdom Revived,* pp. 96–97.

7. Arthur H. Nethercot, *The Last Four Lives of Annie Besant,* p. 29.

8. Gottfried de Purucker, *The Dialogues of G. de Purucker,* vol. 1, p. 145.

9. Gregory Tillett, *The Elder Brother,* p. 105.

10. Nethercot, *Last Four Lives,* p. 145.

11. Mary Lutyens, *Krishnamurti: the Years of Awakening,* pp. 293–297.

12. Pupul Jayakar, *Krishnamurti,* p. 379.

13. Ibid., p. 404.

14. Radha Burnier, "Human Need in the Kali Yuga," *The American Theosophist,* January/February 1994, p. 4.

15. H. P. Blavatsky, *Collected Writings,* vol. 1, p. 133.

Part One: Patriotic Chelas

1. Marion Meade, *Madame Blavatsky: the Woman Behind the Myth,* p. 32.

2. J. T. F. Jordens, *Dayananda Sarasvati: His Life and Ideas,* p. 135.

3. James Webb, comp. *The S.P.R. Report on the Theosophical Society,* p. 316.

4. Ibid., p. 239.

5. Sylvia Cranston, *HPB,* pp. 206–207.

6. H. P. Blavatsky, *Collected Writings,* Vol. V, pp. 267–268.

7. Ibid., Vol. IV, p. 641.

8. H. P. Blavatsky, *H.P.B. Speaks,* Vol. II, pp. 43–44.

9. Ibid., pp. 28–29.

10. Ibid., p. 85.

11. Ibid., pp. 96–100.

12. Marion Meade, *Madame Blavatsky,* p. 259.

13. Ibid., pp. 259–260.

14. *Five Years of Theosophy,* p. 280.

15. Ibid., p. 281.

16. Ibid., p. 282.

17. Ibid., p. 284.

18. Ibid., p. 285.

19. Ibid., p. 286.

20. C. J. Jinarajadasa, comp., *Letters From the Masters of the Wisdom,* Second Series, p. 94.

21. Ibid., pp. 94–95.

22. Ibid., pp. 95–96.

23. Ibid., pp. 96–97.

24. Ibid., p. 99.

25. Ibid., p. 100.

26. Ibid., pp. 115–116.

27. Ibid., pp. 117–118.

28. Ibid., pp. 118–119.

29. Ibid.

30. *Indian Chelas on the Masters,* p. 25.

31. *Indian Chelas on the Masters,* p. 29.

32. Ibid., p. 31.

33. Ibid., p. 32.

34. Ibid., pp. 34–35.

35. Jinarajadasa, *Letters,* Second Series, p. 114; Henry S. Olcott, *Old Diary Leaves,* Vol. 6, p. 389.

36. H. P. Blavatsky, *Collected Writings,* Vol. IV, p. 638.

37. Jinarajadasa, *Letters,* Second Series, pp. 104–105.

38. Ibid., pp. 106.

39. Ibid., pp. 80–81.

40. Ibid., p. 85.

41. Ibid., p. 86.

42. H. P. Blavatsky, *Letters of H. P. Blavatsky to A. P. Sinnett,* p. 62.

43. William T. Brown, "Some Experiences in India," *Theosophical History* 3:7–8 (July—October 1991), p. 214.

44. Ibid., p. 216.

45. Ibid., p. 217.

46. Ibid., pp. 221–222.

47. Ibid., p. 222.

48. H. P. Blavatsky, *Collected Writings,* Vol. VI, pp. 31–32.

49. James Webb, comp., *The S.P.R. Report on the Theosophical Society,* p. 246.

50. Ibid., p. 247.

51. Ibid., pp. 247–248.

52. Henry S. Olcott, *Old Diary Leaves,* Vol. II, pp. 289–291.

53. *Indian Chelas on the Masters,* p. 9.

54. Sven Eek, comp., *Damodar and the Pioneers of the Theosophical Movement,* p. 368.

55. Sylvia Cranston, *HPB,* p. 99.

56. Ibid., pp. 99–100.

57. H. P. Blavatsky, *Collected Writings,* Vol. VI, p. 21.

58. Ibid., p. 22.

59. Jinarajadasa, *Letters,* Second Series, p. 108.

60. James Webb, comp., *The S.P.R. Report,* p. 23.

61. Ibid., pp. 373–374.

62. Olcott, *Old Diary Leaves,* Vol. III, p. 597.

63. A. Trevor Barker, comp., *The Mahatma Letters to A. P. Sinnett,* pp. 367–370.

64. Arthur H. Nethercot, *The Last Four Lives of Annie Besant,* p. 86.

65. Marion Meade, *Madame Blavatsky,* p. 342.

66. H. P. Blavatsky, *Letters of H. P. Blavatsky to A. P. Sinnett,* p. 330.

67. Ibid., p. 325.

68. Ibid., pp. 95–96.

69. Paul Brunton, *A Search in Secret India,* pp. 121–128.

70. Ibid., p. 7.

71. Blavatsky, *Letters to Sinnett,* p. 206.

72. Ibid., p. 291.

73. Ibid., p. 100.

74. Ibid., p. 100.

75. Ibid., pp. 118–119.

76. Ibid., pp. 277–280.

77. Ibid., p. 335.

78. Ibid., p. 336.

79. Ibid., p. 283.

80. Ibid., p. 341.

81. Ibid., pp. 182–186.

82. Ibid., pp. 161–162.

83. Ibid., pp. 300–301.

84. Ibid., p. 302.

85. Ibid., pp. 342–343.

86. Ibid., p. 331.

87. *The Theosophist,* Supplement, May 1883, p. 6.

88. Peter Berger, *The Heretical Imperative,* pp. 60–65.

89. *Encyclopedia of Religion,* vol. 2, p. 299.

90. Ibid., p. 300.

91. David Christopher Lane, *The Radhasoami Tradition,* p. 303.

92. Mark Juergensmeyer, *Radhasoami Reality,* p. 205.

93. Swami Shiv Dayal Singh, *Sar Bachan,* p. 4.

94. Barker, *Mahatma Letters,* pp. 255–256.

95. Lane, *The Radhasoami Tradition,* p. 31.

96. Barker, *Mahatma Letters,* p. 309.

97. Bruce Campbell, *Ancient Wisdom Revived,* p. 172.

98. See Pupul Jayakar's *Indira Gandhi.*

99. Ibid., p. 124.

100. Mark Juergensmeyer, *Radhasoami Reality,* p. 205.

Part 2: The Secret World of Jamal ad-Din

1. Emma Coulomb, *Some Account of My Intercourse with Madame Blavatsky,* p. 102.

2. Manly P. Hall, "Madame Blavatsky—a Tribute," *Theosophia,* May–June 1947, pp. 10–11.

3. Barker, *Mahatma Letters,* p. 116.

4. Wilfred Cantwell Smith, *Islam in Modern History,* p. 48.

5. Ibid.

6. Ibid., p. 49.

7. *Encyclopedia of Religion,* vol. 1, p. 5.

8. M. A. Zaki Badawi, *The Reformers of Egypt,* p. 26.

9. Elie Kedourie, *Afghani and ʿAbduh,* p. 8.

10. Ibid., p. 10.

11. Ibid., p. 22.

12. *Encyclopedia of Religion,* vol. 1, p. 5.

13. Ibid.

14. Ibid., p. 6.

15. Kedourie, *Afghani and ʿAbduh,* pp. 12–13.

16. Ibid., p. 17.

17. Ibid., p. 19.

18. Ibid., p. 20.

19. Ibid., p. 21.

20. Juan R. I. Cole, *Colonialism and Revolution in the Middle East,* p. 135.

21. Ibid., p. 137.

22. Ibid., p. 141.

23. Ibid.

24. Ibid., p. 143.

25. Ibid., p. 147.

26. Kedourie, *Afghani and ʿAbduh,* pp. 30–31.

27. Ibid., p. 40.

28. Ibid., p. 42.

29. H. P. Blavatsky, "Letters," *The Path,* May 1895, p. 36.

30. Felix K. Gaboriau, "Adieu au lecteurs du Lotus," *Le Lotus,* March 1889.

31. Elie Kedourie, *Afghani and ʿAbduh,* p. 43.

32. Barker, *Mahatma Letters,* p. 57.

33. Elie Kedourie, *Afghani and ʿAbduh,* p. 49.

34. Ibid., p. 51.

35. *Dictionary of National Biography 1922–30,* pp. 84–85.

36. Elizabeth Longford, *A Pilgrimage of Passion,* p. 97.

37. Ibid., p. 137.

38. Ibid., p. 164.

39. Ibid., p. 165.

40. Edward Rice, *Captain Sir Richard Francis Burton,* p. 302.

41. Edward G. Browne, *The Persian Revolution of 1905–09,* pp. 401–402.

42. Ibid., p. 403.

43. Ibid., 56.

44. Ibid.

45. Joscelyn Godwin, *History of Theosophy in France,* p. 11.

46. Charles Blech, *Contribution a l'Histoire de la Societe Theosophique en France,* p. 206.

47. Homa Pakdaman, *Djamal ad-Din Assadabadi di Afghani,* p. 45.

48. Ibid., p. 66.

49. Ibid., p. 78.

50. Ibid.

51. Ibid., p. 79.

52. Ibid., p. 98.

53. Ibid., p. 341.

54. Ibid., p. 348.

55. Ibid., p. 346.

56. Ibid., p. 347.

57. Henri Rochefort, *Aventures de ma vie,* tome 4, p. 345.

58. Pakdaman, *Djamal ad-Din,* p. 124.

59. Ibid., p. 327.

60. Browne, *The Persian Revolution,* p. 404.

61. Kedourie, *Afghani and ʿAbduh,* p. 59.

62. Ibid., p. 19.

63. Keddie, *Jamal ad-Din,* p. 279.

64. Ibid., p. 293.

65. Ibid., p. 412.

66. Ibid., p. 413.

67. William H. Hatcher and Douglas Martin, *The Bahaʾi Faith,* p. 13.

68. Ibid., p. 22.

69. Ibid., p. 21.

70. Ibid.

71. Ibid., p. 26.

72. Ibid.

73. Ibid., pp. 32–33.

74. Ibid., p. 33.

75. Ibid., p. 34.

76. Ibid., p. 40.

77. Ibid., p. 48.

78. Ibid.

79. *Dictionary of National Biography 1922–30,* p. 123.

80. Ibid., p. 124.

81. Browne, *The Persian Revolution,* p. 45.

82. Ibid.

83. Ibid., pp. 2–3.

84. Ibid., p. 3.

85. Ibid., p. 12.

86. Hatcher and Martin, *The Bahaʾi Faith,* p. 208.

87. H. M. Balyuzi, *Edward Granville Browne and the Bahaʾi Faith,* p. 25.

88. Ibid., p. 26.

89. Ibid., p. 28.

90. Browne, *The Persian Revolution,* p. 73.

91. Hatcher and Martin, *Bahaʾi Faith,* p. 209.

92. Shoghi Effendi, *God Passes By,* p. 256.

93. Ibid., p. 283.

94. Shoghi Effendi, *God Passes By,* p. 283.

95. Blomfeld, *The Chosen Highway,* p. 154.

96. ʿAbduʾl Baha, *The Promulgation of Universal Peace,* p. 156.

97. Shoghi Effendi, *God Passes By,* p. 286.

98. Ibid., p. 98.

99. H. M. Balyuzi, *ʿAbduʾl Baha,* p. 152.

100. Balyuzi, *ʿAbduʾl Baha,* p. 456.

101. Ibid., p. 368.

102. Wilson, *Bahaʾism and its Claims,* p. 284.

103. Statistics for Bahaʾi membership were reported on soc.religion.bahai, a usenet newsgroup.

104. Peter Smith, *The Babi and Bahaʾi Religions,* p. 149.

105. Ibid., p. 48.

106. Ibid., p. 49.

107. Richard Hollinger, *Community Histories* (Studies in the Babi and Bahaʾi Religions, Vol. 6), pp. xvii–xviii. In a telephone conversation, Robert H. Stockman, director of the Research Department at the National Bahaʾi Center, estimated that one third of the earliest American Bahaʾis had some previous exposure to Theosophy.

108. Juan R. I. Cole, "Iranian Millenarianism and Democratic Thought," *International Journal of Middle East Studies,* vol. 24 (1992), p. 2.

109. Ibid.

110. Ibid., p. 7.

111. Ibid., p. 12.

112. Ibid.

113. Ibid., p. 21.

114. Juan R. I. Cole, "Muhammad ʿAbduh and Rashid Rida: A Dialogue on the Bahaʾi Faith," p. 11.

115. *Encyclopedia of Religion,* vol. 13, p. 244.

116. Ibid.

117. Ibid.

118. Abbas Amanat, *Resurrection and Renewal,* pp. 7–8.

119. Ibid., p. 10.

120. Keddie, *Jamal ad-Din "al-Afghani,"* p. 33.

121. Ibid., p. 34.

122. Amanat, *Resurrection,* p. 15.

123. Ibid., p. 45.

124. Ibid., p. 48.

125. Ibid., p. 50.

126. Ibid., p. 52.

127. Ibid.

128. Ibid., p. 53.

129. Ibid., p. 66.

130. Ibid., p. 107.

131. Wilson, *Bahaʾism and its Claims,* pp. 133–134.

132. Denis MacEoin, *From Shaykhism to Babism,* p. 139.

133. Ibid.

134. Ibid., p. 160.

135. Ibid., p. 161.

136. Ibid.

137. Ibid., p. 415.

138. Ibid.

139. Ibid.

140. Ibid., p. 408.

141. Ibid., p. 364.

142. Ibid.

143. Ibid.

144. Ibid., p. 365.

145. Ibid., p. 414.

146. Ibid., p. 415.

147. Ibid., p. 416.

Part 3: Dharma Heirs

1. Rick Fields, *How the Swans Came to the Lake,* p. 97.

2. Ibid., p. 98.

3. Ibid.

4. Ibid.

5. Ibid., p. 100.

6. Ibid., p. 101.

7. Ibid., p. 117.

8. Ibid., p. 129.

9. Ibid., p. 133.

10. Ibid., p. 135.

11. Olcott, *Old Diary Leaves,* vol. 4, pp. 468–473.

12. Ibid., vol. 6, pp. 16–17.

13. Ibid., p. 338.

14. Ibid., pp. 347–348.

15. C. V. Agarwal, *The Buddhist and the Theosophical Movements,* p. 43.

16. Ibid.

17. Olcott, *Old Diary Leaves,* vol. 4, pp. 486–489.

18. Ibid., p. 60.

19. Ibid., p. 51.

20. William McGowan, *Only Man is Vile,* p. 140.

21. Ibid.

22. Ibid.

23. Ibid.

24. Ibid., p. 141.

25. Ibid., pp. 144–145.

26. Joscelyn Godwin, "HPB, Dorjeff, and the Mongolian Connection," *Theosophical History* 3:3 (July 1988), p. 257.

27. *Cambridge Encyclopedia of Russia and the Soviet Union,* p. 69.

28. James Webb, *The Harmonious Circle,* p. 57.

29. Ibid., p. 58.

30. Esper E. Ukhtomskii, *Travels in the East of Nicholas II . . . ,* vol. 1, p. 2.

31. Ibid., p. 4.

32. Ibid., pp. 168–169.

33. Ibid., vol. 2, pp. 2–3.

34. Ibid., p. 35.

35. Ibid., p. 60.

36. Ibid., pp. 76–77.

37. Ibid., p. 121.

38. H. S. Olcott, *Old Diary Leaves,* vol. 4, p. 288.

39. Ukhtomskii, *Travels in the East,* p. 121.

40. James Webb, *The Harmonious Circle,* p. 58.

41. Olcott, *Old Diary Leaves,* vol. 6, pp. 176–179.

42. Ibid., p. 59.

43. Barker, comp., *Letters of H. P. Blavatsky,* p. 228.

44. Webb, *Harmonious Circle,* p. 61.

45. Ibid., p. 61.

46. Ibid., p. 527.

47. Jeffrey Somers, "Lama Dorjieff and the Esoteric Tradition," *Theosophical History* 3:2 (April 1990), p. 46.

48. Ibid., pp. 47–49.

49. *Modern Encyclopedia of Russia and Soviet History,* vol. 40, p. 161.

50. Ibid., p. 161.

51. Ibid., pp. 161–162.

52. Ibid., p. 162.

53. Geoffrey Drage, *Russian Affairs,* p. 616.

54. Ibid., p. 62.

55. Ibid., p. 63.

56. Ibid., p. 64.

57. Andrew Malozemoff, *Russian Far Eastern Policy,* p. 44.

58. Ibid.

59. John Snelling, *Buddhism in Russia,* p. 35.

60. Ibid., p. 36.

61. Ibid., p. 47.

62. Ibid.

63. Ibid., pp. 47–48.

64. Ibid., p. 48.

65. Ibid., p. 51.

66. Ibid., p. 52.

67. Ibid., p. 73.

68. Ibid., p. 204.

69. Gurdjieff, *Meetings,* p. 90.

70. Ibid., p. 239.

71. Ibid., p. 241.

72. Rafael Lefort, *The Teachers of Gurdjieff,* pp. 139–146.

73. John G. Bennett, *Witness,* p. 256.

74. Ernest Scott, *People of the Secret,* pp. 168–170.

75. Omar Burke, "Solo to Mecca," *Blackwood's Magazine,* 290:1754 (December 1961), pp. 481–495.

76. Kathleen Riordan Speeth and Ira Friedlander, *Gurdjieff: Seeker of the Truth,* pp. 112–116.

77. Webb, *The Harmonious Circle,* pp. 540–542.

78. Idries Shah, *The Magic Monastery,* pp. 84, 186.

79. Barker, *Mahatma Letters,* p. 227.

80. Ibid., p. 231.

81. Webb, *Harmonious Circle,* p. 533.

82. George I. Gurdjieff, *Beelzebub's Tales to His Grandson,* vol. 1, p. 249.

83. Ibid., p. 350.

84. Ibid.

85. Webb, *Harmonious Circle,* pp. 109–117.

86. Maria Carlson, *No Religion Higher than Truth,* p. 75, citing *A Further Record of Extracts from Meetings Held by P. D. Ouspensky Between 1928 and 1945* (Capetown: Stourton Press, 1952) cited in Marrily Taylor, *Remembering Pytor Demianovitch Ouspensky* (New Haven: Yale University Press, 1978).

87. Ibid.

88. Ibid. Despite his disillusionment, in *The Fourth Dimension,* published in Russia in 1918, Ouspensky defended HPB against the attacks of Vsevelod Solovyov and praised the Theosophical movement. See Sylvia Cranston, *HPB,* pp. 299–300. On page 174, Cranston cites a letter in which Ouspensky states that "in spite of all that people can say I always feel that Olcott did not lie, and this is the most remarkable" [aspect of *Old Diary Leaves*].

89. James Webb, *The Harmonious Circle,* p. 198.

90. Reyner, *The Gurdjieff Inheritance,* p. 12.

91. Ibid., p. 39.

92. Robert S. Ellwood, "Madame Blavatsky's Baboon" (review), Gnosis #30, Winter 1994, p. 84.

93. Reyner, p. 96.

94. Ibid., pp. 97–98.

95. Ibid., p. 98.

96. Ibid., p. 97.

97. Henri Corbin, *Temps Cyclique et Gnose Ismailienne,* p. 65.

98. Barker, *Mahatma Letters,* p. 99.

99. Dan Merkur, *Gnosis,* p. 108.

100. Charles J. Ryan, *H. P. Blavatsky and the Theosophical Movement,* p. 23.

101. Mary K. Neff, comp., *Personal Memoirs of H. P. Blavatsky,* p. 131.

102. H. P. Blavatsky, *Theosophical Glossary,* p. 105.

103. H. P. Blavatsky, *Isis Unveiled,* vol. 1, p. 17.

104. H. P. Blavatsky, *Collected Writings,* vol. 14, p. 74.

105. H. P. Blavatsky, *The Secret Doctrine,* vol. 1, p. 288.

106. Ibid., vol. 2, p. 431.

107. S. H. Nasr, *Isma῾ili Contributions to Islamic Civilization,* p. 105.

108. Ibid., p. 105.

109. Ibid., p. 114.

110. Ibid., p. 109.

111. James Webb, *The Harmonious Circle,* p. 73.

112. George I. Gurdjieff, *Meetings with Remarkable Men,* p. 118.

113. Ibid., p. 119.

114. Ibid.

115. Ibid., p. 121.

116. Ibid.

117. Ibid., p. 134.

118. Ibid.

119. Ibid., p. 154.

120. Ibid., p. 156.

121. Ibid., p. 158.

122. Ibid., p. 159.

123. Ibid., pp. 159–160.

124. Ibid., p. 164.

125. Kathleen R. Speeth and Ira Friedlander, *Gurdjieff: Seeker of the Truth,* p. 120.

126. James Moore, *Gurdjieff: Anatomy of a Myth,* pp. 320–322.

Part 4: The Great White Sisterhood

1. *Webster's Biographical Dictionary,* p. 1396.
2. Ian Bruce, ed., *The Nun of Lebanon,* p. 27.
3. Ibid.
4. *Webster's Biographical Dictionary,* p. 1396.
5. Lytton Strachey, *Books and Characters,* pp. 300–301.
6. Ibid., p. 302.
7. *Webster's Biographical Dictionary,* p. 1396.
8. Bruce, *Nun of Lebanon,* pp. 388–389.
9. John Meryon, *Travels of Lady Hester Stanhope,* vol. 1, p. 338.
10. George Paston, *Little Memoirs of the 19th Century,* p. 226.
11. John Meryon, *Memoirs of Lady Hester Stanhope,* vol. 2, p. 254.
12. George Paston, *Little Memoirs,* p. 226.
13. Ibid.
14. Ian Bruce, *Nun of Lebanon,* p. 401.
15. Meryon, *Memoirs,* vol. 3, p. 140.
16. Alexander Kinglake, *Eothen,* p. 77.
17. Ibid., p. 81.
18. H. P. Blavatsky, *Collected Writings,* vol. 1, p. xxviii.
19. H. P. Blavatsky, *Isis Unveiled,* vol. 2, p. 2.
20. Edmonde Charles-Roux, *Un Desir d'Orient,* p. 388.

21. Leslie Blanch, *The Wilder Shores of Love,* p. 296.

22. Ibid., p. 299.

23. Isabelle Eberhardt, *The Passionate Nomad,* p. 4.

24. Ibid., p. 9.

25. Annette Kobak, *Isabelle,* p. 8.

26. Ibid., p. 18.

27. Ibid., p. 28.

28. Ibid.

29. Ibid., p. 137.

30. Ibid., p. 201.

31. Ibid.

32. Ibid., pp. 221–222.

33. Ibid., p. 224.

34. Ibid., p. 238.

35. Ibid.

36. Ibid., p. 245.

37. Barbara and Michael Foster, *Forbidden Journey,* pp. 38–39.

38. Ibid., p. 44.

39. Ibid., p. 87.

40. Sujata Nahar, *Mirra the Occultist,* p. 48.

41. Foster, *Forbidden Journey,* p. 314.

42. Ibid., p. 333.

43. Daniel Caracostea, "Alexandra David-Neel's Early Acquaintance with Theosophy: Paris 1892," *Theosophical History* 3:7–8 (July-October 1991), pp. 209–211.

44. Alexandra David-Neel, *Magic and Mystery in Tibet,* p. 230.

45. Ibid., p. 234.

46. Alice Leighton Cleather, *H. P. Blavatsky as I Knew Her,* pp. 2–3.

47. Ibid., p. 4.

48. H. P. Blavatsky, *Collected Writings,* vol. 14, p. 518.

49. Ibid., p. 519.

50. Alice Leighton Cleather, *H. P. Blavatsky, Her Life and Work for Humanity,* p. 5.

51. Ibid.

52. Ibid., p. 1.

53. Ibid., p. 72.

54. Ibid., p. 118.

55. Ibid., p. 18.

56. H. P. Blavatsky, *The Voice of the Silence,* s.v.

57. Ibid.

58. Ibid.

59. Ibid., p. 113.

60. Ibid., s.v.

61. Ibid., p. 112.

62. H. P. Blavatsky, *Collected Writings,* vol. 14, p. 520.

63. Ibid.

64. Ibid.

65. Leslie Price, "The American Acts of the Apostles," *Theosophical History* 2:4 (October 1987), pp. 134–135.

66. Olcott, *Old Diary Leaves,* vol. 4, pp. 442–443.

67. Ibid., p. 491.

68. Ibid., p. 334.

69. Ibid., pp. 517–518.

70. Ibid., pp. 523–524.

71. Edmund Garrett, *Isis Very Much Unveiled,* p. 45.

72. Ibid., p. 46.

73. Ibid.

74. Olcott, *Old Diary Leaves,* vol. 5, p. 51.

75. Ibid., p. 67.

76. Ibid., p. 69.

77. Ibid., p. 91.

78. Ibid., pp. 98–99.

79. Ibid., pp. 101–102.

80. Ibid., p. 133.

81. Nethercot, *Last Four Lives of Annie Besant,* p. 115.

82. *Dictionary of National Biography* (India), vol. 4, p. 112.

83. *The Theosophist,* supplement, January 1884, pp. 4–5.

84. Blavatsky, *Letters of H. P. Blavatsky to A. P. Sinnett,* p. 19.

85. Norman and Jeanne Mackenzie, *The Fabians,* pp. 45–46.

86. Jinarajadasa, *Letters from the Masters of the Wisdom,* First Series, p. 101.

87. Ibid., p. 44.

88. Ibid., p. 46.

89. Ibid., p. 122.

90. Olcott, *Old Diary Leaves,* vol. 5, pp. 152–153.

91. Ibid., vol. 4, pp. 426–428.

92. Ibid., p. 439.

93. "The 1900 Letter," *Theosophical History* 2:4, October 1987, pp. 116–117.

94. Gareth Hill, *Masculine and Feminine,* pp. 4–12.

95. Ibid., pp. 13–22.

96. Ibid., pp. 26–36.

97. In other areas, recognition of Blavatskian influence has been more widespread. The evolution of modern Western esotericism has been deeply affected by HPB and Theosophy. Neo-Rosicrucianism in most of its current expressions bears her imprint in many of its doctrines, most explicitly in the Rosicrucian Fellowship of Max Heindel. The Thelemic groups, focused on the writings of Aleister Crowley, also acknowledge Blavatsky as a forerunner. Twentieth century Spiritualism has developed in part as a reaction to Theosophy; belief in reincarnation, once rare among Spiritualists, is now commonplace. Many mediums now channel Master figures rather than ordinary excarnate souls. Several of the most controversial twentieth-century guru figures are clearly indebted to HPB. In the 1920s

and 30s, Arthur Edward Wilson proclaimed himself "Brother XII," spokesman for the Great White Brotherhood. Preaching an imminent apocalypse, he gathered followers from around the world to build a series of colonies in coastal British Columbia. After years of abuse, the followers turned against Brother XII and his mistress, Madame Zee, in a successful lawsuit. But the pair had long since vanished with most of the disciples' funds, never to be seen again. In the 1960s, Paul Twitchell created Eckankar, a new religion based on the teachings of the Vairagi Masters. In his study *Making of a Religious Movement,* David C. Lane shows that Twitchell plagiarized most of his writings from Radhasoami sources. With the invented names of Rebazar Tarz, Fubbi Quantz, and Sudar Singh, Twitchell transformed his historical sources into metahistorical myths. Lane acknowledges that Theosophy played some part in inspiring Twitchell's creation of Eckankar; the process of "genealogical dissociation" seems in his case particularly inspired by Blavatsky.

98. H. P. Blavatsky, *The Key to Theosophy,* p. 305.

99. Ibid., pp. 305–306.

100. Andrew Weeks, *German Mysticism from Hildegard of Bingen to Ludwig Wittgenstein,* p. 170.

BIBLIOGRAPHY

ʿAbduʾl Baha.
The Promulgation of Universal Peace. Wilmette: Bahaʾi Publishing Trust, 1982.

Amanat, Abbas.
Resurrection and Renewal: The Making of the Babi Movement in Iran, 1844–1850. Ithaca: Cornell University Press, 1989.

Arya, Krishna Singh, and P. D. Shastri.
Swami Dayananda Sarasvati: a Study of His Life and Work. Delhi: Manohar, 1987.

Badawi, M. A. Zaki.
The Reformers of Egypt. Slough: Open Press, 1976.

Balyuzi, H. M.
ʿAbduʾl Baha. Oxford: George Ronald, 1971.

———.
Edward Granville Browne and the Bahaʾi Faith. Oxford: George Ronald, 1970.

Barker, A. Trevor, comp.
The Mahatma Letters to A. P. Sinnett. Pasadena: Theosophical University Press, 1975.

Bennett, John G.
Witness. Charles Town: Claymont, 1983.

Berger, Peter.
The Heretical Imperative. New York: Doubleday, 1979.

Blanch, Lesley.
The Wilder Shores of Love. New York: Simon & Schuster, 1954.

Blavatsky, Helena Petrovna.
Caves and Jungles of Hindustan. Wheaton: Theosophical Publishing House, 1975.

———.
Collected Writings. Compiled by Boris de Zirkoff. 14 vols. Wheaton: Theosophical Publishing House, 1950–1987.

———.
The Durbar in Lahore. The Theosophist, August 1960—March 1961.

———.
H.P.B. Speaks. 2 vols. Adyar: Theosophical Publishing House, 1950, 1951.

———.
Isis Unveiled. Pasadena: Theosophical University Press, 1977.

———.
The Key to Theosophy. Los Angeles: Theosophy Company, 1973.

———.
"Letters of H.P.B. to Hartmann," *The Path,* May 1895—March 1896.

———.
Letters of H. P. Blavatsky to A. P. Sinnett. Pasadena: Theosophical University Press, 1973.

———.
The Secret Doctrine. Los Angeles: The Theosophy Company, 1974.

———.
Theosophical Glossary. Los Angeles: The Theosophy Company, 1973.

———, ed.
The Theosophist. Bombay, 1879–1882; Adyar, Madras, 1883–1885.

———.
The Voice of the Silence. Vernon, B.C.: H.P.B. Lending Library, 1978.

Blech, Charles.
Contribution a l'Histoire de la Societe Theosophique en France. Paris: Editions Adyar, 1933.

Blomfield, Sarah.
The Chosen Highway. Wilmette: Baha'i Publishing Trust, 1967.

Brosse, Jacques.
Alexandra David-Neel, l'aventure et la Spiritualité. Paris: Retz, 1978.

Brown, William T.
"Some Experiences in India," *Theosophical History* 3:7–8 (July–October 1991): 214–223.

Browne, Edward G.
The Persian Revolution of 1905–1909. London: Frank Cass, 1966.

Bruce, Ian, ed.
The Nun of Lebanon. London: Collins, 1951.

Brunton, Paul.
A Search in Secret India. Rev. ed. York Beach, Me.: Weiser, 1985.

Burke, Omar.
"Solo to Mecca." *Blackwood's Magazine* (December 1961): 481–495.

Burnier, Radha.
"Human Need in the Kali Yuga." *American Theosophist* (January/February 1991): 4.

Burway, Muntasim Bahadur M. W.
Life of His Highness Maharaja Tukoji Rao Holkar II, G.C.S.I., Ruler of Indore (1835–1886). Indore: Holkar State Printing Press, 1925.

Caldwell, Daniel, comp. and ed.
The Occult World of Madame Blavatsky. Tucson: Impossible Dream, 1991.

Cambridge Biographical Dictionary.
Cambridge: Cambridge University Press, 1990.

Cambridge Encyclopedia of Russia and the Soviet Union.
Cambridge: Cambridge University Press, 1982.

Campbell, Bruce.
Ancient Wisdom Revived. Berkeley: University of California Press, 1980.

Caracostea, Daniel.
"Alexandra David-Neel's Early Acquaintance with Theosophy: Paris 1892." *Theosophical History* 3:7–8 (July–October 1991): 209–213.

Carlson, Maria.
No Religion Higher Than Truth. Princeton: Princeton University Press, 1993.

Charak, Sukhdev Singh.
Life and Times of Maharaja Ranbir Singh (1830–1885). Jammu: J & K Book House, 1985.

Charles-Roux, Edmonde.
Un Desir d'Orient. Paris: Editions Grasset et Fasquelle, 1988.

Cleather, Alice Leighton.
H. P. Blavatsky: A Great Betrayal. Calcutta: Thacker, Spink, 1922.

———.
H. P. Blavatsky: As I Knew Her. Newington, Conn.: Sphinxiad, 1976.

———.
H. P. Blavatsky: Her Life and Work for Humanity. Calcutta: Thacker, Spink, 1922.

Cole, Juan R. I.
Colonialism and Revolution in the Middle East. Princeton: Princeton University Press, 1993.

———.
"Iranian Millenarianism and Democratic Thought," *International Journal of Middle East Studies,* vol. 24 (1992), pp. 27–38.

———.
"Muhammad ʿAbduh and Rashid Rida: A Dialogue on the Bahaʾi Faith," *World Order* 15:3–4 (Fall–Winter 1981), p. 11.

Corbin, Henri.
Temps Cyclique et Gnose Ismailienne. Paris: Berg International, 1982.

Coulomb, Emma.
Some Account of My Intercourse with Madame Blavatsky. Madras: Higginbotham, 1885.

Cranston, Sylvia.
HPB: the Extraordinary Life and Influence of Helena Blavatsky, Founder of the Modern Theosophical Movement. Putnam: New York, 1993.

Das, Sarat Chandra.
Journey to Lhasa and Central Tibet. New Delhi: Manjusri, 1970.

David-Neel, Alexandra.
Magic and Mystery in Tibet. New York: University Books, 1958.

Diver, Maud.
Royal India. New York: D. Appleton Century, 1942.

Drage, Geoffrey.
Russian Affairs. London: J. Murray, 1904.

Eberhardt, Isabelle.
The Passionate Nomad. Boston: Beacon Press, 1988.

Eek, Sven.
Damodar and the Pioneers of the Theosophical Movement. Wheaton: Theosophical Publishing House, 1965.

Effendi, Shoghi.
God Passes By. Wilmette: Bahaʾi Publishing Trust, 1969.

Ellwood, Robert S.
"Madame Blavatsky's Baboon" (review), *Gnosis* #30 (Winter 1994), p. 85.

Evans-Wentz, W. Y., comp. and ed.
The Tibetan Book of the Dead. London: Oxford University Press, 1978.

Fields, Rick.
How the Swans Came to the Lake. Boulder: Shambhala, 1981.

Foster, Barbara M. and Michael.
Forbidden Journey: the Life of Alexandra David-Neel. San Francisco: Harper & Row, 1987.

Fuller, Jean Overton.
Blavatsky and her Teachers. London: East–West, 1988.

Gaboriau, F. K.
"Adieu au lecteurs du Lotus." *le Lotus* (March 1889).

Garrett, Edmund F.
Isis Very Much Unveiled, being the Story of the Great Mahatma Hoax. 3rd ed. London: Westminster Gazette, 1894.

Godwin, Joscelyn.
The History of Theosophy in France. London: Theosophical History Centre, 1989.

———.
"HPB, Dorjeff, and the Mongolian Connection." *Theosophical History* (July 1988) 253–260.

Guénon, Rene.
Le Théosophisme: Histoire d'une Pseudo-Religion. Paris: Editions Traditionnelles, 1986.

Gurdjieff, George I.
Beelzebub's Tales to His Grandson. New York: Dutton, 1970.

———.
Meetings with Remarkable Men. New York: Dutton, 1969.

Hall, Manly P.
"Madame Blavatsky—A Tribute." *Theosophia* (May-June 1947) 10–11.

Hatcher, William H. and Douglas Martin.
The Baha'i Faith: The Emerging World Religion. New York: Harper & Row, 1984.

Hill, Gareth.
Masculine and Feminine: the Natural Flow of Opposites in the Psyche. Boston: Shambhala, 1992.

Hollinger, Richard, ed.
Community Histories (Studies in the Babi and Baha'i Religions, Vol. 6). Los Angeles: Kalimat, 1992.

Indian Chelas on the Masters.
Adyar: Adyar Lodge, 1992.

Index to Persian Correspondence of Ranbir Singh.
n.p., n.d., State Archives Repository, Jammu.

"Jamal ad-Din al-Afghani."
Encyclopaedia Britannica, 15th ed. Micropaedia, Vol. 6: 479.

Jayakar, Pupul.
Indira Gandhi, an Intimate Biography. New York: Pantheon, 1992.

———.
Krishnamurti. New York: Harper & Row, 1986.

Jinarajadasa, C. J., comp.
Letters from the Masters of the Wisdom, First and Second Series. Adyar: Theosophical Publishing House, 1973.

Johnson, Paul.
Madame Blavatsky, the 'Veiled Years': New Light from Gurdjieff or Sufism? London: Theosophical History Centre, 1987.

Jordens, J. T. F.
Dayananda Sarasvati: His Life and Ideas. Delhi: Oxford University Press, 1976.

Juergensmeyer, Mark.
Radhasoami Reality. Princeton: Princeton University Press, 1991.

Katz, Martin.
Mikhail N. Katkov: a Political Biography, 1818–1887. The Hague: Mouton, 1966.

Keddie, Nikki.
Sayyid Jamal ad-Din "al Afghani." Berkeley: University of California Press, 1972.

Kedourie, Elie.
Afghani and ʿAbduh. New York: Humanities Press, 1966.

Kinglake, Alexander.
Eothen. New York: Blackeman & Masson, 1863.

Kobak, Annette.
Isabelle. New York: Knopf, 1989.

Lane, David Christopher.
The Making of a Spiritual Movement. Del Mar, California: Del Mar, 1993.

———.
The Radhasoami Tradition. New York: Garland, 1992.

Lefort, Rafael.
The Teachers of Gurdjieff. York Beach, Me.: Samuel Weiser, 1984.

Longford, Elizabeth.
A Pilgrimage of Passion. London: Weidenfield and Nicolson, 1979.

Lutyens, Mary.
Krishnamurti: the Years of Awakening. New York: Avon, 1975.

Maalouf, Amin.
Samarcande. Paris: Lattes, 1988.

MacEoin, Denis M.
*From Shaykhism to Babism: A Study in Charismatic Renewal in Shi*ʿ*a Islam.* Unpublished Ph.D. dissertation, Cambridge University, 1979.

MacGregor, John.
Tibet, a Chronicle of Exploration. New York: Praeger, 1970.

MacKenzie, Norman and Jeanne.
The Fabians. New York: Simon & Schuster, 1977.

McGowan, William.
Only Man is Vile. New York: Farrar, Straus & Giroux, 1992.

Malozemoff, Andrew.
Russian Far Eastern Policy. Berkeley: University of California Press, 1958.

Mathur, Agam Prasad.
Radhasoami Faith: A Historical Study. Delhi: Vikas, 1974.

Mead, George R. S., comp.
Five Years of Theosophy. New York: Arno, 1976.

Meade, Marion.
Madame Blavatsky: the Woman Behind the Myth. New York: Putnam, 1980.

Merkur, Dan.
Gnosis: An Esoteric Tradition of Mystical Visions and Unions. Albany: State University of New York Press, 1993.

Meryon, John.
Memoirs of Lady Hester Stanhope. Salzburg: Institut für Anglistik und Amerikanstick, Universitat Salzburg, 1983.

———.
Travels of Lady Hester Stanhope. Salzburg: Institut für Anglistik und Amerikanstik, Universitat Salzburg, 1985.

Modern Encyclopedia of Russian and Soviet History.
Gulf Breeze, Fla.: Academic International Press, 1976–1993.

Moore, James.
Gurdjieff: The Anatomy of a Myth. London: Element, 1991.

Morris, Robert.
Freemasonry in the Holy Land. New York: Arno, 1977.

Mortimer, Edward.
Faith and Power. New York: Random House, 1982.

Murphet, Edward.
Yankee Beacon of Buddhist Light. Wheaton: Theosophical Publishing House, 1988.

Nahar, Sujata.
Mirra the Occultist. Paris: Institut de Recherches Evolutives, 1989.

Nasr, Siyyid Hossein, ed.
Isma^cili Contributions to Islamic Culture. Teheran: Imperial Academy of Philosophy, 1977.

Neff, Mary K., comp.
Personal Memoirs of H. P. Blavatsky. Wheaton: Theosophical Publishing House, 1971.

Nethercot, Arthur H.
The Last Four Lives of Annie Besant. Chicago: University of Chicago Press, 1963.

Niaz, A. Q.
The Babee and Bahaee Religion. Lahore: Tabshir, 1967.

Olcott, Henry Steel.
Old Diary Leaves. 6 vols. Adyar: Theosophical Publishing House, 1974, 1975.

Oliphant, John.
Brother Twelve. Toronto: McClelland & Stewart, 1991.

Pakdaman, Homa.
Djamal ad-Din Assad Abadi dit Afghani. Paris: G. P. Maisonneuve et Larose, 1969.

Pashkov, Lydia.
Correspondence with Isabelle Eberhardt, Archives d'Outre-Mer, Aix-en-Provence, France.

Paston, George.
Little Memoirs of the 19th Century. London: Dutton, 1902.

Price, Leslie.
"The American Acts of the Apostles," *Theosophical History* 2:4 (October 1987), pp. 134–35.

Purucker, Gottfried de.
The Dialogues of G. de Purucker. Covina: Theosophical University Press, 1948.

———.
Occult Glossary. Pasadena: Theosophical University Press, 1972.

Rawson, Albert L.
"Two Madame Blavatskys.—The Acquaintance of Madame H. P. Blavatsky with Eastern Countries." *The Spiritualist* (April 5 1878). In H. P. Blavatsky's Scrapbook. Archives, Theosophical Society (Adyar) 70–71.

Rochefort, Henri.
Les Aventures de Ma Vie. Paris: Paul Dupont, 1896.

The Sar Bachan.
Beas: Radha Soami Satsang Beas, 1974.

Sarasvati, Dayananda.
Autobiography. 3rd rev. ed. New Delhi: Manohar, 1987.

Scott, Ernest.
The People of the Secret. London: Octagon, 1983.

Sen, S. P., ed.
Dictionary of National Biography. Calcutta: Institute of Historical Studies, 1972–74.

Shah, Idries.
The Magic Monastery. London: Octagon, 1981.

———.
A Perfumed Scorpion. London: Octagon, 1978.

———.
Special Problems in the Study of Sufi Ideas. London: Octagon, 1978.

———.
The Sufis. New York: Anchor/Doubleday, 1971.

Singh, Ganda, comp.
Maharaja Duleep Singh Correspondence. Patiala: Punjab University, 1977.

———, ed.
The Singh Sabha and Other Socio-Religious Movements in the Punjab, 1850–1925. Patiala: Punjabi University, 1973.

Sinnett, Alfred Percy.
Autobiography of Alfred Percy Sinnett. London: Theosophical History Centre, 1986.

———.
Incidents of the Life of Madame Blavatsky. New York: Arno Press, 1976.

Sloss, Radha Rajagopal.
Lives in the Shadow with J. Krishnamurti. London: Bloomsbury, 1991.

Smith, Peter.
The Babi and Bahaʾi Faiths: From Messianic Shiʾism to a World Religion. Cambridge: Cambridge University Press, 1987.

Smith, Wilfrid Cantwell.
Islam in Modern History. Princeton: Princeton University Press, 1957.

Snelling, John.
Buddhism in Russia. Shaftesbury, Dorset: Element, 1993.

Somers, Jeffrey.
"Lama Dorjieff and the Esoteric Tradition." *Theosophical History* 3:2 (April 1990): 44–50.

Speeth, Kathleen Riordan, and Ira Friedlander.
Gurdjieff: Seeker of the Truth. New York: Harper & Row, 1980.

Stockman, Robert H.
The Bahaʾi Faith in America: Origins, 1892–1900. Wilmette: Bahaʾi Publishing Trust, 1985.

Strachey, Lytton.
Books and Characters. New York: Harcourt, Brace and Jovanovitch, 1922.

"The 1900 Letter,"
Theosophical History 2:4 (October 1987), pp. 116–117.

Tielrooy, Johannes.
Ernest Renan: Sa Vie et Ses Oeuvres. Paris: Mercure de France, 1958.

Tillett, Gregory.
The Elder Brother. London: Routledge & Kegan Paul, 1982.

Uktomskii, Esper Esperovitch.
Travels in the East of Nicholas II Emperor of Russia when Czarewitch 1890–91. Translated by Robert Goodlet, edited by James Birdwood. Westminster: Archibald Constable & Co., 1896.

Webb, James.
The Harmonious Circle. New York: Putnam, 1980.

———, ed.
The Society for Psychical Research Report on the Theosophical Society. New York: Arno, 1976.

Webster's Biographical Dictionary.
Springfield, Mass.: Merriam, 1943.

Weeks, Andrew.
German Mysticism from Hildegard of Bingen to Ludwig Wittgenstein. Albany: State University of New York Press, 1993.

Wilson, Samuel Graham.
Bahaism and Its Claims. New York: AMS, 1970.

Yadav, K. C., and K. S. Arya.
Arya Samaj and the Freedom Movement, Volume I: 1875–1918. New Delhi: Manohar, 1988.

INDEX

Note on transliteration: Terms in foreign languages are transliterated in the forms most common in the sources cited, with a few exceptions. Indian place names are given in their contemporary English forms. Names of persons well known for writing in English are given in the familiar forms, e.g. Blavatsky rather than Blavatskaia, but those of lesser-known figures are according to Library of Congress transliteration, e.g. Ukhtomskii rather than Ukhtomsky. Bahaʾi names and terms are transliterated according to the system used in Bahaʾi literature. Cross references from variant forms are provided in cases of possible confusion.